I Came to America

François Alain Borny

EAGLE EDITIONS
2006

EAGLE EDITIONS
AN IMPRINT OF HERITAGE BOOKS, INC.

Books, CDs, and more—Worldwide

For our listing of thousands of titles see our website
at
www.HeritageBooks.com

Published 2006 by
HERITAGE BOOKS, INC.
Publishing Division
65 East Main Street
Westminster, Maryland 21157-5026

Copyright © 2006 François Alain Borny

All rights reserved. No part of this book may be reproduced or transmitted in any form or by any means, electronic or mechanical, including photocopying, recording or by any information storage and retrieval system without written permission from the author, except for the inclusion of brief quotations in a review.

International Standard Book Number: 978-0-7884-3592-2

As I didn't want to involve people I know are still alive, I changed a few names. Some of the names I've forgotten, so I just created them. The characters are true but only in this context.

If someone's name has been used in this story, it would have been only coincidental.

To Aline

FOREWORD

This is an authorized gathering of memoirs. Authorized by my wife, that is. She read it, laughed, shrugged, and then said with tears in her eyes, "Go ahead, Love, you sound better than you look."

So, here am I trying to remember what my life was like before I came to America. It's a long way back in the years ... But that is irrelevant.

F.A.B.

PREFACE

By Matra Kreig
Head of the English Department
at Hargrave High School,
Huffman, Texas

I first met François Borny at a creative writing course I teach at our local community center. It's a typical writing course as far as these kinds of courses are concerned. We meet, I introduce writing techniques, we read examples of good writing, and we share our writings together as a group.

It was in such an environment that I delightfully encountered François's take on the world - that curious combination of comedy and tragedy that can only be successfully pulled off by those writers deeply acquainted with both.

The genesis of this book was from a germ of an assignment that asked writers to explore an event in their lives that changed them in a profound way, whether they knew it or not at the time. François chose an event from his childhood that touched upon his memories of occupied France during World War II. His telling was filled with remarkable detail and an easy narrative style that captivated his listeners. By the time François was finished with his contribution, the class members, through simultaneous laughter and tears expressed great interest in the rest of the story. And so the task was humbly undertaken. This book is its result. (For all the talk of French arrogance, this is one Frenchman whose modesty and humility attest to a kinder, gentler version of the French.)

I was so taken with the original narrative that I asked François to address our high school students at an upcoming Veterans Day Ceremony. He gladly accepted, saying how important it was for young people to realize the greatness of their country and the pride he felt about being an American himself. He was also motivated by the chance to personally thank the World War II veterans who would be in attendance. After a brief history lesson on the background of France's involvement in the war, he told the students of his hunger, his fear, and his country's faith in an Allied victory over the Germans, especially since the Americans were reported to be on French soil. His simple speech, delivered in almost perfect English and expressed through the quiet tears of someone truly grateful, ended with the worshipful phrase, "I love you Americans."

He received a standing ovation that day, as did the veterans he praised. School bullies, cheerleaders, custodians, secretaries, teachers, class presidents, everyone in attendance left the auditorium misty-eyed and tenderhearted, a bit red-white-and-bluer than they arrived. The reader of this story will come away not only knowing François a bit better, but knowing his country and himself better as well.

ACKNOWLEDGEMENTS

I wish to express my gratitude to everyone who helped me in this work.

My son, Jean-François, who found in my prose more mistakes that I would have liked to, his wife Rita, my daughter, Susanne who read the first hundred pages and said she couldn't wait to read the rest of the story, my English teacher, Matra Kreig, who encouraged me from the first day, and some other friends who have inspirited me in the difficult task of writing in English.

Those are —and hopefully I don't forget anyone— my friends Aida and Alex Dyer who are two of the few people who read the first hundred pages of my manuscript, Nancy and Bob Adamski the first acquaintances we met in Crosby twenty-five years ago, Ray McKinney, my golf partner and longtime workmate, Janie Webster, Head of the Foreign Languages department in Hargrave High School, Jane Snead, Barbara Cates, Martha Quaid, Joel French, a Mathematics teacher, who wrote me such a nice letter after he read part of the manuscript, Marty Pipes, Director of the Crosby Community Center and her gentle staff.

1

The oldest memory I have in my life happened long ago when I was two years and nine months old. How do I know that with certainty? Let me explain.

That was the day —September 22— I met with my mother, and the vision I had of that moment is still firmly rooted in my mind. I remember my mother lying on the bed panting, and a woman helping her have a baby.

But that I didn't know at the time. Someone —I don't remember whom— drove me out of the room and asked me to wait there. Wait for what?

It wasn't long after that I saw the same woman getting out of the bedroom holding in her bloody hands a huge baby I hadn't seen before. That's what I was waiting for. A baby! Where did that thing come from? I wondered.

In those uncivilized times, most women gave birth to their children at home with the help of a midwife. Or sometimes, just a friend.

That thing I had in front of me turned out to be my baby sister Juliette, and she was —and still is— two years and nine months younger than me. That was the first meeting I had with her and mother. And I swear I remember it.

Years later I asked Mom, as if unconcernedly, if my memories were accurate. She never believed I was a witness to Juliette's birth, and most of all, she refused to believe that I remembered anything at that age.

Well, yes, I remember and, even today, after so many years have flown away, I can picture the weary face of the midwife and her smile as she said, "That's your little sister, François."

* * *

Mom was a woman of temper, most of the time of a bad one. She seemed to be living in a constant state of anger but no one knew why and, more important, when this particular state of mind would happen. Some days it was worse. Laundry days, pay days (not enough pay), bills days (too many bills), house clean-up days (too much to clean up), and some other days (many of them). One who appeared to know everything about Mom was my father. But he didn't seem to care or to give much importance to the fact that he knew.

He was the opposite of Mom. Never fell anxious about anything. One says that worries turn your hair gray. Well, Dad didn't have any hair for one thing. He always had a smile on his face and a joke going on. He knew so many of them, Mom said he could have been a comedian. Except that Dad stuttered. Not always though, but most of the time. Which didn't keep him from talking.

Physically he didn't match Ophélia either. That was Mom's name but Dad called her Fifi. Which reminds me of a French dwarf poodle we had when I was younger. Mom was tall, skinny as to resemble Popeye's girl friend, straight as a capital 'I', and very intuitive... if not very smart.

My father was rather short, a little overweight, and almost completely bald with the exception of a ludicrous small bunch of dark hair right in the center of his glistening scalp. I have to say that he was the first to laugh at his look. No narcissism there. However, he wasn't too bad looking considering the top of his head. He had a regular face with brown eyes, a straight nose rather small, and two beautiful rows of shining teeth. But, as I already said, Dad didn't give a damn about anything.

It's only many years later that I heard that Pierre Borny was a womanizer. How could he be? Short, bald, and not particularly brilliant. I never understood where he had his charisma. Mom always said that he had a lot of it. His joyous face and his smile, perhaps. His secret died with him in 1978. He was eighty-two.

As for Mom, her only positive features were her beautiful green eyes which prevented her from being totally unattractive. That was probably what trapped Dad into marriage when they first met in Marseille, at the Borelli Park. It was a Friday 13th, Mom said, on a magnificent springtime day with a scent of lavender filling the air. It was noon, and she was having a frugal lunch on a bench surrounded by sparrows and doves cooing their joy. Dad showed up a minute later holding a huge sandwich, then sat next to Ophélia Borgeac. They smiled at each other, Mom recalled with a certain melancholy, didn't say a word, and then they parted on their way to work. Dad must have loved those beautiful smiling eyes. But he must have missed the rest of her attributes. It couldn't have been otherwise.

Mom had large ears and, besides, a nose quite big that seemed to be in a constant motion. Like an elephant trunk, Dad would say much later.

Oh God, that nose! It was the subject of a permanent joke. Mostly from Dad, of course, but also from his friends, his family, and sometimes even from us, the children. But then, we had to be very, very careful. Mom was aware of her Cyrano de Bergerac-like appendix, but could take any mischievous remarks only when she was in a good mood. Which was seldom the case. I heard one day one of Dad's friends saying with a big laugh that if someone wanted to kiss her on both cheeks —the way we do in France— he or she would better go around behind her head which would save time for it was the shorter route. I didn't think it was very funny but Dad didn't seem to be of the same mind.

Again, Dad didn't care anyway. For years, Mom's nose had been his favorite pleasantry to use and abuse. I recall one day we went to the *Galeries Lafayette*, the department store in Nice, and Mom was in a temporary good state of mind as always when she could be on a shopping spree and spend some money. She was smiling, her eyes glittering amid the profusion of light in the store, and her hand in Dad's. They were silent for a while as if they were enjoying that special peaceful time. And maybe they did until Mom had the bad idea to ask, "Is it true, honey, that my nose is so big it deserves to be a laughingstock?"

Dad looked at her, the usual smile on his face. "No, Fifi," he said, and after a short silence, he added, "Watch out, you're stepping on it." Mom made a terrible face, turned to Dad, and said, "Shut up, Hector." She grabbed my hand, volte-faced, and walked out of the store while Dad was sitting on the floor holding his ribs laughing. I squeezed Mom's hand, as I was sorry for her. There was nothing else I could do besides letting tears running down my cheeks.

But it was true that Mom's nose was indeed very large.

Dad's name wasn't Hector, of course. Mom would call him that only when she was upset. That was about all the time. I never understood why. In her moments of joyous lucidity she would call him Pierre. Which was more appropriate.

After the awful scene at Lafayette, my parents didn't talk to each other for a long time. Which didn't seem to bother Dad more than necessary. I was eight at the time, and this was one of my painful childhood memories. Afterwards, I often had the opportunity to mull over those scenes that would be repeated more often in the coming years. Mom suffered of this, and I suffered, and so did my baby sister Juliette whom Mom sometimes called Julia. It would be much later, some time after the war that Dad decided to disappear from our lives.

2

Mom was born Ophélia Borgeac in Cadillac, France. Cadillac is not an American car as you might think, but a little town spreading on the Garonne River's right bank, that was at the time merely a village with a historic past and, mind you, a 17th century castle: the château d'Épernon.

Ophélia Borgeac was born the last day of the nineteenth century. However, not in the luxury of the château d'Épernon, but half a mile away in a little log cabin without electricity or running water. The bungalow, as my mother would call it metaphorically, would be soaking time to time in three feet of muddy water when the Garonne River would turn ugly and invade the defenseless flat banks.

Laurent Borgeac, Mom's father, was a kind of easy going giant with an enormous head topped with a shock of red hair, and a long beard in the same dark reddish-brown color that almost reached his chest. And then, the typical Borgeac's nose that I recognized in the last century picture that hung in Ophélia's bedroom.

Did I say that, unfortunately, I have inherited my ancestor's outgrowth? Not that big however, but I hardly have a turned-up nose.

The hung picture of my grandparents is the only memory I have of the Borgeacs. They were in their Sunday dress and suit, ready for church. Grandma Borgeac was born Sophie Deloret and, according to the same picture, had a gentle pretty face with huge beautiful eyes — Mom said they were green— and only a shadow of a moustache under her cute nose. I had never met them for they had been dead for a while when I was born.

I have never heard much about Dad's parents except that grandpa Borny was a drunk. He never parted from his bottle of wine, which he always carried in his coat pocket. Grandpa's full name was Alphonse Anatole Borny. He married in 1890 Amélie Bonnard who was the daughter of a rich landowner in the island of Ré. I never saw any pictures of them and have no idea what they looked like. Dad recalled that they were nice people besides the invariable drunkenness of his father.

Dad told us with his usual smirk that it was a blessing from God that his father had to sit to work. He couldn't stand up more than a few seconds without the risk of dropping flat on the floor. He was the owner of a small transport company. Which means that he had two horse-drawn coaches and an employee. Both of them would drive the carriages around the island —about eighteen miles— one clockwise and the other counter-clockwise. They would meet in the middle of the island with any passengers or cargo they could find, deliver whatever they had, people or merchandise, and keep going on their respective routes until they would meet again at the stable in Saint Martin, their home base. The trip could last two or three days, depending on the number of customers or on Grandpa's wine supply.

Alphonse Borny died expectedly of cirrhosis at the age of 49. His last words were, Dad recalled, "Give me a glass of wine, Amélie." I believe that was another one of Dad's jokes. Anyway, he left his wife in a lurch, and Pierre Borny had to quit school, find a job at the age of twelve, and sell the two horses and their carriages.

That might explain why Dad was a teetotaler. I never saw him drinking anything but water. Only occasionally a glass of wine.

* * *

Monsieur Borgeac was a civil servant in Bagnères-de-Luchon, a little city a few miles away from the Spanish border. A customs officer who had been exercising his duty in a customs post up on the Pyrenees Mountains. He had spent five years there fighting the Spanish *contrabandistas* —smugglers— who stealthily tried to carry, through the pervious Franco-Spanish frontier, the infamous and illegal absinthe, and the favorite drink at the time of most Frenchmen. Including Grandpa.

It was there that he met, on a Christmas Day, with Sophie Deloret who happened to be the city mayor's daughter, married her, and then moved to Cadillac where the government sent him for a while. There, Ophélia Borgeac was born on December 31, 1900. The next day, the twentieth century was born.

The happy Borgeac family enjoyed life in general and in good humor, except when the raging Garonne River flooded the banks and invaded their property ruining their kitchen garden along with the little orchard where two fig trees and grapes supplied the household with fruits and wine. For a while they wouldn't have any vegetables or fruits unless they bought them at the local market. And the money was tight in the early 1900's.

Ophélia went to school in Cadillac. Not too long though, in spite of her goodwill. She brought home bad report cards, and Laurent and Sophie Borgeac decided to send her to the château d'Épernon. Not to marry the count, however, but to learn the highly appreciated trade of cooking. Ophélia became the best cook a husband could dream of. Mom was still a *Cordon Bleu* —a very skilled chef— until the late stage in her long life.

When Mom was fourteen the Borgeacs move to La Rochelle on the Atlantic coast. No more river, no more flooding, but instead the awesome ocean right in front of their small house, with the cute little harbor on the left side where the vestiges of Richelieu's defense walls could still be seen in 1914, after three hundred years standing there, useless and unaesthetic.

In La Rochelle, Mom could express her culinary talents and learn a few new recipes in a region where food was the first concern. Until she married a guy from the Island of Ré, whose name was Pierre Anatole Borny.

The island can be seen from La Rochelle when the morning haze has disappeared above the ocean and the sun shows up through a clear sky. Many years later I visited Ré. Saint Martin is the main city where my father was born along with a little over 2000 inhabitants. But the main curiosity is that a high percentage of those people are named Borny. Why so many of them? You can stroll on almost any street of the town and find at least one Borny. And they swear that most of them aren't even related. How can that be? I also know that about seventeen Borny families are living in the United States as legal residents. And probably a few more illegally. I've had all those names and addresses since the eighties, but I believe the list can't be accurate any longer. Those families must have procreated. Which should have increased the number of legitimate Bornys in the United States as well as the illegal ones.

But it was in Marseille that Pierre Borny met with Mom. Dad was born almost at the end of the nineteen century, four years before Ophélia's parents decided to have their only child. He was the only boy amongst six children, all born on the Island of Ré long before a penal colony was installed there in 1946 in replacement of the infamous Devil Island in the French Guyana.

None of the girls had a formal education having dropped out of school after the third or fourth grade. My father was the scholar of the family. He could read.

They all lived in Marseille where the family had moved after the Great War. World War I that is.

* * *

Dad was eighteen years old when a certain William II of Prussia decided to declare war on France and England on August 3, 1914.

So Pierre went to the war, I'm sure with his usual smile across his face as if he were the happiest man in the world, his backpack full of military clothes, a puttee around each of his spindly legs, and a huge 1896 Lebel rifle he had no idea how to make work.

Private Borny didn't care. There would be plenty of time for him to learn how to handle the weapon.

But Dad never had to know how. He became the company's barber, and he loved to tell how that happened. The drill sergeant — we call in France *adjudant*— asked for a barber at the new recruits first morning assembly. There were none. So he demanded if, by any chance, someone had an idea how to cut hair. Again no one. Finally he noticed my father's irresistible smile amongst stern faces and asked him to approach.

"What's your name?"
"Pierre Borny, Sir."
"You can cut hair, can't you?"
"No, Sir, I can't," my father answered.
"Can you shave?"
"You mean myself? Yes, sure."
"You're the new company's barber."

The whole company howled with laughter. Pierre shrugged then said loud enough to be heard by everyone, "You'll laugh less louder when I'll cut your hair."

"Don't you worry, Borny," the adjudant said with a funny expression on his face. "He who laughs last .... Well, you know."

I heard that story over and over when Dad was still living with us.

After the Prussians were kicked out of France with the help of General Pershing's American Expeditionary Forces, Dad returned to Marseille, worked for a while in a barbershop, met again with Sophie

Borgeac, married her, and moved to Nice where he opened his own barbershop and where I was born a few years later.

3

I was approaching nine years of age and I remember, with an acute recollection, the talks about the incoming war. I didn't participate in any of the discussions, of course. The first thing you learned in the Borny's family as soon as you were born is that, when you are a kid, you don't say a word in a grown-ups' reunion. Not even open your mouth to yawn for mother Borny would fulgurate flashes through your brain that would freeze you like a fossilized insect. And if you were lucky you might get spanked too. Mother was very agile with both her hands and possessed an acquired aptitude to find my butt.

But no one could shut my ears, could they? I kept them wide open and tried hard to understand what was said, pretending I wasn't listening. Now, as to comprehend all of the various aspects of the talks was another story. I wasn't sure what war was except that people got killed and countries ruined and destroyed.

* * *

It was a little bit more than a persistent rumor about that guy whose name was Adolph Hitler. A German idiot who, besides, was completely insane. He came from nowhere at a time when Germany was in a big mess. Moreover, that moron wasn't even German. He was born in Braunau, Austria, sometime the previous century. I believe in 1889. So, what the hell was he doing at the head of the Third Reich? A Nazi State he had help to create with his friends, Goebels, Goering, Himmler, and their clique.

That's what I'd hear in those joyous reunions that would turn into a bacchanalia of drinks, food, all wrapped up with my father's jokes. Most of them bad as usual.

Dad was 43 years old at the time and had already experienced war. War World I that is. Well, perhaps to say that he was in the army during that war would be more accurate for Dad never confronted the rigor of the enemy's real fire. "If mobilized again," he often repeated, "I would end up in the same barber salon I quit in 1918." One thing was sure: those four years he spent in a military salon had helped him improve greatly his trade. He was now a real professional barber.

In the period he had cut hair for his fellow soldiers, he had avoided, sometimes barely, to be lynched on the spot. That was the only danger Mister Borny had encountered while defending the fatherland. He faced way more danger at home when Momma was in her congenital bad mood.

So, what about those rumors of war? Edouard Daladier, our chief of government, and his British counterpart, Prime Minister Neville Chamberlain, went joyously to shake hands with the Nazi dictator. No war was in view, both believed and said when they returned to their respective quarters.

* * *

It was July or August 1939. We lived on *rue* Mirabeau, in a two-story building that was only a few years older than a century. It was a square construction, all in a decrepit state, with an interior paved court where a bunch of assorted kids played, pooped, got spanked, cried. All of the aforementioned with an irritating noisy agitation. A gallery ran all around inside the building on the second floor overlooking the tumultuous quadrangle. No apertures on the façade save for three small businesses, one of which was my father's barber salon. At that time I hadn't paid much attention to what the other two businesses were. I'd find out later that one was a grocery store, and the other one a storage for a banana wholesaler, a huge African guy from the Ivory Coast.

Our apartment —directly under the roof— had windows in each room opening on the gallery and overlooking the courtyard. No air conditioning or heater, of course. In August it was incredibly hot, and in winter we would freeze our French buttocks off, mostly when the Mistral would blow from the north and funnel between the Massive Central Mountains and the Alps through the Rhône River Valley to drop on our city a shower of ice cubes. No snow though. Just cold.

Dad's salon was pretty busy. Not much money from it but it kept Dad out of trouble and Mom on her own self, deep in her familiar bad mood. Pierre Borny worked hard five and a half days a week, from early Tuesday morning to Sunday around noon. In summer time, Mondays were devoted to the beach, swimming or fishing. With Mom or without her. Juliette would follow sometimes, but she wasn't a beach fan for her very pale complexion would turn lobster-like in a few minutes. Even on a rainy day. Never understood that.

My hometown has miles of beaches. Not much sand however, but pebbles, nice, round, clean little damn stones that twist your ankles when you walk on them unless you are a kangaroo or an Arabian dromedary. However, when you'd get used to those stupid rocks, it would be all right. You would even like them for you wouldn't have to dust off the sand before you got home to prevent Ophélia Borny from jumping at you, hands towards your butt. Moreover, pebbles kept the ocean cleaner than sand and the waters in Nice were crystal clear all yearlong.

With Dad, we would swim long distances hugging the beach from one end to the other. I was used to it, since I was a trained swimmer from the local swimming club since I was six. And Dad was a fine swimmer too.

Or we would go fishing on the rocks of Saint-Laurent-du-Var, a gentle small fishermen village lying at the western end of Nice. Fish were scarce for amateurs like us, but none of us cared. I enjoyed spending the day with my father and, in spite of the fact that he and Mom didn't get along very well, we loved getting together. I have sweet memories of the time when, leaving home in the wee hours of the morning, we would walk six miles to Saint-Laurent in the coolness of a new day carrying our fishing rods.

Even after Dad had left us, I never held a grudge against him for what he did to Ophélia and to us. But it took a while before I thought of him in a more rational way. Who gave us the right, we children, to judge our parents? No matter what Pierre Borny did, he was my father and, notwithstanding his caustic humor not always fun, I loved him and respected him as a son is supposed to. I kept in touch with him until his death. He lived in Paris at the time, and I in Monaco.

My sister Juliette was not as forgiving as I was. After our father disappeared from our lives, in 1948, she never saw him again. To this day she still refuses to talk about Dad. And God knows how hard I tried.

Father remarried a young woman. Thirty years younger than he was. Her name was Raymonde. And still is for she's alive and well at eighty-seven. We talk to each other once in a while on the telephone. Besides, I have news from Paris by the daughter she had with my father in 1950. My half sister's name is Liliane. A pretty name for a pretty girl. The only one who has blue eyes in the family. I wondered where those eyes came from. No offense, Dad. I met her when she was ten. I didn't even know I had another sister. But obviously she knew everything about me for Dad told her about his son. One day, while visiting with my father in Paris, he asked me embarrassed, if I wanted to meet his daughter.

For a second I thought it was another bad joke. It wasn't and of course I met with Liliane the same day. And while I was in Dad's apartment, I met with Raymonde, who was hiding in another room before coming out at Dad's request. He first didn't dare ask me to talk to his wife. I always wondered why. Raymonde is one of the sweetest ladies I have ever met. Since that day she had considered me as her son, and Dad was so proud of that.

They lived in Paris after Dad left his barbershop in Nice to open another one in the capital.

What a mess. Mom was desperate and so were we. Money was extremely scarce. Mother had to look for a job. The second time in her married life. The first time was after Dad went to war in September 1939. But she was a good cook so she found a job in a small restaurant, in the train station, called prosaically *Café de la Gare*, Café of the Train Station. Juliette and I were still going to school. She, in a middle school and I attending Lycée (High school) Jules Renard.

But that was after the war.

* * *

I still remember the sad period before that damn war. At home it was a fake happiness in which Dad, Mom, Juliette and I lived during the months that preceded World War II.

No much talk between us except when Dad and I went swimming or fishing.

And in spite of the rumors of war we managed to survive day after day in a creeping atmosphere avoiding in the house rough contact and big dramas among us. Dad would work, Mom would cook and take care of the house with an unbroken rhythm and, I'm sure, a passion for what she was doing. I don't remember seeing my mother idle, never saw her relaxing on a sofa reading a magazine or listening to the radio. As soon as she was up in the morning, she was busy. Even at lunchtime she was more often on her feet than sitting.

And making ends meet was another problem Mom would have to face more and more. But she was very much used to her misery and she was tough.

4

The rumors of war started making people nervous all over Europe. At the end of August 1939, Hitler and his Waffen Schutzstaffeln (SS) were ready to invade Poland to annex the city of Gdansk (Danzig for the Germans) and its corridor to the sea, which, the mustachioed dictator said to be a part of Germany that was given by mistake to the Poles after the Treaty of Versailles in 1919. That, of course wasn't true, but an excuse to rip Poland apart and share the remnants of it with Russia.

Smart Russia who believed they had foreseen the aggression long before Hitler himself had even thought about that. Well, that's not quite true either, for it's a common belief that the Austrian-born Nazi was thinking about Poland since he was a quack painter in Vienna after World War I.

Russians were, for decades, interested in a piece of Poland. They thought that, at least, the oriental part, if not the whole country, belonged to them.

In April 1939 Hitler met with the other dictator, another mustachioed: Joseph Stalin. Hyenas never eating each other, the meeting went smoothly and happily. And at the end of it, the Pact Germano-Sovietic was born.

And what a pact! Astute Stalin would wait for Germany to be Russia's cat's-paw and then, crush Poland and split the country.

Within a few days Poland would be erased from the political map of Europe.

But France and Britain's prime ministers had stayed alert. They spied on the negotiations, and jumped on their feet as soon as they knew the contents of the Pact sealed with the signatures of the two jackals.

France was first to bellow through the voice of Edouard Daladier, our prime minister. A long, loud roar that Chamberlain echoed with anger from his office, 10 Downing Street in London.

"If you enter Poland, Mister Hitler, we'd be obliged to declare war on Germany," both ministers yelled convinced they could face the ogre any time without fear.

What a miscalculation! Rather a mistake. The German army (Der Wehrmacht) was a formidable beast, armed to the teeth, extremely well trained, and having the will to eat anyone around them.

Hitler, of course, ignored the ultimatum and, on September 1, 1939, at five o'clock in the morning, without prior official mobilization, and without any declaration of war, he attacked Poland on the western part of the country and started his expansionist plan. The struggle for the *Living Space* much needed for the expected one-thousand-year-long life of the Third Reich had begun.

The perverse Stalin had waited until September 17, to make sure Germans had done the dirty work first. And only then he gave his Cossacks the order to enter the eastern region of Poland and massacre the remnants of the already crushed people.

* * *

And that was it. War was on its way.

If I close my eyes, I can picture, as on the big screen of a movie theater, the unforgettable scenes of that infamous day. It was September 3, 1939, and I was nine years old. We all knew something very wrong was going on since Hitler's blunt rejection of the French and British ministers' ultimatums.

I recall every detail of that infamous Sunday when my Dad came home from work around noon. We watched him walking through the door, his usual joyous face having an exceptional severe look. And I remember the first words out of his mouth. "That's it," he had said with a shrug, "We're at war. Mobilization bills are posted all over the city. Let's go down the street and look at them."

Rue Mirabeau was unusually crowded that Sunday in spite of the driving rain and the cold wind that blew from the Var River Valley down the street. Winter seemed to be precocious that year.

Faces were stern; eyes were full of tears staring at the gruesome poster. We approached the throng and read. I also remember the exact words: *Mobilisation Générale. Tous les réservistes sont appelés à rejoindre immédiatement leur corps.* (General Mobilization. All members of the military reserves are ordered to join their regiments immediately).

We went back home. Mom was crying and I believe it was the first time that tough lady had tears in her eyes. I wasn't sure I understood the whole occurrence. One thing was certain: Private Pierre Borny was going to war for the second time. He was forty-three years old with the experience of the First World War.

But that was twenty-five years before and, at that time, Dad and I hadn't met yet. So I wouldn't have known his mental state when World War I began.

What were we going to do without him? Mom would have his pay directed to her, but soldiers know how ludicrous military pay is.

My father left the next morning. We walked him to the train station crammed with a large number of civilians soon-to-be-soldiers.

There was a song at the time, a song of which I still remember the words.

Quand un soldat s'en va en guerre il a
Dans sa musette son bâton de Maréchal.

*Quand un soldat revient de guerre il a
Simplement eu de la veine, et puis voilà.*
(When a soldier goes to war he has in his backpack a field marshal stick.
When a soldier returns from war he was just lucky enough, that's it.)
How many times that has been proved true. I knew a few young neighbors who ran out of luck and never came back.

* * *

For almost six years —September 3, 1939 - May 8, 1945— we had experienced horrible happenings, incommensurable pain in our bodies and our souls, and the horrendous ordeal of a people under the yoke of a barbaric nation. That was what the Nazi Germany at the time deserved to be called.

My family had lived on a certain level of poverty in those years as far as I remembered. After Dad left for war we were much poorer than we had been before. Mom could bring home some francs from the little restaurant she worked for, as well as some food left over by scarce customers. Most of the men were at war and women usually didn't enjoy going to a restaurant by themselves when their spouses were fighting somewhere near the German border.

During World War I Dad had been given an obsolete Lebel rifle. He didn't pay much attention to it. He was promoted barber of the company and the sole weapons he used then were a sharpened razor and a pair of scissors.

My father wasn't that lucky in 1939. He had to learn how to use the same old 1896 Lebel rifle. He went to the shooting range, tried to understand what to do, but missed all his shots. He claimed nobody had told him he had to shoot at the targets in front of him.

He then returned to the barracks with bruises on his right shoulder from the recoil of his rifle, and deaf from the whistling of the bullets around him. He considered himself a lucky man not to have shot anyone on the shooting range, and fortunate not to have been shot either.

How do I know all those details? Well, as I already said, Dad was a compulsive storyteller in spite of his occasional stammering, and he enjoyed telling the account of his first day in the real army when he returned from war after the armistice was signed with our *beloved* Adolph Hitler.

However, at that time, war wasn't over yet. Dad returned to the shooting range the next day. He was then told that the series of huge squares in front of him, with a large red circle in the center, numbered one to ten, were meant to be targets, and were there to be shot at. Not solely to harmonize the landscape. Your target, he was told, is number four. That time, one of Pierre Borny's bullets managed to shave the upper end of a square missing the bull's-eye by about four feet. He was happy though the objective wasn't the one he was supposed to shoot at. It was number one, three targets away from his on his left.

But he was excusable for he had shot only twenty-four rounds to achieve that remarkable feat.

* * *

Germans were through with the trashing of Poland, so they turned their attention to the western front where the French and British had made a timid attempt in the forest of Warndt, towards Germany's border. A timorous undertaking though, that didn't scare Hitler and his fanatic Nazis in the least.

On October 16, Germans counterattacked violently to push back the French and British forces where they had started. Back to the Maginot Line.

The Maginot Line? Another joke that kept Dad laughing for a while. The German army reached the Line, stopped there for a minute or two wondering what in the world was that stupid wall for. "It's the Maginot Line *Herr Standartenführer,*" (Colonel) said an officer from the *Abwehr* (Wehrmacht's secret service). When asked where the wall ended, the officer answered, "Two hundred kilometers from here, sir. At the Belgian border."
"Let's go and bypass that."
That was a gag told among the German troops. Bypassing the Maginot Line wasn't that easy however, but almost. The aforementioned *Standartenführer,* and everyone else in Germany, knew exactly what the damn Line was. A real joke.

The Panzerdivisionen bypassed the Maginot the same day and the French were driven back like animals at bay. Nowhere to go but south. The British chose Dunkirk to escape by sea. And the stampede started; French soldiers running for their lives without any orders or even any commanding officers, and British trying to cross over the Channel in a desperate retreat, helped on their way to England by amateur boatmen who came from England with their own boats.

Germany had accomplished what they called *Der Kriegblitz* (the Lightning War). They had run over France as if it were a Marathon, only much faster.

The Nazis had already invaded two thirds of France, from the Rhine River down to south of Lyons and, on the west side, in a narrow corridor from Vierzon to the Spanish border.

Meanwhile, a horde of French civilian refugees were running southward trying to put the most distance they could between them and the German invasion armies. All the roads north and south were jammed with a very unique traffic. Horse carriages, narrow drays, wheelbarrows, bicycles, were used to escape the war zones and to carry useless belongings that would be abandoned sooner or later in the ditches along the road.

Children, women, old people, and also, hiding among those human wretches, a few have-been soldiers who were nothing but the shadow of a not so proud army.

And to make the horror worse, German Messerschmitts and Stukas (war planes) harassed the refugees along clogged roads shooting at them and killing hundreds.

That was the time when we were down on all fours, that Benito Mussolini, the fascist Italian dictator, chose to declare war to France and Great Britain. Wasn't that a nice parting shot?

That same day, Italian planes joined the German friends to shoot at civilians on the road of exodus.

It was obvious that France and Britain weren't prepared for war. Nazi Germany was. It was a very costly lesson for the two allies.

Fortunately, it happened that Nazi Germany would also pay the high price for its ignominy, but much later, and thanks, one more time, to the Americans.

5

We have an old saying in France, *"It's in the oldest kettles that one makes the best soup."* It was probably what the beaten government had in mind when they called an old legendary figure: The eighty-three years old Maréchal Philippe Pétain who defeated the Germans at the battle of Verdun during World War I.

They called him back to the front stage from Madrid, where he was Ambassador to Spain, for he was a venerable soldier, with a sympathetic face people would like and trust. He had a twinkle in his blue eyes, beautiful features, and a white mustache that gave him a geniality that attracted the respect and the sympathy of ordinary people like you and me. In other words, his bearing was at all times majestic.

Albert Lebrun, President of the Republic since 1932, summoned Pétain to Paris to be the head of his new government in replacement of Edouard Daladier who had been the one who had yelled on the rooftops, only a few months before, that there would never be any war between Germany and France. Why yes, of course.

And finally, they called the old marshal for they needed a scapegoat to take the blame for the bitter defeat our army had endured, and negotiate with the enemy to obtain the best terms possible on the incoming armistice.

The Germans accepted the truce but, naturally, under their own conditions. They stopped their progression towards the south —a curious mistake from the victor— and recognized the appointment of Philippe Pétain and his own cabinet.

The new government couldn't stay in Paris where the Germans

were already established. Pétain and President Lebrun decided that the city of Vichy would be adequate for it would be off the occupied northern zone, although close enough to stay in contact with the occupants.

For Philippe Pétain would keep a gracious ear, listen to the orders of the German High Command, and transmit them to the people of France. He was convinced that France and Great Britain had irremediably lost the war and there wasn't a damn thing anybody could do about it. And the only way to save what could be saved and end the killing, was to collaborate with the Nazi commandment.

Obviously, they all forgot about a certain general whose name was Charles de Gaulle.

Germany had laid down its own rules that would be enforced by the French police organizations —mostly the *Gendarmerie*— and their own Gestapo. But first they imposed on France the payment of an outrageous war debt. Which meant that the French people would be responsible to produce enough to feed the whole German army that was spread all over Europe. Not a single product of any kind could be directed to the population.

Within twenty-four hours the grocery stores were emptied of all kinds of food. They closed their doors not to open again for the next five years. Bakeries, butcheries, dairies, cloth and shoe fabrics, gas stations, did the same. Those allowed to remain open would see their production strictly controlled and directed, by Pétain's clowns, to the German army.

No more bread, milk, sugar, coffee, meat, vegetable, heating fuel. One couldn't think about anything we had had on a regular basis not long ago.

But war had ended for the routed French army. Dad came back home though some of his friends never made it. In our own apartment buildings two young men never returned home. I've forgotten their names but I remember their faces. Many more soldiers I didn't even know, never showed up at their native places.

Pierre Borny reopened his barbershop, but Mom lost her job at the restaurant for there was no food to serve. Ration cards made their first appearance in July. We could buy once a day a small piece of black bread I always thought was made from sawdust. Once a month two pounds of potatoes for a family of four. An egg for each member of the same family for the same period of time. But we didn't care much about those eggs. Most of them were rotten anyway and had to be thrown away. The list of things we missed was endless. Dad would say, *"Hey folks, we have no nothing."* Name it and you would know right away that we didn't have it. Germans had taken everything from us. But not our dignity.

School reopened only a few days after the armistice was signed. My best friend in the fourth grade was Sylvain Bénichou, a Jew from Morocco who lived with his parents on the top floor of our apartment building. He was as poor and destitute as I was, but more confounded than me for it was a bad time to be a Jew in those years. Why didn't he stay in Morocco, which would have made a huge difference a few weeks later when the Americans came to North Africa and reinstalled freedom?

Sylvain and I wouldn't have given much thought about the harshness of the uncivilized period of time, and wouldn't have cared much about the condition of life if we had something to eat, and some shoes to wear. I recall mornings when we would go to school in the darkness of the early hours with no food in our stomach and no shoes on our feet.

We finally got lucky in our misery. The grocery store that was forced to close in the basement of our building at the signature of the armistice, reopened as an *espadrilles* fabric. That was a kind of shoes with a canvas upper and a sole of twisted rope. At least we weren't going around barefoot for a while. But those espadrilles didn't last too long and were somehow expensive for our small income. The shoes started cutting on the top, then the rope untwisted, and we had to walk barefoot again until Mom had enough money to buy a new pair.

* * *

Soon after the reopening of our school, Sylvain was abruptly told by our principal that he wasn't welcome in the establishment any longer per order of the legal authorities, which meant the Nazis through our dear Marshal Pétain. Sylvain was suddenly the happiest kid in the district, and I envied him, of course. No more homework, lessons to memorize, punishment to endure, and no more walk in the cold mornings with no shoes on his feet. Why wasn't I born a Jew?

But it wouldn't be long before I changed my mind on his luck to be a descendant of the ancient Hebrews. To be a Jew was a very dangerous state under Hitler's dictatorship, which extended to the whole Europe.

* * *

I lied when I said Germans took everything from us. They didn't like Jerusalem artichokes we called *topinambours*. We had plenty of those. Have you ever tried them? Don't. If Germans didn't like them, it was for a good reason. Topinambours tasted like shit though I don't really know what feces taste like. Lucky me. But even starving we couldn't eat those weird looking vegetables. Spaniards have a saying, *"Para la hambre no hay pan duro."* For hunger there is no stale bread. Yeah, right! Who said that never had to eat Jerusalem artichokes. And we also had tons of turnips, the tasteless vegetables Germans didn't like either. Mom made miracles with those rutabagas.

She would cook them in different ways to give them some taste. Good taste as strange as it seems. How did she manage that remarkable achievement? No one in the family had ever figured it out, but we ate turnips every day. Twice.

I tried, during those years of general food shortage, not to crave anything for I was afraid to miss those things.

* * *

But while we all starved, the aforementioned General Charles de Gaulle was putting together in the country a secret apparatus —not secret to everyone though, and certainly not to the Germans—to liven up the morose state of the French people. Groups were formed in secret places, each with specific tasks. Mainly killing Nazis.

Germans soldiers were usually transferred by trains or by trucks from one point to another with equipment, armament, and ammunitions. So, those groups of men —we called them *résistants*— blew the trains, the trucks and the Germans up.

The occupiers retaliated, of course, with rage and the blessing of Philippe Pétain, our infamous traitor, who sent the gendarmes along with the Gestapo to arrest suspicious Frenchmen. They were executed by firing squads, which executions begot more blowups and, of course, more firing squads. A very scary vicious circle.

* * *

Dad closed his shop one day without notice, and the next thing we knew, he was gone. And we hadn't the faintest idea where he went, though Mom seemed to know something we didn't.

Years later we all knew. Dad said, "It was no reason for me to tell you where I was going and why I was doing that stupid thing."

When, at the end of the war my father received the *Military Cross* from General de Gaulle himself, I'm sure Mom was proud of him. And so was I.

6

And then, what happened December 7, 1941? Another idiot in the Pacific named Hiro Hito, whose subjects believed he was a deity (what a joke! Sounds like one of my father's), decided to attack Pearl Harbor without any provocation whatsoever from the United States or from anybody else. This was a huge miscalculation from the Japanese. How huge? They found out later the hard way.

And that was the straw that.... The whole world exploded.

Americans, in their gentleness and confidence, were not prepared for that kind of surprise attack. But they realized rapidly what they had to do to get on their feet.

Eventually the Japanese would pay the price for their treachery, as would the Nazis on the other face of the world, but some time later.

* * *

On November 8, 1942, and I remember very well that day, the Americans landed in Morocco and Algeria, helped by a small group of résistants that had destroyed the whole heavy armament supposed to be used to prevent the landing.

Two days later the enraged Germans occupied the so-called *free zone* like a flow of deleterious lava, so they could balance —or so they thought— the military forces on both sides of the Mediterranean Sea.

And to deteriorate the already rotten climate, Pétain offered the Germans Tunisia, which was at the time a French protectorate. The Nazis invaded the central-eastern part of North Africa to get closer to the Allies.

A few days earlier, France's warships went down in Toulon by the deliberate actions of the crews who fled afterwards to join de Gaulle's forces in London. Germany wouldn't be able to take over the French fleet, now disabled, and use it against the allies.

* * *

Everything then turned from bad to horrible in the now occupied South France. I still remember the ominous day the Nazis arrived in Nice. We were awakened early in the morning with the sinister grating of tanks' caterpillars on the paved streets. Scattered here and there, small groups of people watched in silence the dreadful invasion with disgust and an incommensurable fear.

A big sign 'KOMMANDANTUR' (German Army headquarter) was hung on the city hall's frontispiece. And above, a huge swastika flag was attached to a long staff. What an ugly sight! But that wasn't the only distressful vision. Within a week Gestapo (short for Geheime Staats Polizei), made their first appearance, and at the same time the infamous black-dressed Waffen SS (Schutzstaffeln) were seen all over like rats on a landfill.

Six months later, at the brink of summer 1943, France had unwillingly become German in her entirety.

For almost two years, Germans had stayed in the northern part of the country. We heard, of course, about the brutality of their retaliations against our *résistants*, their shooting and their trains crammed with people sent to concentration camps in Germany. Buchenwald, Mathausen, Dachau, were sinister in all minds.

But the fate of the northern part of France was somehow remote from our own city and, though what we heard wasn't pleasant, we felt selfishly almost happy. We didn't talk much about the ordeal the

Northerners were living. We didn't know really how bad it was for them. We were about to find out.

* * *

Dad was —I know I've already said that— a compulsive storyteller like most barbers. They get bored cutting hair. Nothing fun about that. So they talk about anything that comes to their minds and bore their customers. Most of the times with insipid stuff no one is interested in, and certainly not the clients. Years later, after my Dad retired of sort I found a barber I was happy with. He was mute. Real mute though a very gifted craftsman. I didn't know if he was deaf as well. I never asked. And he never said a word to his customers.

My father talked a lot albeit his stammering. But he had never said a word about what he did after he left home to join the *résistance* in the mountains with two other men of our apartment complex. Not a word until the war was well over. And even then he was reluctant to talk. Bad memories, he would say, are even worse when we call them back.

At that time no one knew where they were though Mom said, much later, that she had then an idea of their whereabouts. We were not supposed to talk about, but everybody knew what they were up to.

And so did the gendarmes who came once to our home and asked for my father. I was terrified and I believe Mom also was. But she kept her composure and said with —I learned later— a fake anger, "I wish I knew where the bastard is. He forgot he has a son and a daughter. Not talking about me."

I asked her, after the gendarmes were gone, why she called Dad a bastard. She smiled, one of those rare smiles filled with the compassion that, once in a while, showed in her beautiful eyes. "I don't believe, François, they will come back soon, after my outburst," she whispered as if the policemen were still in the room. "At least they pretended to believe me. Did you see their smile? I think we still have good people among them, people who think like us and will try to help us."

* * *

The first time I heard about the usual line of work of those called résistants, was a few months after the end of the war. Alphonse Renard, one of my father's companions during the war, told us a story that would give anyone the creeps and a deep feeling of uneasiness. I was then fifteen, I believe. But even then, Alphonse didn't give any names. Real names I mean. Mouth shut was the rule during the war and even for some time after. First names only were used to communicate and most of the time they were false. No one liked to prate about his business during the war. Some boastful idiots bragged about what they had done, here and there, in the résistance. Most of the time, if not all the time, it was only lies for no one was proud of what the war had made of them: terrorists and murderers, as the Germans called them, although heroes, as the French named them. No matter who they killed and for whatever reason, ending the life of human beings was still a terrible action.

Alphonse was clear about that. He had no self-pride or boastfulness for what he had done. He didn't like blowing up trains or road convoys but, as he said, Germans started the cycle. They first came to France uninvited, imposed their inflexible laws, their brutality, their hatred of the French people, and other people as well, and executed in cold blood whoever didn't observe those laws.

The résistants retaliated as brutally, killing Germans and the Germans reciprocated executing civilians who, for most of them, had nothing to do with the onslaught. The SS's and the Gestapo would surround an area in the city, then search a building at random for men. And sometimes women would do. Seldom would those men or women be sent to a prison to be executed the next day after a severe and brutal interrogation. Most of the time there would be summary justice, and people would be shot in front of their own apartment building leaving the cadavers where they had fallen, to be taken away by relatives or friends. I've seen once those dead. It was bloodcurdling. It was the first time I'd seen dead people and it terrified me.

Alphonse came home invited on a Sunday. That was when I'd heard what Dad and his friends had done between 1942 and 1944. Then the allies landed, and everything became legal. Or sort of.

"It was in the wee hours that morning," Alphonse said after dinner, and Dad was listening without a word. "We came into town six of us, six goddamned crazy people moving like ghosts in the *Vieux Nice* (Old District of Nice). A woman was amongst us. Odette, you remember, Pierre?"

"She was a tough lady with huge brown eyes, and her hair cut like a boy, and she was adorable," Dad replied. "What a pity."

"Yes. She was arrested that same night," Alphonse said with a shrug, "as we parted to rejoin our camp in Lantosque. Along with two other friends. What were their names, Pierre?"

"Two brothers, Antoine and Fernand. We knew they were tortured before the Germans shot them."

"How did you know that?" Mom asked.

"We had one of our guys there, in the prison; Louis. He was a gendarme appointed as a guard. He's still working at the jail. Louis wasn't his name, of course. He was the one who told us that Major Shultz had the habit to visit a certain nightclub in Nice every Friday after dark. Curfew didn't apply to German officers."

"Antoine and Fernand were indeed tortured," Alphonse continued, "before they were shot the next morning. So, we assumed they had talked about our place, and us and indeed they had. We moved from one site to another on our mountain. It wasn't easy in a middle of a moonless freezing night. We came down from the hills six of us, and returned three. Fifty per cent. Not bad for all accounts."

"Not too bad indeed," Dad said, "except for them."

Mom had got on her feet to pour some wine into the men's glasses. She was shaking and spilled some on the table. "It could have been you."

"Yes, it could. That's what we called luck. It was a risk we had to take. We all six volunteered for that dirty job."

"We arrived around two in the morning," Alphonse kept going as he ignored Mom and Dad's private dialogue. "No movement whatsoever in the darkness of the streets but the occasional SS patrol and the animation of a little club named *Le Chat Noir* (the Black Cat), a popular bar before the war but now frequented only by German officers and their French mistresses. Outside the club were a line of khaki Mercedes-Benzes with dozing military chauffeurs at the wheel, who waited for their drunk officers and their sluts."

Then, it was a long silence as Alphonse turned his glance around.

I remember, Dad got on his feet obviously moved by the memory, and left the room. We were all ears and Mom was now crying in silence. She knew what was coming up and, even after that long elapsed time, she had shuddered recalling what my father had probably told her in the privacy of their bedroom when he had stealthily visited us.

"We were there, as we waited deep into the shadow of the narrow streets. We could hear the music from the club, and the sound of German voices singing *Lily Marlene*, the song made popular by the German actress Marlene Dietrich with her strange raucous voice.

It was cold that night, enough to freeze water in the gutter, but no one complained and no one said a word.

"Then, here he came, the dignified though inebriated officer. A *Sturmbannführer*, a Waffen SS major, the collar of his shirt wide

35

open in spite of the cold, staggering toward us, a cigarette between his lips. He was the man we waited for. *Herr Major* was looking for a dark spot in the street, behind the club, to release his surplus of beer."

Another long silence as Dad returned to the dining room. I would have sworn he had cried. He shrugged as he glanced at Mom, and then sat down near Alphonse. "You grabbed the German with your hand on his mouth," Dad said, "and Antoine was the one who killed him. All in silence except for the sigh of the dying officer's last breath.

"That was three years ago and I still can't imagine what we'd done that night." Dad smiled joylessly at Mom with another shrug as if it wasn't his fault. "Right after the war," he said, "I returned to the Vieux Nice Quarter, and I looked for the street corner where we had killed the major. I'd swear I could still see some dried blood on the curb. I wonder whom he left behind in Germany. Wife, kids, mother?"

No one spoke, amazed and terrified by the story.

Dad kept on. "We had blown trains and trucks, and barracks, and even once a plane for it was war. But I never had such a bad feeling like that night. To kill someone in cold blood was, at the time, beyond my toughest Christian thoughts."

"The rest was easy," Alphonse continued. "We wanted to make an example of Sturmbannführer Shulz for he was responsible for hundreds of dead among the French population of Nice. We put a long rope around his neck and his body and lifted him at the top of a telephone pole. A macabre vision. Blood was still dripping from his wound. We left him there for everyone to see at daybreak.

"We parted when we left the premises with one objective: Gather in the mountains in our secret place as soon as possible. It was three in the morning and we had a long way to go and SS patrols to avoid. But three of us didn't make it. Up in the mountains, we waited for our friends for over an hour. And then, we knew they had fallen into a German trap somewhere in the city."

"And what about the explosion that night of April?" Mom asked.

"Well, that was fun or sort of," Dad said with a quick glance at Alphonse.

That happened a few months before the Americans landed a hundred miles from Nice. And meanwhile, we still lived in a city infested with Germans.

7

December 23, 1943. What a chilly day it was! The Mistral was blowing like crazy down the Rhône Valley to reach Nice with one hundred-mile gusts. No one dared to step out in this wind and moreover, in this kind of cold. No snow or rain for over twenty-four hours. The fringes of the roofs held stalactites, which were like dangerous daggers.

The next day would be Christmas Eve. But who cared? Perhaps the Germans or at least those who had kept their Christian faith. To tell the truth, couldn't be many. But this is perhaps a personal opinion.

It's, in a normal time, a French custom to lay our shoes in front of the fireplace before going to bed, light a nice, comfortable fire, and wait for Santa Clause to bring toys while we are asleep.

But this was war. No toys, no Santa Clause, no joy. The only gifts we had were the krauts. And we hadn't asked for them.

So, what were the options? Light a fire on the hearth ... if you had any firewood, and lay your shoes down ... if you had any shoes.

We had neither one and after Mom had cooked some turnips for dinner, we went to bed keeping all our clothes on to stay warm, and trying to forget that we hadn't much in our tummies.

Dad was at war somewhere in the mountains above Nice making the Germans miserable. We didn't know his whereabouts except that time to time he would come home in the middle of the night for a few minutes and return to his business leaving behind a few francs and the little food he could have gathered on farms.

We didn't expect him for Christmas. Everyone knew that the Germans were particularly alert expecting that those men, missed from home, would try to spend a little time with their families for the holidays. And we couldn't even attend Midnight Mass for the curfew was strictly enforced. But religion wasn't the main concern for Mom. She wasn't a regular churchgoer and only once in a while she would take us, my baby sister and me, to the Cathedral Saint Charles. I didn't believe she knew any prayers, but as she told me once, "It's with your heart you pray, not with words."

I saw her once enter the nave alone, as Sylvain and I played in the church backyard, and I wondered what brought her there. Back home I asked why she went to Saint Charles. "Only to pray for your father," she replied, "and for the war to end. I don't know if God heard me, but I hope so."

"He heard you, Mom," I said hugging her, "He heard you."

Unlike Mom I was a churchgoer, though I don't believe I was a very religious boy. But with my friend Sylvain Bénichou we had a great time serving as altar boys. I wasn't sure Sylvain ever understood what was said at Mass, but he was my friend, and he didn't care what was going on at the church as long as we were together and we had fun.

The priest of the parish, Father Schiaffino, was a very gentle old man. He was skinny and dirty with a long gray beard and rheumy eyes and dragged behind him the smell of a sewer. The fun, for us altar boys, started when we would steal his hosts and drink his wine while he dozed on his rocking chair in the sacristy snoring like a motorboat. I don't believe Sylvain's parents were aware of their son ignoring the religious laws of the Talmud. And if they were, they never said a word, for synagogues were closed anyway in occupied France and Jewish people were forced to read their Torah at home where no one could hear them.

Across the street, and two blocks down from the cathedral, was a minuscule Baptist church, the pastor of which was a lanky middle-aged man with an amiable smile. He would welcome us, the neighborhood kids, into his backyard where we would play the little war —as if the big one wasn't enough— until our mothers yelled for us to run home. I've forgotten the pastor's name, if I ever knew it.

Sylvain, like all the boys we knew, was a familiar with the Baptist church, and I always wondered which religion he liked better besides, of course, his own which he wasn't allowed to worship.

At two in the morning on Christmas Day, I finally received my Christmas present. My father came home for a short visit. We imagined how hard it must have been for him to sneak between two SS patrols in the darkness of a freezing night during the curfew. But he managed somehow. He brought some food and a little money for Mom.

Just before he left that same night, I told Dad that I would like to join him in the mountains. I thought Mom would hit the roof. "Are you insane or something?" she yelled, and then started crying. I would have sworn Mom's nose had swung, even so slightly.

Dad was much calmer. He smiled and said with a shrug, "You might have a chance —or should I say the disgrace— to be part of this damn war, son." And after a short time of reflection, he added, "If the Americans across the Mediterranean don't make the right move now, this war might last forever. You are thirteen years old, François. May God prevent you from seeing what we endure in the mountains."

"I know what a gun is, Dad," I said split between the pain I caused to Mom and the desire I had to be with my father. "And I sure know what a German looks like."

Dad smiled, a disarming smile I knew so well. "Let me tell you," he said, "If the Germans are still here on your next birthday, you'll come with me. Deal?"

Not everything that happened during that very same night was a

Christmas gift. Just before dawn, two Gestapo men along with two French gendarmes came to our building. The racket was loud enough to awaken everyone in the apartment complex. Dogs barked and kids cried in the courtyard.

I watched my friend Sylvain taken away with his parents. I didn't know what would happen to them except that they were probably heading to Dachau, the place we all called the *Camp of the Death*.

* * *

A few months later the American Expeditionary Corps landed a few miles from Nice. That day, as if by magic, the Germans disappeared from our city. All that was left of them was a despised swastika, which was emblazoned on a flag draped on the City Hall's frontispiece. And the nightmare was over. Several hundreds men and women in the prisons in Nice knew they had their life back. And so did my father.

But that was another story.

8

I'd lost my friend Sylvain and I felt like an orphan, forlorn in the middle of nowhere. Like a twin who had lost his brother.
Dad had returned to his duty in the mountains above Nice or somewhere else. Nobody knew. And it was better. We heard about trains derailed, bridges blown up, German convoys pulverized, and I knew Dad was somewhere around and part of it.
And I, poor me, had to return to school. Without my friend and without any hope that war would end some time soon.
I was in the eighth grade and willing to drop out the next day if I were allowed. But then I recalled Mom who had said once, that I'd attend school as long as she lived, I like it or not.
Germans were still there, but the cold weather was gone. Spring is a marvelous season on the Mediterranean coast. The Côte d'Azur, some call it Riviera, had always attracted the vacationers —mostly British— all year-round. But not for a few years now when another kind of tourist stormed the country. We could see them everywhere distinguishable with their verdigris uniforms and their stern faces. Gestapo swarmed the place, also recognizable with their black leather coats and their felts down to their eyes, driving black *Tractions-Avant* (front wheel drive) *Citroën* whose sight everyone dreaded. Gestapo meant people arrested, dragged to the prison or, sometimes, just shot in front of an apartment unit. Most of the time their own building. Years later one could see the scars of the bullets on the walls. People refused to fix those holes. They wanted to remember.

* * *

In North Africa things were going well for the allies. Dad came one night for a short visit. As usual he had brought a little money and some food. He had also a map folded in his pocket. He unfolded it showing Algeria and Tunisia where American, British and French flags were drawn. "Here are the Americans," he said showing a red line in a middle of Tunisia. "Under the command of General Patton, they are kicking Germans' butts one at the time. "Never heard of him, huh Son?" Dad said.

"Not lately, no," I remember I replied. "Who's that guy?

"We know him in the mountains. We helped two American paratroopers that brought us some good equipment. A radio, among other things, where we can listen to the American broadcasting in French."

"Would that be good?" I asked with a glance at Mom.

"You damn right, it's good," Dad replied. "They will be here before you can say shit."

"Oops!" Mom shouted. "Watch your mouth Hector."

Here we go again, I thought. Mom must be mad again or she wouldn't have called Dad Hector. "Pierre," I said smiling. "Pierre is his name, Mom."

"Yeah, right. It's Hector for me when he talks dirty," Mom said, but then smiled.

"Well, the kid has to learn some day, no?" Hector said.

Yes right, I thought, Mom and Dad would be surprised to hear how much I knew. I even smoked a cigar once, which Sylvain stole from Father Schiaffino. I didn't like it. Mom must have known for she asked me, when I got home, if I'd been smoking. "Not me," I lied, and then ran to the bathroom and threw up for ten minutes. Mom did me the favor not to ask again about smoking. An experience I didn't repeat.

There was a short silence, and then Mom said, "You know, Pierre,

Monsieur Farelacci died yesterday."

"I'm sorry to hear that," Dad replied looking at me. He used to cut his hair when he was still a barber. "I know how you loved the old man. What happened?"

Monsieur Farelacci was one of our teachers at Jules Renard High School. He was a Corsican who had retired years before from teaching but was recalled for duty for all the young teachers were away, at war with de Gaulle, prisoners in German camps or, just like my father, in the mountains killing krauts like crazy.

The teacher was an envoy of God; it couldn't have been otherwise. All my friends loved him for his gentleness, his caring, and the stories he liked to tell, with his heavy Corsican accent, about the island and the city of Ajaccio where he and Napoléon were born a century apart. He would always recall how he admired the emperor, and how he would have enjoyed life during the prestigious era of Napoléon Bonaparte. Every day he would have a five-minutes break for an anecdote about the great Corsican and his life.

But he was an old man. Probably over seventy years of age, head and shoulders bent forward, gray hair, and a pair of half-moon spectacles over which he would watch us with a false expression of severity.

We never knew for sure about his age except that he was a widower and lonely for many years. He didn't have any children or relatives, and when he died, that Friday morning as he taught History, I'm sure no one missed him but us, his pupils.

I ran to the principal, monsieur Forestier (Yes, I still remember his name) after monsieur Farelacci collapsed between two rows of tables. When we arrived in the classroom, our teacher was dead, eyes closed, his back on the floor, and his crotch stained with his lax bowels.

It was the second time I had seen a dead man and it was much more disturbing than the first time. We were struck with sadness for that sudden death left us almost orphans. The class was called for the day, and we all left school with tears in our eyes and thoughts in our little minds. Who's going to replace our dear Monsieur Farelacci?

The following Monday we had the most agreeable surprise — we're so sorry Monsieur Farelacci, wherever you are— when we met with the new teacher. It was a lady, an extremely beautiful lady. Her name was Ms. Barbier, and all of a sudden, the whole classroom fell in love with her. And I believe the whole school also did including the other teachers.

Twenty years later, I was then living in Monte-Carlo, I met accidentally a former classmate I hadn't seen since I left Jules Renard High. I've forgotten his name, but I remember his first words. "Do you remember Ms. Barbier?" he asked me with a smile knowing that no one could forget the gorgeous teacher.

Although she didn't have our late teacher's gift to be a good raconteur, she was a fine Geography and History educator. Her constant smile helped us to comprehend and to love the two difficult subjects. I didn't worry much for any subject was difficult for me, anyway. I think I started being interested in those matters the day Ms. Barbier began teaching at Jules Renard. Where did she come from? Probably from heaven. We never knew, and we didn't care as long as she was there.

I read every book on History I could put my hands on. And I decided, already in the eighth grade that I would be a teacher, whether in History or in Spanish for I was equally fond of anything related to the Iberian Peninsula. But first I wanted to marry Ms. Barbier.

9

Early one morning in April 1944, around four o'clock, we were awakened by a frightening explosion that shook up the whole city. Mom ran out of her bedroom as she put a robe on her shoulders. "What happened?" I asked. "You think it could be Dad?"

"I don't know but probably, him and his crazy friends," she replied shaking. "You know they think they can win the war by themselves. Let's go down the street and check out where that comes from."

"Mom!" I stopped her, "it's still dark out there and you know how Germans love to shoot people who dare to be on the street in the middle of the night. Curfew, remember, Mom?"

"Yes, sometimes I forget," she replied, "after such a long time I'm still not used to it. Let's wait until daylight. In the meantime I'll make some coffee."

We could hardly wait. Mom brewed the usual ersatz coffee made of roasted date seeds. Didn't smell like coffee and didn't taste like coffee. I never could figure out what that ersatz tasted like. Perhaps manure, but I didn't try that either so I wouldn't know for sure. We were used to that kind of crap since the Germans invaded our country and took everything from us. No one complained any more. It was that or nothing. We added some goat milk —the kind our visitors didn't like— and it would do.

When finally sunbeams filtered through the curtainless windows of our apartment, we went down the street. Almost everyone in the building was awake and wondering what the explosion was about.

In the courtyard young toddlers had started their traditional clamor as the continuous and disturbing bark of a half dozen dogs covered the angry voices of scurrilous moms shouting obscenities to their young offspring. A rooster was crowing on the top of an overfilled garbage can as a couple of chickens cackled around. We never knew to whom the chickens belonged but they disappeared one by one probably eaten during a worse food shortage. We didn't know by whom.

What a mess our apartment unit was early that morning. But it was nothing new. No wonder the residents of the other buildings on Mirabeau Street called it *La Cour des Miracles* (The Courtyard of the Miracles) in relation with the infamous area in Paris, in the sixteenth and seventeenth centuries, when vagrants had the right of sanctuary. Victor Hugo vividly depicted the infamous Cour des Miracles in his novel *Notre Dame de Paris*.

It was perhaps not as bad but still our courtyard was a terrible place to be at any given time, day or night. In a way, it was a blessing for even Germans didn't care much about checking on us in our building. Except for the day two gendarmes came home asking for my father, the only moment I'd seen police and Gestapo in our courtyard was when Sylvain and his parents were taken away in the wee hours on Christmas Day.

* * *

Rue Mirabeau crossed rue Meyerbeer that reached, on its north end, the train station, and on the south, the *Promenade des Anglais* (Englishmen Promenade) that overhung the beach. The Promenade was famous since its construction in 1863 for it was the site of predilection of numerous English people, hence its name, —as well as many other nationals— who looked for nice weather in south France during the rigor of cold months in their own countries.

From the promenade, just across rue Meyerbeer, was a wooden jetty which stuck out into the sea about two hundred feet. At the end of the pier was a large platform on which a sumptuous building in rococo style stood for the last fifty years. It served as a public room for entertainment, dancing, and gambling. We knew it as *Le Casino*. Before the war it was a gathering place of rich and famous people, but since the Germans arrived in Nice the high ranked military personnel and their female companions only frequented it.

We arrived on the Promenade where official vehicles were parked at the curb and the casino was no longer to be seen. Instead, a nice fire was consuming the remnants of what had been a glorious landmark on the Riviera. Debris was washed onto the beach where, not long ago, Dad and I used to come for a swim. German soldiers were everywhere. The explosion, everybody knew, happened at four in the morning. The casino couldn't be crowded at the time and the casualties couldn't have been significant.

When we met with Alphonse and Dad some time later, they were laughing. "The explosion was fun in the middle of the night," Alphonse had said, " but it wasn't us."

"What do you mean it wasn't you?" I asked disappointed. "Another group?"

"Yes. The Germans themselves," Dad said with a chuckle. "We have thought about blowing up of the casino for some time. But we would have done that in the middle of a party, not at four in the morning."

"And why would the Germans do that?" Mom asked. They seemed to enjoy the casino."

"Germans considered the building as a hazard," Alphonse said, "an insalubrious hazard. So they decided to blow it up. It's too bad. We would have done better."

10

I recall one day, in the period between the release of Dad from the army after the armistice was signed by Marshall Pétain, and the day he left us to join the Résistance, we went for a swim as we usually did in summer time. I asked him, as we were floating, how far was America. He had looked at me with a smile and said, "Not that far, just across the Atlantic."

"Well," I said, "I won't go today, not swimming anyway."

"Why not? Keep swimming we might get somewhere."

That was the first time I've talked or thought about America. "Have you any idea how it is over there?" I asked my father. He had no idea besides that America was way on the other side of the ocean.

Watching movies at the Empire Theatre near home before the war we'd learned a handful of tips. Those films showed what was the normal and common life for the average American. Great life that was if we believed the images sent by Hollywood; huge mansions, with flocks of servants moving swiftly around, offering cocktails to idle young men and women casually dressed with designer clothes, dawdling around an Olympic-size swimming pool. Yes! Beautiful.

Then, of course, those same young people would take a quick promenade on board a sixty-five foot cabin cruiser. This would be on a lake that mirrored the snow-crowned mountains where they had been skiing early that morning in company of the movie stars Sonja Henni and John Payne, and the famous Glenn Miller orchestra.

It would be then time to return to the mansion, and dress up for dinner. Men would wear tuxedos and bowties, and ladies elegant evening gowns. The women would smoke cigarettes with long ivory holders, hands gloved up to the elbows, and a smile across their perfectly made-up faces.

Everyone spent his or her time that way in America, Dad had said. I knew that.

And that was the life I wanted to live by any means. That was the country I wanted to go to. But not swimming though.

In France it was another story, as expected. No swimming pools, no cocktails, no tuxedos, and no young men for they all were at war.

I thought about the Americans being not so far south of France. Just across the Mediterranean were those same people who, we knew, used to enjoy the huge mansions and the great life I aforementioned. What were they doing in North Africa? Why didn't they come where they were the most needed? Well, Dad told us that it wouldn't be long before the allies showed up on our shores. They had already kicked out the Germans from Tunisia and Sardinia, and were now strolling toward north Italy making short work of the Wehrmacht.

So, what were they waiting for? We were in the middle of June, and school had ended a few days before. Nothing to do until October when classes would resume. Dad was still in the mountains unless he had joined the allies in Normandy where they had landed a few days before.

British, French and Americans now stormed the northwest part of the country pushing the enemy eastward. And it was a nice feeling for everyone. Part of the German occupation forces in south France had joined their brothers in arms somewhere in Normandy keeping here just enough military forces and Gestapo to harass the population for the last time. More French were arrested, and more executions carried on.

And, in the meantime, members of the organized underground were preparing the landing of the allies.

Unfortunately, the last blow from the Germans was a brutal one and the most terrifying cold-blooded assassination by the Nazi army in France's occupation history. That happened in a little village named Oradour-sur-Glane that lay twenty miles north of Limoges in the Haute-Vienne *département* among peaceful rolling farm country. For two days German troops were passing through the village, not even slowing down, heading north towards Normandy.

One unit wasn't in a hurry: the fanatic SS division *Das Reich* under the order of Obergruppenführer Rolf Stundt a psychopath who told as a joke that he never ate human brains with a silver spoon as someone had said. He used a gold one.

The SS arrived at Oradour a little after noon on June 10, 1944, four days after the allies had landed in Normandy. It was a magnificent day in the village. The sky was of a sumptuous blue and the little breeze that came from the hills was refreshing. On the streets no one, for the inhabitants were listening to the good news on the radio that gave the latest on the advance of the allies on the Normandy front. Soon they would be in their village and the war would be over for them.

There was happiness and hope among those men and women. War's end would finally come to their village.

But the SS were a few hours ahead of the allies. American, British and French troops were after them. Nonetheless, Germans had plenty of time to check on the villagers. They gathered all the men and shot them without further ado. The women and children were brought together in the only church of the village, and brutally shot. Then the SS set the old construction on fire.

What a sad end of the war for those villagers. Nothing was left but forty acres of charred houses and 642 cadavers.

* * *

And the miracle happened on August 15, 1944. The first Franco-

American assault waves landed between Fréjus and Saint-Tropez. On August 28, the humiliated German garrisons of Marseille and Toulon handed their weapons to the allies. September 3, Nice was liberated and, as by enchantment, the whole population was on the streets, and this time with exultant joy and pride.

We have seen for many years, before that day, trucks full of soldiers, tanks rolling their caterpillars on the streets pavement, canons towed behind armored vehicles, and flags hung all over. And I remember it was a dreadful spectacle.

But this time they were American. So why did the people seem so happy? What was the difference between one army and another one?

"For one," Mom said as we watched the friendly invasion, "look at those faces. Look at their smiles. Remember the stern faces of the Germans? Remember how frightening they were? Their ugly flags displayed on their tanks and trucks didn't help to welcome them. We knew what they were up to, and we already hated them."

I was fourteen years old at the time, and I wondered why and how our lives could have changed so drastically within one day. September 3, 1944.

Of course, Germans might have forgotten the amazing feat of that glorious day. One thing's for sure . . . I'll never forget.

11

Life had resumed except that Dad was still at war somewhere up north with General de Gaulle's army. He was no longer an army barber, and I was pretty sure he could use a rifle by now. In World War I he learned to be a hairdresser. In World War II he studied the art of killing Germans. What a difference a war made. "I thought it was awful but that was life," Mom said. Or was it death?... I wondered.

A few days after the allies landed on the southern coast, we received a letter from my father. That was what we thought. He was fighting the Germans though he didn't say where. Of course we assumed he battled in Normandy for our enemy opposed a fierce resistance there trying to prevent the allies from getting to Germany. "Futile effort," Mom had said. "Our men will kick those damn Germans out of our country and even into theirs. Hitler has no way out. There is no other issue to that war. Five years now, and we aren't through yet. But we'll be there soon." It was the first time I heard Mom use the word *damn*. War had changed her too.

After a short silence, my mother grabbed my arm and smiled. "Let's go to the church, we have to pray for your father, Charles de Gaulle and a guy named *Douait David Ensenover*. We have to thank them for what we have today. Freedom."

Some time later that day I knew who Mom was talking about. It was General Dwight David Eisenhower, the Chief of Staff in Europe.

Mom was back to the little restaurant where she had been working since Dad went to war. Food wasn't yet in profusion, but not any longer scarce. We could buy bread —delicious American bread—

eggs and milk, and meat, and chocolate, and all kinds of food we hadn't seen in the store for almost five years. We could find various products imported or brought from America. Peanut butter, I never had before, was one of them. Our own products weren't going to the Germans anymore but distributed among the French.

For the first time, on September 4, the day following the arrival of our American friends, we had real coffee at home. Mom would make some *café au lait*, an entire bowl of milk and a few drops of coffee. I wasn't sure I remembered the taste of coffee before the war, but this was delicious. And when I left for school, Mom gave me a small flat wrapped strip that looked like a bandage. "What is it?" I asked.

"Chin-chin gone," Mom said with a grin. "I got it from an American soldier at the restaurant. You will like it."

Some time later I found out that Mother meant to say *chewing gum*. I didn't remember if I had any before the war, though Mom said I did, but to the best of my knowledge it was the first time in my life I was chewing gum. And I was already fourteen years old.

* * *

The Café de la Gare where Mom was a cook was busy with American soldiers. She made a nice living there, brought home more money than I ever saw and good food which was not leftovers. Mother looked, for the first time in months, almost happy. She smiled and even laughed a lot, though her beautiful green eyes had kept their usual sadness. I believed Mom was crying in her bedroom, but she never showed her tears in front of Juliette and me. She was a tough lady as she had proved oftentimes.

* * *

On a Sunday morning I was on the beach, a few blocks from

home, as were many people since the German occupiers had disappeared from our lives. The weather was gorgeous as is supposed to be on any day in October. Not a cloud in the azure-blue sky, and the little breeze that blew from the south wasn't strong enough to ruffle the surface of the ocean. I was in paradise though I missed Dad fighting somewhere with the French army.

That was where I met Jimmy Gunn. I'll never forget his name, or his face. He was next to me lying on the pebbles, his shirt off, his forage cap on his face, and already as red as a boiled langoustine. That guy, I thought, was going to have a tough time in bed tonight.

When finally he sat up and I could see his face, I discovered a young soldier, very blond with very blue eyes, a little mustache that failed to give him the look of a mature man, and a huge scar across his narrow chest that was still held by stitches. He reached into a haversack and pulled a large sandwich made of that American bread I loved so much. He looked at me and, smiling, he said in an approximate French, "You want some?"

I was starved but I couldn't accept. I asked him what he was doing on the beach. "I'm a convalescent," he said showed me his scar. "And now sun bathing in your beautiful city."

"Sun bathing? Rather sun cooking I believe."

He laughed and I ran to the water for a little swim, regretting already that I had turned down his offer. He stayed there watching me, finishing his sandwich, and broiling a little more.

* * *

School had resumed a month before and the first thing that stunned me and, I conceded, even shocked me, was the disappearance of Marshal Pétain's portrait that was hung above the blackboard. We have been watching the gentle face of the marshal for over four years. All that time we, children in the grade school, had been told that he was the greatest man in the world. And all of a sudden he was declared persona non grata, a traitor and an assassin. It was surprising and disappointing but I believed, ineluctably. Pétain, we were told, has done enough damage to deserve this.

As soon as I could, I volunteered to enroll in the English class now allowed. That was the most important thing for me to do if I wanted to go to America and enjoy the big mansions and the way of life we all heard of. So, as I learned a little English —about a dozen words the first week— and as the young G.I. could speak a little French, we communicated almost like old pals.

I wanted to practice the little I'd learned in a month, and he was happy with that. He told me he was almost nineteen years old and fighting in Italy for the last three months. That was where he got his wound, he explained. For the time being he was convalescing after being treated in the hospital Saint-Roch in Nice for the last month. But good times came to an end, he complained. He had to join his company somewhere in northern Italy, "To pursue the Germans until they surrender," he said laughing.

I saw Jimmy Gunn after school at the beach the following ten or twelve days. He always had something for me. A sandwich, a chocolate bar, chewing gum, of course, and even a jar of orange marmalade he brought me to take home.

I was going to miss my new friend, for sure. We started understanding each other quite well. I was learning from him, and he was from me.

Two days before he left for Italy I asked Mom if I could invite Jimmy home so he could have a decent meal instead of sandwiches before he went off to war.

That was the way Mom and Juliette met Jimmy Gunn.

My mother had cooked a beautiful *Canard à l'orange*, Jimmy never had before.

That day I met him on the beach and we walked home. He carried his usual haversack and I wondered why since he didn't have to bring his lunch that day.

I found out why when we got home. Jimmy filled up our pantry with all kind of food in cans, in bottles, and in jars. Mom was confused and embarrassed, but Juliette had smiled the whole time Jimmy was there, and one could read in her eyes that she had suddenly fallen in love with my friend. She was almost twelve years old.

Jimmy Gunn was from a little town in Georgia, I had at that time forgotten the name. A few years later, after he disappeared from our life, I tried to find that city with the help of maps and almanac books. To no avail. I was thinking that, if he hadn't been killed in the war, he might be alive and living in his hometown. But we didn't know.

* * *

After Jimmy had left, late that evening, Mom said something I didn't think about. "We never had a German guest with us, have we? I wonder why."

I meditated for a long time on my mother's statement. After so many years have flown away, I'm still not sure why. You can't explain friendship and love, can you?

12

Jimmy wasn't gone a month yet that we received a letter from Italy. It could have been a nice letter —and probably was— if we could have decrypted at least a few words, but my knowledge in that damn language didn't go beyond those brief common expressions; the sky is blue, good morning, thank you, chewing gum, bread and chocolate.

I brought the letter to school to show my teacher, Ms. Falk, an old English lady, tall and skinny, who looked like a dry vine shoot but much less attractive. Yet, she was a nice person as I found out some time later. The students had done to her what they shouldn't have done; horrible practical jokes, making fun of her, drawing cartoons on the blackboard supposed to represent her, and being insufferable ninth grade assholes.

Oh, I've done my share of stupid things too. I remember a day when she walked into the class —in France high school teachers move from one class to the next, not the students, unless it has changed since my years— and she sat down on her chair where I had emptied my inkpot a few minutes before. Of course she found out when she got home that her skirt was stained with black ink. But she had no idea in which class she had deserved such a sad treatment. And, of course, much less who did it.

Well, in my supreme obnoxiousness and stupidity, I repeated the same brainless joke the next morning. Ms. Falk walked straight to her chair, stared at it, and knew right away in which class the offense had originated. The rest was easy. "Who did it?" she asked. "I want an answer before I discipline the whole classroom. It's that simple."

I got caught like the slow-learning jackass I was. I had to confess my crime for my classmates would have lynched me at the morning break if I didn't. But, at my astonishment, she didn't punish me, and I always wondered why. She just shrugged and cleaned up the chair. I knew then that she was a great lady though very, very ugly. She never got married and we never knew if she ever had a boyfriend. How could she? We couldn't picture her with kids. How ugly they would have been?

Of course, I never spilled my ink again and Ms. Falk was grateful for that. She told me once when I met her in the local library.

Nevertheless, she kindly translated Jimmy's letter, wondering how I could have made an American friend in such a short time. "Actually," I said, "It was him who befriended me."

I wrote back to him...in French, being sure he would find someone who could speak my language. We wrote to each other during the following months, and, all of a sudden, I didn't receive any more letters. Americans, French, British, and even Russians were in Germany finishing up those poor Germans who were also fed up with the lengthy war. Adolph Hitler was dead in his bunker and so was his wife, Eva Braun, both burnt beyond recognition and wizened like two marshmallows. How convenient: *beyond recognition*. But that is another story and I'm not sure that they were really dead. A rumor ran for a while about Adolph and Eva stealthily leaving Germany and ending up in a country in South America. I promise myself to make some research though I believe the official truth was that they were burnt to a cinder. But...But.

As for our beloved Marshall Pétain, he was tried and condemned to death. Finally the judges changed their minds and sent him to jail at the venerable age of eighty-eight. He was transferred to l'Île d'Yeu where he died in 1951 at the respected age of ninety-five. Poor fellow. He was the ambassador to Spain minding his own business when they summoned him to Hell.

* * *

Prisoners of war began to return home, few in good health. One of my neighbors, Julien Mendès, died two weeks later from tuberculosis he had contracted during his captivity. Another of Dad's friend, I've forgotten his name, also a tubercular, was sent to the Alps Mountains for a cure of pure air. He came back home almost two years later, in a coffin to be buried next to his wife who passed away after he had been taken by the Germans and sent to Auschwitz, in December 1943. He was a Jew.

13

War had ended, of course, in April 1945 and life resumed for a world rid of Germans and associates. We still had a few of them for a little while, but they were harmless prisoners of war, now ready to return home or to join the Foreign Legion. Home, that meant what was left of their homes in their beaten up country, was not appealing for all. Germans had been irremediably crushed in their bodies and souls by a universal coalition headed by the United States of America. It would take some time before they could emerge from their downfall.

Italy had gotten rid of their fascist dictator Mussolini in a way not very nice for the Duce. He was shot to death and hung by the feet for a few days for everyone to see; and Hiro Hito of Japan had disappeared into anonymity in the maze of his palace in Tokyo. But he never made amends on behalf of his fanatic military geniuses that were in fact responsible for the aggression of Pearl Harbor.

So, everything seemed to be going well.

On October 18, 1945, twenty-four German individuals were charged with war crimes and crimes against humanity, and prosecuted in an international trial in Nuremberg, Germany. The trial began on November 20 of the same year and the judgment was handed down on October 20, 1946. In France, as well as in other countries which had suffered from the German invasion, we were waiting feverishly for the irremediable condemnation of the barbaric Nazis.

That was what the judges in Nuremberg offered the world.

I returned to school and finished three years at Jules Renard. A few teachers returned from war to their favorite occupation but we were fortunate to keep Ms. Barbier. For me it would be until the end of the twelfth grade three years later.

* * *

May 1948. War had been over for three years and the Nuremberg Trials concluded long ago with the conviction of the main defendants.

Juliette had dropped out of school and started an apprenticeship in dressmaking and I was the proud holder of the Classic Baccalauréat diploma from Jules Renard High School. I always wondered how I could achieve such an exploit, being rather indolent and even a little lazy for schoolwork. But, as Mom always said, "you're a lucky rascal." Yeah! Lucky. Maybe it was Ms. Barbier and her smile.... and her beautiful legs that encouraged me.

Unfortunately I was through with her. I was leaving Jules Renard and my favorite teacher. Only my love for History and Spain remained in my heart.

What was next for me? I wasn't sure. First idea was to enroll in a journalistic school. I liked to write but I also loved History, Geography and the Spanish language and culture. That might help the writer I wanted to be. But, the only school of journalism at the time was up north in Lille deep in a snowy country, five hundred miles from the sun of my hometown.

So, I might move only west of Nice, in a little coastal city named Sain-Laurent-du-Var, only twelve miles from home. There was a cute little university whose campus extended out on a piece of land, fifty yards from the ocean. And I won't have to move. Home would be still rue Mirabeau in the infamous *Cour des Miracles* where new dogs still barked, children, not the same, still ran and cried and pooped, and mothers still yelled the same obscenities over and over.

But I was born there, and my best friend Sylvain had lived there, and my father had been there until the day he had vanished into thin air.

Moreover, a local train ran back and forth from Nice to Cannes twenty-five miles away, and stopped at all the stations between, including Saint-Laurent. I lived two blocks from the terminal in Nice, which was convenient for me, inexpensive and fast.

* * *

Mom had kept her job at the restaurant. She loved cooking and the money was good. Dad was still cutting hair in his barbershop, and telling bad jokes to his customers. But, now and then he would disappear for two or three days at the time, and Mom would worry though she had started getting used to it.

My father would return home after those escapades as if nothing happened, without any word of excuse, and Mom wouldn't articulate a sound. She wasn't fit for happiness, I believe. We were silent at lunch and supper times. No jokes bad or otherwise, and my father's smile had fainted away.

And one day, what we all expected, happened. Dad was gone, and this time for good. He didn't say goodbye to me or to Juliette, and of course, to my mother. It took a few days to realize that Pierre Borny was never to return. Mom knew the reasons and, after a while, we all knew. Dad had a mistress, and her name was Raymonde.

For some time I checked in the morning at the barbershop until a sign that said *For Sale* was hung at the door by a real estate agency.

I swore that same day that, if I ever get married, God forbid, I will never, ever do that to my wife and my children.

It took a long while to readjust to our widowhood and orphanage. Mom kept working and I began to look for a summer occupation. Vacation time had begun. A long one; three months.

I found a job at a small printing shop, not far from home, in the photoengraving department. It was an interesting work I liked right away.

I always wondered how a picture could be reproduced on a newspaper by the thousands of copies. Well, I found out within minutes in my new job.

The foreman, a lady, explained to me, "The photograph to be reproduced is shot in a huge camera —holding 20"x 24" film— through a screen made of dots. A negative is obtained with those dots that are of different sizes according to the nuances of tones; light gray, dark gray, black and white. The result of the process is a negative called a halftone. Then, this negative is just printed, as an ordinary picture, but on a zinc plate. That plate is engraved with a solution of water and nitric acid. The result is mounted with lead types in a square form that is put on a press and submitted to an inking. The dots only take the ink and therefore print the picture."

Wow! That simple. I can do that. It was my first day at work and already I knew everything. My salary was a solid ten francs a week that was ten francs more than I ever made. Mom didn't need the money, she told me. So I opened a bank account with my first pay. The employee at the bank teller looked at me with what I believed was a smirk. "Your account opening will cost you ten francs. So, you have an account, but no money." He smiled then said gently, "That happens all the time, boy. Don't you worry. Bring some more money and we might even give you a checkbook. For now, no checkbook but as you have no money, you don't need one."

I left the bank and the laughing employee with a hangdog expression. So much for my ten francs. A week's work down the drain. Well, not quite since I was the proud possessor of a bank account.

That lasted almost three months, the remainder of the summer vacation. And my bank account swelled to a huge sum of one hundred francs. Enough to go to Spain, spend two weeks over there, and return just in time for college. That, I mean going to Spain, was one thing I wanted to do before I returned to studies, if I ever decided to. Wasn't sure yet. For Spain, I didn't care where I was going as long as it was on the peninsula beyond the Pyrenees Mountains. I would ride the train from Nice as far as my money could take me, perhaps find a small job somewhere in the middle to make a little more money and find a cheap place to stay in a small Spanish city where I can enjoy *churros* and *café con leche*. Doughnuts and coffee and cream. That was all I needed in those times of destitution: doughnuts in a coffeehouse. I could stretch my money as far as two weeks and, if I were lucky, I could find myself a señorita who would help me stay in Spain a little longer. If she can afford to feed me, of course. But as I say, churros and café con leche would be just fine.

14

Sunday morning, September 15, 1948. Borders between France and Spain have been opened for an over a year now. Only thing one needed was the visa. The Spanish consulate in Nice was also new after general Franco opened his heart and his land to the appreciation of the European countries. Diplomatic representations were opened in the main cities in France with the blessing of our president, Vincent Auriol.

I was eighteen and I couldn't wait to go through the Pyrenees Mountains.

I boarded a train at seven o'clock in the morning, on a third class car for there was no cheapest fourth class. No restaurant on the train nor sleeping car, but Mom had prepared a nice lunch to take with me and I wouldn't sleep not to miss the countryside from Nice to Port-Bou on the Costa Brava. It was the first time I rode a train and, I have to admit it, I was a little frightened. What if the car went off the rails? Huh! And what if I missed the station where I'm supposed to get off? Huh!

Well, the train didn't derail, and I was thankful about that, and the station to get out was simple. Everybody has to abandon the train at Port-Bou for it was the terminal for us French before pursuing our trip. Port-Bou is right on the border on the Spanish side. In Spain the rails gauge is narrower than most of the European countries'. Spanish tracks do not accommodate other wider cars. So we had to ride another train. But the commutation was somehow troublesome.

First it was the mandatory police check, both French and Spanish. It seemed that the French gendarmes did not like to see the nation's travelers crossing to Spain where they were going to spend good, true money earned in France. Then, the Spaniards in their great wisdom apparently hated those strangers who crossed the Pyrenees to spend time spoiling their fellow countrymen with their offensive riches and their objectionable French mentality.

At least it was what the *Guardias Civiles* looked like to me with their three-point glistering hat. I wasn't aware of how bad my objectionable mentality was, but I knew my offensive riches had peaked at the time at the extraordinary sum of two hundred and twenty francs: roughly fifty dollars. And I didn't intend to spoil anyone with it, Spaniards or others.

I had a glance at the *Guardias*. They really looked dreadful. I expected them to cry any minute, "What don't you go spend your vacation and your money somewhere else." Yeah! I thought, why not in Germany. Those words never came, and I was grateful to them.

First impression of Spain wasn't that good. The Guardias' bad attitude set my teeth on edge like the noise made on a board by a piece of chalk.

But that wasn't enough. The next post was the customs' department. Another set of ugly guys. They first opened my suitcase looking at me —not at the suitcase— as if I were a *contrabandista*, a damn smuggler.

For ten minutes they tried to find something wrong —I had no idea what— in my only piece of luggage. I don't believe that at the time they were looking for drugs. I'd never heard of such a thing, and I had no idea, I recall now, what drugs were used for. Nowadays, my two year old grandson knows what we're talking about, thanks to the publicity made on national TV, in the movies, and everywhere else. *Don't do drugs!* Yeah! Right.

When I was about fifteen, Dad talked to me about those drugs and their devastating effects. I didn't know what in the world he was talking about. I said yes as if I understood his words, and it was the end of it.

As the customs agents didn't find anything they would have liked to find, they gave me back the suitcase for me to shut it. It was a mess. Shirts and socks hanging out like overflowing from a garbage can. I looked around for someone to help me. A fat person would do.

A gracious lady came to me. She was pretty, smiling, fat, and without a word, sat on my luggage. That left me happy and thankful. Then she walked away without any comment.

The travelers trudged to a café of sort inside the station. It was crowded, smelling like cooked olive oil, fried something, and *anisete*, that sweet liquor which had legally replaced the forbidden absinth since the end of the Spanish Civil War.

We had to wait for the Spanish train to come, but no one knew how long we'd be waiting. It could be an hour, we were told, or five hours. It depended. "On what?" I asked. "No idea." was the answer. So I sat there and order a café con leche. It was one in the morning.

The fat lady, who helped me with my suitcase, sat at the same table. She was still smiling and I wondered if it was to me. I turned round. Nobody seemed to have noticed her. I guessed I was the recipient of her smile. Was she making a pass at me? A lady at least thirty years older and a hundred pounds heavier than me. I couldn't help but think of Ms. Barbier. Why didn't she make a pass to me? Of course she was engaged to be married the last time I saw her and looked very much happy.

But that lady in front of me? Yet, I conceded she had a very pretty face and her smile was engaging. But I wondered, engaging to what? "My name is Doña Filomena de Escobar," she said in French with a slight Spanish accent, her facial expression still showing an unusual pleasure. I'm not quite sure her last name was Escobar. If not it must be close. I just can't really remember, but Filomena is right; that I recall. Later I noticed that no one ever called her but by her first name.

Even her children. Some others, I heard, would call her Doña Filomena. A supreme mark of respect.
I wouldn't have liked to give her my name though I felt obliged after she had mannerly and freely put her big butt and her two hundred and fifty pounds on top of my cardboard valise. I thought I might have to buy another one as soon as I stopped somewhere in a civilized city.
"My name is François," I said reluctantly, not daring to add my last name. What did she want my name for? Actually I didn't need hers either. I didn't ask for it, did I?
Well, I was very wrong. I discovered some time later that I needed that nice lady more than I had thought. "Where are you going?" she asked matter-of-factly as if she didn't care.
That's it, I thought, it's not a pass but a whole bunch of free tickets she's throwing at me. "I don't know yet," I said glancing around as if looking for help. In a corner of the room were two young men who couldn't be but French. They were smiling eyeing me. They had probably experienced that kind of adventure in their life. I didn't, and I had no parry for it. Naïve, I guess, but to a certain point.
"I have a round-trip ticket for Madrid" I pursued. "It's valid a month. I can stop anywhere in between and continue my trip any time within the month."
"So, you're going to Madrid?"
"Yes, some time this month. Don't know when."
"I think I would give you my card. That can help you if you happen to be in Madrid this month."
"Thank you," I mumbled staring at the card. I read it aloud. "*Hotel-Pensión de Familia Filomena. 13 calle Cervantes.*"
"It's very easy to find. It's a well-known street, a few blocks from the Prado Museum and the Botanical Garden. Not a very long artery that reaches Cánovas del Castillo Square with its magnificent Neptune Fountain."
"I had no idea what she was talking about: Prado Museum, Calle

Cervantes, Cánovas del Castillo Square. Those were Hebrew for me.
"It's a convenient start for a tour of the city," she continued. "And the hotel is rather inexpensive for students. You are a student, aren't you?"
"Correct." I was afraid I had already said too much. I checked the two Frenchmen with a glance. They were walking up to my table. Thanks God.
"Hello, Filomena," one said, and sat down uninvited.
"Hello, handsome." She smiled then looked at me. "I met those gentlemen last year in the same train. Students. Means broke." Her accent was barely noticeable unlike the makeup that colored her face.
"Right, we're still broke," one of them said. "The Sorbonne is an expensive university. We were broke last year, we are this year, and probably we'll be for the next ten years," he said laughing. "I am Robert Valois, and my friend is André Delatour. Both from Paris, the Latin Quarter."
They didn't have to say they were from Paris. Their accent was explicit enough.
"I'm François Borny, from Nice," I replied still a little suspicious. Did I say I disliked Parisians? Well it's not quite true. I have numerous friends from Paris and they are decent people, but generally speaking, Parisians are commonly pompous, arrogant, obnoxious, and full of themselves. They have a saying that gives the measure of their self-importance: *Il n'est bon bec que de Paris*. That could be roughly translated by; there is nothing good that doesn't come from Paris. It was an old poet from the middle Ages, François Villon, who said that first. He was a crook, a thief, an assassin, and frequented the rotten *Cour des Miracles* amid vagrants of all kinds. But he was one of the most talented poets of the French litterature.
We provincials are, according to Parisians, and no matter where we come from, just good enough to lick their boots.
They have what they are so proud of: the *Titi*. (Pronounced Tee-

tee). It's a child, eight to ten years old. He's insolent, likes to make fun of people, mostly provincials he recognizes at the first sight, smart like a fox; he's a cunning kid, mischievous, witty.... and adorable. He's the one who would say just for fun, with a croak of laughter, "Good morning, Madame," to a priest wearing a cassock. And if the priest has a big belly, like most of them have, he would add, "It's your fault, Madame, if you got pregnant."

But he would get profoundly hurt if someone calls him *kid*.

I loved Paris since my first visit years later. I like the city, the monuments, the eccentricity and the beauty, but, sorry folks, I still don't trust Parisians a hundred percent. But I repeat, some are very nice people. I've met a lot of them.

Those two young men smiling in front of me seemed to be amenable and charming. They shook my hand, and said, "We're going to Madrid. Want to join us?"

"Don't know yet." Something told me to get away from them. Perhaps my natural suspiciousness when it comes to Parisians.

I looked again at the business card. Calle Cervantes, near the Prado. Filomena. Curious name, but it fitted perfectly to the fat lady. I didn't know why.

* * *

It was not quite three in the morning when the narrow-tracked Spanish train entered the station. Within a few seconds the restaurant emptied like a washbasin whose pipe had been unblocked, with the same *swoosh*. And everyone hurried to the empty train. There were one first-class and two second-class cars. Out of my reach. I jumped into the first third class coach, threw my luggage on the shelf, and sat down puffing seconds before Robert and André sat at their turn in front of me. "We couldn't keep up with you," Robert said. "Why such a hurry?"

"Just want to make sure I have a seat at the window. I like to watch the panorama." I looked towards the corridor. "Where is the lady?"

"Filomena? Oh, she is on a first-class car, of course. But she'll be here before long. She doesn't give up easily."

"She's a good lady, I believe," André said. "We've known her since last year. We've spent memorable moments at her hotel. It's a small one, a dozen rooms at the most, but clean, nice and close to the Prado Museum. We came last year as soon as they opened the border. Pension Filomena would be the perfect place to be if it weren't for the cooking. They fry everything in olive oil."

"Pure olive oil," Robert added. "Yecch! But it would be the same everywhere, even in the four-star hotels. You can smell olive oil everywhere in Spain. And you never get used to it. You return to France and, for a month, you'll keep the horrible smell up your nose. But we can endure that for the rest is worth a million."

"Do you speak Spanish?" André asked.

"Enough to find my way, I guess. Though I never came to Spain. I studied the language for a few years, and I will be still learning if I decide to go to the university."

"You don't know yet?" André said.

"Not yet, and if I do I would have to find a job to pay for it. And if I don't I would still have to find a job."

"Let's try to sleep a little," Robert said as he lay down on the wooden seat.

We were three people in the car that could hold eight. Which was good for us. Plenty of room.

* * *

"Hello young men!" Filomena was here, smiling and sharing with us her perfume she must have been bathing in. It was daylight already, with a cloudy sky, which meant that we would have some rain before

long. I'd been dozing most of the time, but not really sleeping. André and Robert awaken with several yawns, rubbing their eyes as if they'd had a good night of sleep. "Good morning, Filomena," one said.
"Let's go to the restaurant car, I'm starved," the lady proposed. "I buy."
That was good news. I was famished too and not inclined to spend the little money I brought. Not yet. Mom's sandwiches were gone long before we reached Port-Bou.
We stepped into the restaurant when the train stopped at a station. I could read *Gerona* at the main gate. On our way to Madrid we were.
"We still can see the disaster of the Civil War," Filomena said. "Look at those buildings and that church over there. Nothing left. The communists have done that before they left the city. There is not a single church standing, but we are rebuilding. You'll see this kind of ruin all over, though it's been nine years since the war ended. Madrid has been hurt too while fighting Franco and his nationalists. The city finally surrendered in July 1939. Hence the end of the war, and the political climate we're living in since."
"We still have that kind of scars on our own buildings in Paris" André said. "War has ended only three years ago for us. But it's nothing in comparison to what happened in Germany. Ninety per cent of Berlin has been destroyed and not close to be reconstructed."
"They have looked for that," I said. "They are the one who started it, weren't they?"
"Right," Robert said. "They got what they deserved. But let's forget Germany and the Spanish communists. War is over and in the back of our minds, if not forgotten."

15

I was back to France on October 1, after my first extraordinary trip to Spain. Two weeks in this wonderful land, and I was ready to do whatever I was going to do in my own country. When Mom asked me what? I said I didn't know, but probably I'd enroll at Ardaillon in Saint-Laurent."

"You better hurry up. School starts on October 15, I believe. Two weeks to register."

"I'll do that, Mom. Tomorrow," I said wondering how she knew about the deadline.

"Do you need any money?"

"I still have some left over from Spain. Filomena has been very nice to me. I told you about her."

"Yes. She seems to be a pretty decent lady."

"A very warmhearted lady. Perhaps a little too fat, but lovely. And amusing too."

"Amusing?"

"Witty, and fun that is. She invited us, Robert and André, my two French pals, and me, to a *boda*—"

"Which is?"

"A wedding. Actually her daughter's wedding. It was fun, the food was great, and my friends could have told you that the *Sangria* was galore and superb. They slept their hangover into the afternoon the next day wasting a whole day of vacation."

"And you were?"

"Back to the Prado for the third time. Before the wedding I spent some time there by myself."

"The museum?"

"The museum. I went first with my friends, then by myself twice before the wedding. In fact, you need more than two days to see the thousands of paintings hung on the walls. Velasquez has his own room, Goya has over one hundred paintings, El Greco, Murillo. All extraordinary artists. By the way, I've even seen a portrait of our king Louis XVI by Callet.

"Before he was beheaded," Mom asked laughing. Mom seldom offered any kind of humor, but every time she did it stunned me.

"So, why don't we talk about your trip?" Mom continued. "How was it, besides the wedding and the museum?"

"Thrilling. I can't wait to return. Perhaps next year. I might have my summer job back at the printing shop. That would help me for the university and for my next journey to Spain."

"I'm sure you will get it back, but don't forget school. This is more important. I'll help you if need be. Juliette is doing very well as a dressmaker. She lives in a sort of boarding school and, already, makes some money. She's a gifted young lady, I believe. So she won't need much from me and I need little for myself. Now, tell me about Spain."

* * *

I wondered how it all started: my passion for Spain, my desire to visit the country and what really did prompt the earnest craving to learn more about it.

It probably began during the German occupation, when I was in the seventh grade. I enrolled in a Spanish class for there was not a foreign language to study besides German and Italian. Spanish was the only other language permitted at the time. No English, of course, Norwegian, Swedish or Russian. Since the Spanish Civil War, *El Caudillo* Franco was Hitler's close friend, though the General had always refused to take any part in the world conflict. Smart! Franco had probably anticipated the coming of American capitalists in his land after the war.

For two years I studied not only the language, but also the history and the culture of that country that would be, a few years later, the source of an enchantment for me. I read avidly Cervantes, first in French of course, and much later, and with enormous difficulty, in Old Spanish. Almost undecipherable. Yet, I discovered the craziness of Don Quixote and the gentleness of his credulous squire Sancho Panza. I still remember a few lines of that extraordinary masterpiece. I always have a great pleasure, and probably a certain degree of boastfulness, to say the following sentence when asked if I spoke Spanish: *Los que seán entrepuesto en mi camino durante estos ultimos años lo han pagado de sus vidas. Algunos de forma nada placentera.* Those who have interfered with my life during the past few years have paid for it with their lives. Some in a way not pleasurable at all. That impresses most people .... Save the Spaniards. The latter have two reasons for that. First, not many natives have read Don Quixote, and second, my accent doesn't fool any of them.

Nevertheless, I got familiar with other masterpieces; the daring and delicate poems of Frederico Garcia Lorca who was assassinated by Franco's fans at the start of the Spanish Civil War, and whose work has been for many years prohibited in Spain. I'm not sure that one can find, even nowadays, the subtle *Blood Wedding* or any work by the writer.

Vicente Blasco Ibañez was one of my favorite authors. His famous *Arena Y Sangre*, translated into English by *Blood And Sand*, conquered the world when Hollywood made a movie with Tyrone Power, Linda Darnell, Rita Hayworth, and Anthony Queen. It was a great movie from a great book.

* * *

The nocturnal Spanish life had stunned me the moment I arrived, though my friends seemed to be blasé. Parisians are seldom impressed by anything outside Paris, and Spain was nothing but a pale copy of the nights in the City of Lights. At least that was what they said for I had yet to go to Paris to compare.

Madrid lives a semi-lethargic life during the day, but it wakes up around seven o'clock in the evening. The *paseos*, the boulevards, regain the strange animation they have lost in the wee hours of the morning. From seven p.m. to one or two in the morning, an incessant human flow reanimates the streets and boulevards from their daytime dullness and sluggishness to an extraordinary and insane commotion. Thousands of people of all ages just stroll back and forth the main arteries of the city. For Madrid it was, among others, and I believe still is, *Callé de Alcalá*, Alcalá Street, to *Callé Mayor* through the *Puerta del Sol* with a left bifurcation towards *Plaza Mayor*. A walk of about a mile that left you filled with enthusiasm and respect for those Spaniards who, not long before, were in the midst of a brutal civil war.

But Madrid is worth a tour in any direction and on any street. One will always find interesting subjects in any path. *Paseo del Prado* will take you to one of the most impressive museums in the world. The Prado holds hundreds of invaluable masterpieces from past Spanish artists as well as some treasures from Flemish, French and Italian painters.

One of the things that surprised me was the mix of the styles of classical antiquity and modern work. I've never seen anywhere else but Spain that amalgamation which seemed quite inappropriate and yet magnificent.

* * *

The Hotel-Pensión Filomena was a little two-story yellow building in a short street two blocks from the *Paseo del Prado*, across from the museum.

We arrived in the middle of the night after a trip —in the slow choo-choo train that brought us from Port-Bou— which was all but boring. For me the journey took two days from Nice and I guessed it was two days for my Parisian friends as well. A big chunk off our vacation. But it was the best time we had in a train that was supposed to be tiresome and monotonous. It wasn't.

We had breakfast, lunch and dinner, all paid for by the lovely Filomena. She had been an unexpected host; gracious, always generous which we, impoverished students, had appraised at its true worth. She was a pleasant travel companion who seemed to have no thought in the back of her mind and no ulterior motive. We shall see, I told myself.

Lunch in the restaurant car was another experience. Filomena had ordered wine, Spanish of course, which she drank with an evident pleasure. Robert and André proved to be two very polite and obliged guests as they accepted the rounds of wine that seemed to be endless. I tried myself without being convinced of the quality of the drink. The wine was too sweet for my taste though I didn't have a great experience in the field of oenology. The Parisians appeared to like it. I found out later that they liked any wine and liquor as long as it was in abundance. And much more when it was free.

And on the train, Filomena provided the wine in ample amount. She even offered to sing which began to embarrass me until I heard her voice. A beautiful, crystalline and, in the meantime, a powerful soprano modulation that suddenly kept us dumbfounded.

Five minutes later, the whole train was in the restaurant car, applauding and singing in unison. A man materialized from nowhere with a guitar, then another one. All of a sudden it was a *fiesta gitana*. A Gypsy festival. There is always a guitar player in a train, explained Filomena. That day we had two.

* * *

The room smelled a mix of furniture wax, fresh soap and cheap perfume. The curtains were drawn closed on the windows overlooking Calle Cervantes. It was ten p.m. and I was exhausted. I smelled like an entire flock of pigs, needed a shower after two days in the train and craved for a good night of sleep. I'll see tomorrow what Madrid looks like. But a knock at the door gave me a start. Without waiting for an answer, Robert and André stormed in. "What are you doing, François?" Robert asked frowning.

"I'm going to have a shower and go to bed."

"Are you crazy? You don't sleep at night in Spain. You might sleep late in the morning, or even until the afternoon, but certainly not at night. That is when you want to visit Madrid; that is when Spain is alive. People work and live sluggishly from ten in the morning to seven or eight in the evening, and then begin to enjoy life, the real Spanish life. Come on, let's go."

I didn't know how those two people managed to be so energetic. They still had some wine in their body. Their eyes showed a level of alcohol that must match Filomena's. I was looking for an excuse to get away from that night outing. Just didn't feel like taking a stroll.

"It's raining," I said. "Look."

"Raining? Where?" André laughed. "It's only a sprinkle. That won't stop Madrilenians from enjoying the usual nocturnal walk. Come on, come on."

It was raining more than a sprinkle when we stepped out. It was cold too. Filomena was nowhere to be seen when we got to the lobby. "She had too much to drink," Robert said with a smirk. "Women! Can't hold liquor. But God she was good, wasn't she?"

"She was indeed," I replied, "but why does she do that?"

"What?"

"Be so nice to us. In the train she bought our breakfast, our lunch, our dinner—
"And she entertained us as well," Robert said. "Yes, she's something else. We met her last year, and it seems that she couldn't wait to see us again. She was so happy to meet us in the train. She comes from Paris where she has a son, an engineer who works for the Renault Company. That's where we met her last year, on the train I mean, and as a strange coincidence, we met her again this time. But we were heading to her hotel anyway. It wouldn't have been that much fun to travel by ourselves if she weren't on board. We've been lucky one more time."
"And wait to have your bill before you leave," André said. "I'll be surprised if you have to pay for your room."
"You're kidding, of course," I said. "Why would she do that?"
"Because she's a nice lady. I believe she sees in us her missing son. The one who died during the civil war. He was hung by the neck along with others by Franco's fans in 1936. He was eighteen years old. She doesn't talk much about him. Her maid told us when we first came."

Paseo del Prado was crowded both on the asphalt and on the curb. Cars had a lot of problems trying to drive through. Walkers won't move from the center of the street ignoring the imperious and blaring sounds of warning made by the motorists. Just kept walking. On the sidewalk pedestrians had the same difficulty to move. Everywhere the high pitch of the Spanish language, a sound I didn't recognize, the sound of a tongue I thought I had mastered. Yet, I could understand only a small part.
"Do you understand what they say?" Robert asked.
"No, I'm afraid. Perhaps if I talk to someone in particular I might comprehend that damned language."
"So, let's talk to someone, anyone. You have a preference? Man or woman? Blond or brunette?" Without waiting for an answer, Robert

grabbed a young woman's arm. "Sorry he said. Do you speak French?"

She had the most beautiful eyes I've ever seen. Green, my favorite color. She looked at Robert, a little befuddled, but not that much. Then she stared at me and, embarrassed, I turned my gaze in the opposite direction. That pretty face wouldn't be interested in me speaking Spanish. She smiled as I pretended not to look at her. "I am French," she said, and then laughed.

"Oops! Wrong person," Robert said laughing at his turn. "We're looking for a Spanish lady. My friend here wants to talk to a local. Maybe you speak Spanish. Do you?"

"Yes. I've lived in Madrid for the past two years."

"Two years? What are you doing in Spain? Certainly not on vacation or you would have to give me the combination."

"I work at the French embassy. My father is the commercial Attaché."

I was standing ten feet away staring at the ebb and flow of the crowd, but I didn't miss a word of hers.

"Sorry," she said, "but my friends are waiting for me over there." She pointed at two young girls smiling at us.

"Wow! André said impressed. "Are they French too?"

"No, Madrilenians. But they understand some French. They are at the Madrid University where they study our language."

"I can teach them," André offered.

"Why don't we walk together?" Robert asked.

"Why not," she replied amused. "You come to Spain, on vacation I assume, and you come across a French woman. Funny."

"Not to mention two beautiful Madrilenians." Robert turned in my direction, and yelled, "François, come on. What are you doing over there?"

"Shy?" she asked.

"More likely stupid, I believe. Not yet a college student. He said

next month he would be. In Nice. Can you believe that?"
"Nice, hum, I love Nice." She looked in my direction and I stared somewhere else. "I see," she said, "timid."
"Come on François, we're waiting for you."
I waved my hand and said, "I'm returning to the hotel. I want to visit the Prado early in the morning."
"Don't hold your breath," André yelled. "Not early in the morning. Come on, François."
"See you tomorrow." I turned and walked away, as Robert and André shrugged in desperation.

* * *

"And you didn't go with them?" Mom said. "What's wrong with you, François?"
"Mom! This girl was too beautiful for me. What could I have done with two professional Don Juans like André and Robert?"
"What are you talking about?"
"Wait, Mom. Let me finish."

* * *

The next morning I got up at six, as I usually do in Nice. My friends were still in bed and I didn't want to awaken them so early. But, it appeared that six o'clock was not a time to be alive in Spain. No one was up in the hotel. The night watchman was dozing on his chair behind the counter. I went to the dining room. It was a small cubicle with four tables, and read with horror the sign hung on the door: *Breakfast served from 9:00 to 11:00.*

Nine o'clock? I'll be dead by then. I'm starving. I need some coffee and something to eat. I dropped my key on the counter without awaking the watchman and walked out. Cervantes Street looked like my hometown in the middle of the night under the German occupation. No one seemed to dare to be there. I looked right, left, and I decided to walk to Cánovas del Castillo Square and Paseo del Prado. No one there either with the exception of street cleaners with their hoses washing off the previous night's trash. I asked one of the men where I could find a café or a restaurant. He laughed and said, "*No hay, señor, no antes de la ochos.*" Not before eight o'clock. Where was everybody? I'm going to have to prepare myself for those dull mornings without breakfast. I'll buy something the night before and keep it in my room.

I returned to the hotel for it was useless to wander in a deserted city. Pompeii must have looked like this after the eruption of the Vesuvius

The square Cánovas was worthy of anyone's attention, but the starvation began to take a toll on my enthusiasm. First day in Spain and I'm already bored....and starved.

I decided to wake Robert and André. They were less than happy but got on their feet. "How was it last night?" I asked not sure I wanted to know.

"You missed a good walk. The girls were terrific. Mostly the French one. She asked a lot of questions about you. Like what's wrong with you? I said you were an idiot from Nice. What could one expect from a provincial?"

He laughed happy to have made a joke on me.

"What do you want to do so early?" André asked.

"Let's go to the museum."

"All right, but let's have some coffee first."

Filomena was awake and the watchman gone. "Hola!" she said then smiled. "What are you all doing so early? You might be arrested if the *Guardias Civiles* find you wandering in the wee hours of the morning."

"Wee hours? It's almost noon," I said.

She laughed. "It's only eight and you would find no one alive in the whole of Madrid at this time of the day. So, what are you up to?"

"I'm famished," I said. "I was looking earlier for an open place where I could eat something. I might be dead of starvation before my vacation time is over."

"I just made fresh coffee. Want some?"

Robert and André rushed to the dining room. A pleasant smell of coffee filled the air. On the table, a large dish full of doughnuts. "Don't look at these," Filomena said, "they are from yesterday and very much stale."

"Who cares?" I took one and sat down. Filomena brought some coffee. "This doughnut is the best I ever ate," I said.

She smiled, a gentle smile that illuminated her pretty face. "We call those *churros*," she said. She turned to the Parisians and said, "I've never seen you up at this hour."

"That guy," Robert pointed at me, "is crazy. He wants to see the museum. We were on the paseo with three fantastic girls last night, and he decided to return to his room."

"Three girls? One too many for you two. What about you, François? You don't like girls?"

"I love girls, but I didn't feel those were for me."

"May I ask why you feel that way?"

"I don't know. Perhaps too beautiful for me. Besides, Robert found them. I want to find mine by myself, and only when I'll decide."

"You're full of.... you know what? André said"

"Wind. That's what we say in Nice. Full of wind."

"*Plein de vent*. We say the same in Paris. Stir wind but incapable of anything else."

I shrugged and waved to dismiss the dialog.

"What time do they open the Prado?"

"It's open from nine until seven in the evening."

"Oh yes, seven. Time for everyone to wake up and suddenly attack upon the streets. Time for life to resume in Spain."
"Don't you mock," Filomena said laughing. "You'll love it. Like owls, humans are nyctalopic. They can see better by night."
"Well, by night I usually sleep. Unless something very interesting happens." I got up and walked towards the door followed by my friends. Then, I changed my mind, walked back to Filomena and kissed her on the cheek. "I love you, Filomena."
When we reached the door, we turned round. She was crying silently. "I love you too," she said with a broken voice.
"Her son," whispered Robert.
I must ask her, sometime before I leave, what really happened to her son.

16

The massive building of the *Museo del Prado* loomed in front of us as soon as we reached the corner of Cánovas del Castillo Square. On the right hand side of the construction was an entrance facing the statue of Goya who seemed to watch that part of the museum where most of his masterpieces are hung.

"That's the entrance most commonly used for a first visit," Robert said.

The Prado was open when we arrived around 9:15. About a dozen visitors were in the entrance hall waiting for the tour to begin. A guide showed us the stairs on the left hand side and said, "The best way to visit the museum is to start on the upper floor. Then you follow the sign and gradually find yourself on the street floor. Enjoy your visit."

We strolled across a series of halls where the works of Renaissance painters were displayed. The portrait of *Carlos Quinto*, Charles V, by Goya, attracted my attention. We had studied the life of the king, I believe in middle school, and then I didn't like him. He fought, not always fairly, my own king Francis I to whom he disputed the crown of the Saint Empire which was finally given to him and for which he took the title of Emperor.

Well, I still didn't like him but I enjoyed Goya's talent. Two other works by the painter figured among the riches of the halls. The 2nd of *May* and the 3rd of *May* also called *Firing Party*. Two impressive renderings of the Napoléonien era. The first one depicted the insurrection of the Spanish patriots against Napoléon's troops at the *Puerta del Sol in 1808*, and the second one, the terrible execution by night of those patriots.

That the French Emperor had sacrificed hundreds of thousand of human lives in Spain and elsewhere to put his brother Joseph on the Spanish throne was inconceivable at the time and still is. Napoléon had no idea who he was confronting in Spain. He paid the high price of greed for Europe.

We kept moving towards the south end of the building. There was El Greco hall with its masterpiece *The Adoration of the Shepherds*.

After a long moment I didn't even care about my friends. I didn't know where they were, but I didn't really need them.

I spent over an hour on a portion of the second floor, walking back and forth to make sure I didn't miss anything before I headed towards the Velasquez collection. The work I came to Spain for. Or almost.

The place was large and well lit through a glass roof. Two large mahogany benches were set in the center of the room; one in front of the painting of the Count-Duke of Olivares, and the other one facing the portrait of the King Philippe IV.

I walked slowly around, with a glance at each painting, then I stopped at the *Surrender of Breda*. The name reminded me of something we had worked on in my years in high school. If I'm not mistaking, and if Ms. Barbier's History class had had an impact on me, Breda is a city in Holland conquered by the Spaniards in 1625. I always wondered what in the world the Spanish army was doing so far north in that cold Europe. There was, of course, a political reason. Something about a succession interest on the French throne. I was there in awe, looking at every detail of the Velasquez masterpiece; the Dutch on the left hand side handing the key of the city over to the Marquis Ambrogio de Spinola, an Italian nobleman who had no business being at the head of the Spanish army. But, it was the way it worked at that time. Spanish army with German and Russian mercenaries, some Barbarians too, under the command of an Italian marquis. Made sense.

It was then, as I was deep in thought and oblivious of my

surroundings, that I heard my name whispered at my back by a melodic voice. I turned around slowly, not being sure the call was for me. It was. The most beautiful green eyes, in the most beautiful face, were staring at me. The young lady I briefly saw on the paseo del Prado the night before with Robert and André, was there, even so incredibly it may appear. I was speechless. She stood there in front of me, smiling, and I was shivering like a kitten out in the snow.

"Hello," she said, "nice to see you again."

"This is a nice coincidence," I finally managed to say.

"Are you sure it's a coincidence?"

"It is for me. What about you?"

"I knew you were coming here this morning, and I just wanted to tell you that my friends and I missed you last night."

"How did you know I was coming here? And how do you know my name?"

"You remember when Robert tried to convince you to come with us, you said you were coming here. And he called you François."

"I remember. But aren't you working today?"

"It's Saturday."

"Yes, right. I don't even know what day we're living in. I am in Madrid for two days and it seems to be already a long time. My friends must be somewhere in the museum. They came with me, then they disappeared."

"They left the museum. I saw them leaving through the front entrance."

"Already? Probably looking for a *bodega*."

She laughed showing a superb row of white teeth. I shamelessly scrutinized her smiling face. She had a cute upturned nose, a well-designed mouth I almost rushed to kiss, and short auburn hair surrounding the perfect oval of her visage. "You have an advantage on me," I said, "you know my name."

"*Me llamo* Aline Delheuil," she said laughing. That, I understood.

Both the Spanish language and the laughter.
We walked together around the Velasquez room not even seeing what I was looking at. Her perfume enveloped me like an aura as I felt the happiest man in the world. Here was this very attractive woman, and there I was, agape with admiration.
"Do you want to start over the visit of the museum?" I asked.
"I've seen it several times, and I probably will see it again. You are never through with the visit to the Prado. So much to see. Why don't we walk outside? The weather is gorgeous and there is a beautiful garden just on the other side of the museum."
We stepped out and turned left. The garden was visible from there.
It was nice indeed under the trees of the park. "It's called *El Jardin Botánico*," she said, the Botanical Garden.
We strolled through the shadowy alleys, not saying much, just enjoying being together. At least I did. I looked at her and it seemed that she also took pleasure in the moment. My hand brushed hers by accident, —or was it?— which made me pluck up to grab one of her fingers, then the whole hand. My heart began to pound wildly in my chest. I stared at her and I believed she had blushed. Without a word I led her to a bench and we sat down. "I'm enjoying every minute of this," I said staring at the sky through the green foliage of the trees.
"So am I," she said after a short pause, and her voice didn't sound the same. I leaned towards her and, with all the courage I still had in me, I kissed her with all the passion I could muster. She responded to my kiss with the same emotion and the same fervor.
God, what was I doing here?
I have found my girl, I thought, by myself, and in my own time, without the help of anyone. Well, I had to concede that Robert had something to do with it. If he didn't have stopped Aline the previous night, I wouldn't be here in this magnificent garden with the most beautiful girl in the world.
We spent two hours in the Botanical Garden. We only stopped

kissing to get our breath back.

When we got up, I took her hand and we walked out of the park.

"Let's eat something," I said.

"I'm starving," she said laughing. "I buy."

"No you don't. Do you think I can't afford?"

"I don't think, I'm sure. You're a poor student who hasn't yet gone to college. I'm a rich girl who makes a living in Madrid, whose father is the commercial Attaché at the French embassy and whose bank account is certainly larger than yours. Can you match that?"

"I sure can," I answered. "You're looking at a student who has no idea how he's going to pay for his tuition, if he ever decides to go to college, whose father has left home and abandoned his family several times for the past year, and whose mother is struggling to raise two kids —which includes me— cooking in a small restaurant in the train station in Nice, France. What about that?"

"Wow! And you want to pay for our lunch?"

"Yes, I still have around one hundred and ten francs. How many pesetas that makes?"

"A little over one thousand. Just enough to have *café con churros* every day for the next two weeks."

"That was my intention. I'm not eating my fortune on anything else. And I can even afford to buy you the same."

"I love coffee and doughnuts, but only in the morning. So, if I wanted to eat a decent lunch, I'm going to have to buy. This is final."

This lady seemed to know what she wanted. Must be from Brittany. One says that they have a stubborn attitude there.

"I have my car in front of your hotel."

"A car? Why, yes, of course. In front of my hotel. Why I'm not surprised that you know my hotel. Robert, right?"

"Right. I stopped by this morning. I saw a charming lady. The owner I assume. I asked her if you were still in your room."

"Filomena is her name. She's fantastic, a great lady."

"I know. She said she knew about me. How could she?"
"I have not the faintest idea."
"Don't lie. She said you told her that Robert and André were having a walk with three beautiful girls, and you didn't want to intrude. Well, I guess you were talking about my two friends and me. Right?"
"Women talk too much. Filomena must have guessed you were the beautiful girl I was talking about."
Aline laughed and said, "You still don't want to intrude?"
I didn't answer not willing to look more stupid than I already looked.

* * *

"So, you finally found a girlfriend," Mom said, "and you had to go to Spain for that heroic act."
"She's so gorgeous, Mom. You might see her someday if she keeps her word to come to visit with me next year."
"Is she?" Mom said skeptical. "Girls on vacation promise anything."
"She wasn't on vacation, Mom. I'm the one who was. She had a job in the French embassy."
"Yeah, and her father is a commercial Attaché, you told me. Did you tell her what your father was?"
"I did, Mom, and I wasn't proud. She laughed and bought me a lunch."
"Hum! A rich beautiful girl with green eyes—
"And a car."
"Forget about the eyes, the car, and her for now. You go the Saint-Laurent and enroll in the university. Ist das klar?"
Mom speaking German is not a good sign. She looked like an SS in those moments. Must be already upset. "Jeder einzelne Wort, every

single word," I replied laughing then ran out of my mother's sight.
German occupation of France had not been totally useless. At least I'd learned a small fraction of Goethe's language that hopefully, I wouldn't have to use ever in my life. I was wrong, of course.
But let's be clear about that. After the war, I had some thought on the occupation, the Gestapo, the SS, and the ordeal we had managed to overcome; and I don't believe any of us living in an occupied country, French, Norse, Dutch, Poles or whatever, hold a grudge against the German people. They were just like most of us, hoodwinked into that misery. And, subsequently, they paid the high price for the presumptuousness of their leaders. Twelve years of Nazism was more than enough even for the tough German people.

* * *

When Aline came to the hotel the following morning at eight o'clock I was already in the lobby. Filomena was there too, pretending to have some paperwork. She was sitting at her desk watching me with her motherly look.
"She'll be here soon," she said as if I worried. "Your friends were stunned when they discovered you were dating Aline."
"How do they know that?" I said almost shocked, "I didn't say anything about."
"I told them. It was fun to see their faces." After a short silence she added, "Here she is. She has just parked her car at the curb."
I was right, I told myself. Women talk too much.
Filomena had brewed some fresh coffee and offered us a cup.
Aline kissed me on the lips which made Filomena smile. "Where in the world are you both going so early in the morning?" she asked.
"To the *Escorial*," Aline replied joyful. "Hopefully we can make it to the *Sierra de Guadarrama* with my old car."
"It's only thirty miles away, but the visit can last the whole day."

"We'll be back before dark," Aline said, "and then it will be time for the *paseo*."

Before we left the Hotel Filomena, Aline crossed the lobby, passed behind the counter, and kissed the Spaniard. She was befuddled but managed to simper. I already knew that her smile most of the time came with tears. That woman was so emotional that it must hurt her.

It started raining as soon as we slid into the car. So much for a pleasant ride, I thought. As if Aline had read my mind, she said, "I'm sorry about the weather, but it's only a thirty-mile drive. Fifty kilometers. And the visit of the Escorial is indoor, unless you want to take a look at the gardens, which are beautiful by the way."

"No gardens, I've already seen many in my hometown."

Aline's car was a 1938 convertible Renault in good condition for a ten-year old vehicle she came from Marseille with, and kept enjoying it in Madrid for the last year or so. She drove carefully for the winding narrow road looked dangerous in the rain.

The Renault rolled sluggishly towards the foot of the Sierra where El Escorial stood massive and overwhelming.

It seemed that we had left Madrid half a century ago when we first caught sight of the heavy dome that overlooked the stately construction, former royal palace of King Philippe II who lived in his apartments on the west aisle of the castle.

We hadn't talked much during the drive. Aline was very cautious, sitting close to the wheel trying to anticipate any surprising turn of the road. The windshield wipers squeaked intermittently as the cloudburst turned out to be a storm. We couldn't see much beyond the hood.

"Are you scared?" Aline asked.

"No," I lied, a shiver crawling along my spine.

"Good. I am terrified. I feel like I'm driving a submarine. We might have to stop somewhere if we found a dry *somewhere*, I mean. Do you want to drive?"

"No license yet. No time for it, but as I don't own a car, it doesn't matter."

After so many years I still recall the unpleasant ride from Madrid, the rain and my girlfriend's heedful drive.

I tried to relax with the thought that the worse that could happen to us was a road accident, yet Aline was driving at about thirty miles an hour. Which couldn't be too bad if she missed a turn and we drove into a ditch.

To relax the atmosphere I talked about the dinner we had the night before. Aline had chosen a small restaurant called *El Bodegon Logroñes* on a small street near calle La Magdalena.

"The *Cochinillo asado* —roasted suckling pig— was delicious." I said. "It was a first for me. I even like those ugly things, what did you call that?"

"*Calamares a la tinta*, calamari fried in its own ink," she answered keeping her eyes on the road.

"That also was a first for me. Mom cooks the same baby squids but cleans up the ink before. I liked that too, though I'm not sure I'd try it again as long as they keep their ink."

"And you also liked the young waitress, didn't you?"

Jealous, I thought. Nah! "You mean Rosita. She was very pretty."

"Pretty? She's gorgeous with her fine features typical Spanish, her thin waist, her big, you know what, her huge brown eyes—

"I like green eyes better," I cut smiling unequivocally.

"Yeah, you manage to come out on the top. But I forgive you."

Twenty years later, back from a business trip to Africa, I stopped in Madrid. The French air-traffic controllers were on strike and our plane couldn't fly over the Pyrenees in French territory. We had to stop in the Spanish capital. We would be commuting the next morning by train. The same train I rode back to France on my first trip to Spain, but that time I was in first class. My hotel that night, paid for by the airline company, was the *Villamagna* one of the most prestigious hotels I ever spent a night in.

I called for a taxi and went to *El Bodegon Logroñes*. It was still there and so was Rosita. She was pretty as before with her huge eyes and the red carnation in her very dark hair, but she had gained some weight —too much for my taste— and her left hand wore a wedding ring. She didn't remember me, of course, but it was a nice memory from my first voyage in Spain, and my first dinner tête-à-tête with Aline. I didn't dare to go to Filomena's hotel. I wasn't sure what I would find there. The last time I'd seen the nice lady was in 1952 when I was off college, spent six months in Spain, and tried to be ready to start my adult life.

* * *

The rain had stopped by the time we parked the car near the northern entrance of the Escorial which was, Aline said, the usual start to a methodical visit of the palace.

It was huge, awe inspiring and absolutely gorgeous. We spent the next six hours strolling back and forth through the countless rooms, watching the unnumbered pieces of art by the most prestigious painters, but were mostly amazed, and somehow stupefied by the beauty and the riches of the Royal Pantheon. Twenty-six sumptuous sarcophagi lined the walls. Marble, gold and bronze were the main materials of the lavish sepulchers.

Aline read the little pamphlet she had picked up at the entrance, and translated for me. "All the kings since Carlos I —and also the queens who bore kings— are buried here but four of them. Philippe V whose remains are at *La Granja* palace on the northern side of the Sierra Guadarrama, Ferdinand VI lying in a grave in Madrid, Amadeus of Savoy, buried in Turin, Italy, and Alphonse XIII who died in exile in Rome."[1]

"The visit of this sole room is worth the trip from Madrid," I said. "Now we can have lunch and return to Madrid for the evening paseo. Right?"

"Right if it doesn't rain. For the paseo, I mean. I wonder what your two friends are up to."

"Probably sleeping off their last night drunkenness. They like beer and wine, and I believe this is their main reason for coming to Spain."

"They are La Sorbonne students, François. Wait till you're in college."

"Yes, let's wait and see. For now, let's have lunch. No beer and no wine."

"Fits me," Aline said then laughed. "I buy."

"No, you don't." I said with determination.

---

[1] Years later, the remains of Alphonse XIII were brought to the Escorial.

17

When I returned home late in the afternoon from Saint-Laurent-du-Var, I was happy and, at the same time, a little frightened. Early in the morning I rode the train from Nice, went to the university, and started filling up the long and annoying three-page application. I handed over my high school diploma as if I were the only one to have such thing. A secretary copied it, rolled it back the way it was then, smiling, gave it to me asking ten francs for the registration, and told me, when I asked, that there were no tuition fees as is usual in public school in France. I should have known that. It just didn't cross my mind.

As money was my first concern that was a relief. The only money I needed concerned the books. I could find some used ones at a fair price on campus. As I didn't have to live there, I would be fine just with a part time job at the printing shop where I already worked if they hired me over. Then we'd see.

Waiting for me at home was a letter from Aline. I had two the day before. She was still working at the embassy, *calle de Salustiano*, and driving her convertible Renault from her new apartment near the Puerta del Sol.

It was a week ago that I left Madrid and already I missed Aline. We had a good time together going out by ourselves with the exception of Filomena's daughter's wedding when we gathered with a bunch of people including Robert and André who seemed to have drunk already half of Spain's wine reserve. Their eyes were bulging and red even more than when I made their acquaintance at the train station in Port-Bou.

We came across Robert and André at the hotel a few times but they went their way, and we, ours. However, before I left the hotel I wanted to say goodbye. The two Parisians were leaving the next morning with a week or two of hangovers and a promise to return to our host for the next vacation.

Filomena was sad. I've never seen her in a regular mood like a regular person. She would go from joviality to gloominess within minutes. When I asked for my bill she cried and waved her hand as to say forget it, and when I left, she even cried harder. "Come back," she had said with a broken voice, "I'll be here waiting for you and your girlfriend."

"I'll come for a visit now and then," Aline said kissing her before we left towards the train station. We were both dispirited as she drove past Christopher Colombus Square towards Chamartin train station north on Paseo Castellana. Not much to say besides our sadness to part after those so glorious days we had spent together. We probably won't see each other again, and for me it was a terrible thought to mull over. Aline seemed even less cheerful, and when I got out of her car, and kissed her for the last time, she had tears in those beautiful eyes I'd never, ever forget.

As I didn't fill comfortable with lengthy goodbyes, I didn't let her come to the platform with me. I picked up my luggage, walked straight to the station, then turned round at the gate and waved *hasta la vista* with a smile. "Write to me," she yelled. I nodded incapable to say a word. We wrote to each other every day for the next ten months, until June arrived and it was vacation time again.

In her letter Aline recalled the Filomena daughter's wedding. Maria Teresa must be no more than eighteen, just like me. I couldn't picture myself getting married now. But I believed women could do that much younger than men.

It was a very special event I wasn't familiar with. It had been fun, that's for sure. First, Filomena's behavior. She had been cute despite her two hundred and fifty pounds, funny, adorable, entertaining, and pathetic. All the above in a single day. But indeed we had a great time as we always had when Aline and I could spend some time together, which was every day for the two weeks I stayed in Madrid.

The wedding was held in the picturesque village of Chinchón, about thirty miles southeast of Madrid. We had left the Saturday morning on a bus Filomena had rented for the occasion. Filomena's son, José, came from Paris with his flamboyant girlfriend, Jacqueline, to attend the wedding. He was a tall, very handsome young man of twenty-five, always smiling like his mother.

Jacqueline was —and probably still is for she married José the same year at Christmas time— a typical *midinette*[1] born and raised in the capital, impudent and showing no shame or shyness in any circumstances. She talked a lot, most of the time to say nothing, with a very pronounced Parisian accent, and a crystalline laughter that made everybody laugh jointly. She was a very pretty young woman of twenty-two, sharp and witty as Parisians can be, with dark brown eyes, a nose that could have tolerated to be a little shorter, and a body to damn any male around her. In other words, she had the gift to please everyone. Including me, Aline had said more than once.

We rode the bus along with about thirty people, all apparently Filomena's relatives enjoying life like Spaniards can do. They need not much; a guitar, a singer, male or female, a tambourine, a pair of castanets, and a *bota* or two, —that kind of leather flask full of good Spanish wine. The *boda* —the wedding— had started already in the bus. Guitars and tambourines appeared from nowhere as soon as Filomena's voice began to fill the air with flamenco songs.

---

[1] In Paris, a young woman working for a fashion designer.

Gorgeous weather accompanied us to the village along with the typical Spanish music and unnumbered *botas* copiously filled up to the necks with Xeres wine.

On our arrival, we stopped next to a church at the *Plaza Mayor*, a picturesque square lined with typical Castilian multi-story houses displaying their flowered balconies over the covered market.

"Sometimes, they block all the streets around the square and use the plaza as a bullring," Filomena said between two hiccups, a glass of wine in her hand.

Next to the bus stop was a standard Spanish restaurant, with bullfight posters on the wall, toreros' hats hanging from the ceiling and castanets everywhere. "This is where we'll have the reception, after the wedding at the church," Filomena explained. "First God, and then enjoy food and drinks, and songs."

I believed it was the other way around. But what the heck, we had a good time. Aline grabbed my hand and we walked into the church. It was cool inside. A few people were on their knees on their prie-dieus as a priest lit candles on the altar.

"Let's make a wish," Aline said, as she closed her eyes. I knelt next to her and closed my eyes. When I opened them she was staring at me smiling. "Did you make a wish?" I asked

"It's none of your business," she answered laughing and trudging towards the door.

"It's an old church dedicated to Saint Cecilia," Aline said once we were outside. "If I'm not mistaken, it has to be from the twelve or thirteenth century. Spain is scattered with old churches, very little of modern age. One day we'll go to Barcelona. There is a very special cathedral. *La Sagrada Familia*. Not old but weird architecture. It's worth the trip."

It was a nice religious service at Saint Cecilia. The priest, a little red-faced man, seemed to be a cheerful guy using a lot of humor during the ceremony. I couldn't understand half of what he said, but Aline translated as the padre gave his blessing.

Then, we strolled to the restaurant where a number of waiters were expecting us seemingly impatient and enthusiastic.

Filomena, her daughter and her brand new son-in-law sat on a small table next to a narrow stage where five musicians awaited the order to start the music.

Maria Teresa was a pretty girl with huge eyes like her mother and, like a mother, a tendency to get on the fat side. Her husband, Leonardo, on the contrary could have afforded to have a little more weight. His tuxedo seemed to be cut for a two-hundred-pound man when he only must weigh a hundred and fifty. But his smile was contagious and his talking serene, courteous and intelligent.

He said a few words to thank his mother-in-law and every one of us for attending his wedding. "And now," he said raising his glass, "*Aproveche. Bon Appétit.*"

The food appeared to be great and so was the wine. Filomena was more than a little inebriated by the time we reached the dessert. I couldn't think about how much wine she had drunk within the last few hours. Her eyes were ready to pop out, but she kept singing and laughing and crying. All at the same time.

I approached her and sat on the next chair. She looked at me, then, without stopping singing, she hugged me with tears rolling down her pretty face. When she was through with her song I said, "Filomena, I want to ask you something. I heard you lost a son during the civil war."

She stared at me then blew her nose into a handkerchief just slightly larger than a bedsheet. The trumpeting reminded me of those old Tarzan movies with running elephants.

"Yes," she uttered, "and not a day passes without thinking of Mariano. That was his name. He was eighteen and a close friend of Garcia Lorca. You heard about him?"

"Yes, Frederico Garcia Lorca, the poet," I replied. "I know he has been assassinated by Franco's Nationalists when the civil war began. I've read some of his work translated into French."

"That's the official outcome of the investigation. But I know better. Mariano has been killed along with Lorca by the Caudillo's secret police on August 19, 1936."

"The Caudillo?"

"Franco. That's what everyone calls him. El Jefe. The Chief."

She blew her nose one more time with the same sonorous trumpeting.

"Their bodies were found along with two others in a ditch near the Prado Museum. Mariano was your age when he died. He would be thirty years old today. He was my first child, then José was born, then Maria Teresa."

I gave her a kiss on her cheek, patted her gently as she went for another cry. Aline was watching me from our table which we shared with José, Jacqueline and the two Parisians. It was the only table where French was spoken, and it fit me well, though my Spanish was improving by the hour.

We returned to Madrid late that night after the newlyweds disappeared furtively in the middle of the *fiesta*. Filomena had sunk into an armchair and was sleeping, head tilted backward, her mouth agape, and her nose vibrating with a resonant snore. We had to carry her onto the bus where she continued her sleep until we reached Madrid.

18

The university seemed to be crowded on Monday October 15, 1948. I went to the principal's office for I was lost in the building. The same secretary who took my application a few days before, was there smiling at my disheartened face.

"It's always like this the first day," she said. "We get lost and feel abandoned and miserable in the maze, but it won't take long before you find your way through the campus and some friends who would help you in your solitude. Here's the booklet with a map and the list of the different classes and teachers. You have until tomorrow to choose amongst the classes you will attend, yet you won't have the choice on the mandatory courses or on your teachers. You'll have a choice for the minors."

I thanked her and trudged out more lost than before I got in the office.

Seven o'clock chimed on the big clock of the neighboring church.

On the first day nothing started before eight. I went to the library where used books were on sale by older students. All I needed was a college first year math, French, Philosophic Analysis, Biology, History, Geography, English and Spanish. I looked around the crowded library. It was easy to separate the freshmen from the seniors. The latter walked through the campus with arrogance and self confidence, always with a girlfriend hooked on their arms, a smirk on their face, staring at the neophytes with an air of condescension as if they were telling you, "Hey, kid, you're going to be sorry to be here."

I was already sorry. I looked at the main entrance wondering if I could just walk away to never return. But Mom would be so disappointed that I felt sorry for even having the thought.

The freshmen were called over to the amphitheater where a few professors were to give lectures. Strangely, it wasn't crowded. I sat near a young student who couldn't have been older than fifteen. "My name is François Borny," I said.

"I am Gaston Lambrech," he responded with a shy smile and a voice that must not be much lower than mezzo-soprano.

"What are you doing here," I asked.

"Just like you. I'm a freshman."

"Are you sure it's the right school? This is Ardaillon University."

"Yes, I know. I belong here, believe it or not."

"How old are you?"

"Nineteen. It's a good age to start college, isn't it?"

"It sure is. I thought you belonged rather to a high school." I shook his hand. "Well, I guess you don't know anyone here. I don't."

"I met a nice girl this morning, Denise. She's over there on the last row, and she's from Menton."

"Let's meet her. I'll buy a drink at the cafeteria."

We walked up to the last row of seats, and put our butts down next to Denise's. "This is François," Gaston introduced, "and this is Denise." She smiled gently, but didn't say a word, obviously also embarrassed and scared to be here for the first time. I looked around and I could tell that she wasn't the only one. I had included myself amongst the feverish people waiting, under the sword of Damocles, to see what our fate had in store for us. Not sure if the future would be brilliant or boring.

One of the professors began to explain what Ardaillon stood for, how long the university had been there, and what were the main subjects taught here. He talked for an hour in a deep silence, and I noticed that no one had left the amphitheater during his speech. It was Mozart playing music with words. A long silence ended his talk and the cheers that it created came like a thunder. We all stood in appreciation. That man was great.

"When you leave the amphitheater," he said scratching his nose after the applaud ceased, "pick up a form on the table over there, fill it up, and give it to the dean's secretary. You will find the class numbers and the names of the teachers in the subject you have chosen. Classes start tomorrow, seven a.m. Be on time. Good luck to you all."

He was a little man with long hair, large spectacles, a bow tie larger than his narrow face, and a fine mustache under an aquiline nose. From where I was in the amphitheater, it seemed that the professor had a slight strabismus. He looked funny in his general aspect and not at all like a scholar though he was a Ph.D. I found later that he was one of the best teachers I ever met in my life. His name was Schwartz, a Jew who survives Mathausen to become one of the best writers in modern French literature. I met him again many years later. He had the same pathetic aspect and the same slight strabismus that, however, was overpowered by a sparkle in his eyes. He had retired and lived in Valauris, near one of Picasso's workshops, where he was writing his memoirs. A month or so later I read in the paper that Professor Schwartz had passed on abruptly without finishing the story of his life. It was too bad for the world could have learned a lot from his experience.

Two years later his memoirs were published under the title *I've been in Mathausen*. Of course I hurried to buy it. It was a horrid compilation of what happened to him and his fellow-prisoners during the years of captivity. He couldn't finish the story of his life, but a well-known author, and friend of his, wrote the end of his work.

* * *

Denise, Gaston and I walked down the steep stairs of the amphitheater, picked up a form on the table near the door, and trudged to the cafeteria where we sat near the counter. I bought the drinks and returned to the table. "Where are you from, Gaston?" I asked.

"Grasse, the city of the thousand perfumes," he said proudly as if the city belonged to him. "Near the Fragonnard Museum."

"I love Grasse and its smell," Denise said. For the first time I heard her voice. It was a girlish, almost childish, voice with the usual southern drawl of the region. Yet she looked a lot like a grownup woman to me. Taller than I was, blond with a twinkle in her blue eyes, and a pretty smile that seemed to be unalterable. But I'm not crazy about women who have to bend over to kiss me. No offense, Denise, I thought.

"What are your subjects?" she asked.

"Let's see." I picked up the single sheet form and read. "French, compulsory of course, teacher, Ms. Antonin; How does she look?" I asked.

"Beats me," Gaston said with a shrug. "I don't know any of the teachers besides those we have seen here a moment ago. And there were no women amongst them."

"Math," I continued, "also mandatory, teacher, Mr. Klein, Philosophy, Mr. Schwartz. This one we know. He doesn't look very good, does he?" I made a check mark in the little boxes in front of each course I chose and so did Denise and Gaston.

I've forgotten the names of my Biology, English and Spanish teachers, an oblivion I'm not very proud of. But I recall my History-Geography professor, Mr. Gouhaux, a short man always smiling and making strange noises with his hands stuck together. He wore a toupee that seemed to have its own life, always threatening to fly away but, to my knowledge, never heard of such a thing. The professor was, we found out quickly, an inexhaustible source of History as well as Geography. His erudition was undeniable. He knew Homer's Iliad and Odyssey as if he had lived in Greece in the 8th century BC. He had a pleasant way to teach that reminded me of Monsieur Farelacci, my high school teacher at Jules Renard.

"I'll try Spanish and English for the minors," I pursued. "I want to go to Spain so I need to learn the language. As I hope to go to America one of those days, I need English."
"What would you do in America?" Denise asked.
"Live the American way. Rich and famous." We all laughed at my impossible dreams.
"I'll be in Spanish class with you," Denise added, and then smiled. And in History. Maybe some others also.
"Hum!" whispered Gaston with a wince.
"What?" I said.
"Never mind," he mumbled impishly, then looked down at his form and read, "English, Math, French, etc., but no Spanish. That's all for me. Anyway, we'll be together in a few classes—"
"For the next four years," Denise cut in laughing.
"Oh, shut up, Denise," I retorted. "For now let's have something to eat and don't think about the next four years," I said. "And then we go home. I know a cute little restaurant on the beach, I used to go there with my father on fishing days, when I was a kid."
"We'll do that," Gaston said. "Then you'll ride the train to Nice, François, and you, Denise, to Menton. And we'll see each other in the morning. I'll take the bus to Grasse. I would have to find an apartment here in the area. I don't want to travel every day to Grasse."
"I'm sure that must be easy," Denise said, "if you have the money."
"I would have some help from my dad."
Lucky you, I thought. Mine doesn't even know I'm here.
The small restaurant on the beach was called *Le Pêcheur* —The Fisherman. It lay about three blocks from the university. It was noisy inside. Fishing nets, buoys, anchors, propellers, and other boat devices, were hung or set everywhere. "Rather dark in here," Gaston remarked. "Only storm lanterns give a semblance of light, but no one seems to care."

"You cannot inspect your food in this kind of dimness," Denise muttered. "But perhaps it's better that way."

It smelled deliciously of fresh fried fish when we stepped in. Three young women were waiting a dozen tables where a bunch of happy and boisterous students seemed to have fun. No one older than twenty or twenty-two in the restaurant besides the owner. A smiling middle aged short and fat man behind the counter sitting next to the cash register. I didn't recall him from before the war. There was at the time a young lady named Isabelle who owned the restaurant. She was gracious and sympathetic with her young customers from the university. Then war came that turned everyone's life upside down. I approached the counter and said, "I knew the former owner, Isabelle. I used to come here with my father for dinner after we had spent the day fishing on the pier over there. What happened to her?"

"You knew Isabelle? Not many people remember her," he said erasing his smile from his face. "I'm Emmanuel, her brother. The Germans killed her on the beach."

"Oh, I'm sorry."

"She hid two Americans parachutists in this restaurant when it was disaffected. No food at the time, so no business. You remember? I was in London with de Gaulle. When I came back home I heard about her fate. I knew she had passed away but I had no idea how it happened."

"Poor Isabelle. She was such a nice lady."

"The Germans caught her and her friends," Emmanuel continued. "They tried to escape shooting their way out through the back door, killing two or three Germans —I never knew for sure— but they were overwhelmed by the SS's fire power. They got killed right here, on the beach. You can see the three crosses in front of the restaurant."

"I noticed the crosses, but I didn't know what they meant. I'm sorry about Isabelle," I repeated before I returned to Denise and Gaston at the table.

The waitresses were three young college students, making some money for their studies. The three were seniors and on their second year working at the restaurant. "It could be a good way to make some money," Denise said. "To pay for an apartment here at Saint-Laurent, for instance. Besides, food would be free."

"There is the owner over there," I said pointing at the fat man. "Why don't you ask him for a job?"

Denise didn't wait for this to be repeated. Perhaps she was waiting for encouragement. She got up then walked to the counter. A minute later she returned to our table all smile. "I'll start tomorrow night, three to eight, just in time to take the last train to Menton. All the day-jobs are already taken, of course, but I'll be fine."

"While you work here I'll be working at my printing shop. I've been re-hired for the part-time job I had last summer. Perhaps we could put our money together on a rented small house, Gaston, you and me. We could share the apartment so we won't have to travel to Nice, Menton or Grasse every day. My printing shop is on the road to Nice. A little stroll from here."

"That's a great idea," Denise said as she jumped to her feet and kissed me on the cheek.

"Hum! That's what I thought," Gaston murmured with a smirk.

"What did you think?" I asked.

"I mean, I agree with Denise.... But I won't kiss you."

19

No news from Dad. He had disappeared now for more than a month without a word of his whereabouts. The barbershop was still open but only the employee worked, an old man called Tintin for the lock of blond hair he had straight up on his head like my favorite hero of the cartoon *The Adventures of Tintin & Milou*. The old barber had thick glasses on his nose —I always wondered how he could see through them— and a mustache he probably hadn't trimmed since World War I.

He had no idea where my father was, he said, but I'm sure he knew something. He was my father's coworker for years and I believe friends have secrets they don't share with the family. Dad had always loved to brag about his conquests, though not to us, of course.

Mom had made up her mind. She knew then that Dad wouldn't return home soon. She decided to sell the shop. And the hell with Tintin. He should have chosen a better employer. I didn't know Mom's intentions, so every morning I checked the shop, said hello to Tintin —I never knew his real name— and walked by towards the train station.

And one morning, I saw the sign *For Sale* stuck in the window. Mom had taken the bull by the horns and Tintin was gone. We didn't know where, nor did we care.

* * *

It was Saturday on a cold November with mistral blowing down the Rhône Valley, one of those cold days in wintertime. Usually it's never cold long enough on the French Riviera to be bothering. The temperature sometimes falls to the thirties, and the next day, you found yourself in shorts, strolling the Promenade des Anglais bathed with sun and temperatures up to 80°. Crazy weather but more enjoyable than in Paris or Strasbourg where November and December bring snow and freezing temperatures that last for weeks.

But cold in Nice may come suddenly in December and January, dropping below the freezing mark of 32°. That was the Riviera. Not many people on the beach with the exception of crazy Swedish or British tourists wearing shorts and T-shirts while we turned to ice when the temperature dared to go below the fifties.

I had been in college now for a month and, I had to concede, enjoying it. I love the teachers, the classes, and the company of my friends Denise and Gaston. Somehow I managed to be through with my classes at two o'clock, and have a quick sandwich on my way to the shop where I joined the night shift for a few hours. Roger was the old man in the photoengraving department. He was a nice Marseillais in his middle fifties, very fat and very bald, who kept singing all day and all night, as long as he was working, old songs from his hometown. I learned from him all the melodies from before the war by successful composers I never knew, who would have been on the French Hit Parade, if there were one.

Although over fifty years have passed I still remember the lyrics and the tunes of most of those beautiful songs.

* * *

My friends Gaston, and sometimes Denise, were kept busy after school looking for a small house in Saint-Laurent. They still had to return home every night. Long way for both of them. Up in the hills to Grasse for Gaston, and an easier hour-route by train to Menton for Denise.

Each morning we would gather together at the cafeteria before we started our school day. Denise worked at *The Fisherman* restaurant every night but Sundays. On her way home she would do part of her homework for the next day. That was the convenience of the railroad.

* * *

Mom sold the barbershop pretty quickly. A young couple bought it with a plan to build up a business for men and women. They were both hairdressers, energetic, and gracious. And she was beautiful. Mom invited them for dinner one night, cooking one of her master dishes she had the secret of. The sale made a little money to put in the bank for Mom, Juliette and me. My sister was still an apprentice in dress making but doing quite well. The shop owner, Mrs. Martini, had adopted her full time, so we scarcely had Juliette visiting us. Now that she had part of the barbershop money at her disposal, she was relaxed. As for me, I knew then that I had my next year of college secured.

And the news came one morning by the means of a letter. Dad was in Paris. The letter was addressed to Juliette and me. It was a list of reasons why he had left us, a kind of distasteful nomenclature I didn't want to know. As for Juliette, she ignored even the fact we had received something from our father. "Throw it away," she had said, "or send it back to him. With a grenade inside."

Mom had looked at the letter, tears in her eyes, hesitated a few seconds, then tore it to pieces without reading it. That was it. Dad had disappeared from our lives, and I wondered if it wasn't the best thing that could happen to us.

It took me a few years before I forgot those gloomy days and I agreed to meet with my father again.

20

I rushed through the arch at the university gate as Denise arrived under her umbrella. A pouring rain had fallen on the French Riviera for two days now, which happened about once or twice every decade. Niçois —the people from Nice— are not used to so much rain in so little time. The sun shines about three hundred and twenty days a year which leaves not much room for rain. But we are happy that way. Rain is good for Paris or Lille or Strasbourg, but not here. That's why I stayed where I was born.

Denise smiled at me and I could feel in her look that she remained a happy girl despite the flooding.

"Did you work late last night?" she asked as if the answer didn't make any difference.

"At the shop? No, till about nine. Why do you ask?"

"You look tired."

"It was two this morning when I went to bed. I had to finish my homework for this morning."

"History/Mythology?"

"Yeah! Fascinating. Never get tired of those legends. Come on. Let's go to the cafeteria. We still have thirty minutes before the bell."

"I buy," she offered.

I looked at her, smiled and, without a word, I hooked my arm in hers. "What about you?" I asked. "You look tired too."

"Same old stuff. We're swamped with Mr. Gouhaux homework. But that's all right. I love his class."

Gaston got up when we stepped into the cafeteria. "I thought you were skipping school today," he said laughing.

"We still have thirty minutes," Denise said. "Time to have a cup of coffee."

"Who buys?" Gaston inquired. "I'm broke."

"Come on moneybags. What's the matter with you? Where did you put your money?"

"Into an apartment, a brand new one I found last night after school."

"What?" Denise yelled getting on her feet.

I noticed since we'd known each other that she had an inclination to stand when she is happily surprised. She looked taller like this, but still pretty. Who is she going to kiss this time, I wondered? She leaned over Gaston and kissed him on the head, then got close to me and hugged me. No kiss today. She ruined my day.

"Where did you find that?" she finally managed to say as she sat down all excited.

"Charles de Gaulle Avenue. Not far from the train station and from the university."

"They already have an avenue named after General de Gaulle?"

"Yes. The War has ended three years ago, François, remember? They've had plenty of time to give or change the names of the streets. Every city and village has something called Charles de Gaulle. A street, a boulevard, a stadium or a building. No more Philippe Pétain streets, or boulevards or whatever."

"Vive de Gaulle," I yelled. Everyone in the cafeteria froze then stared at me. One senior student come close to our table, pretended to have a gun in his hand, and shot me.

"That's all right," I explained. "A mistake I won't do again." We all laughed as the student walked away and pretended to put his gun in his belt.

"So, when do we visit it?" I asked.

"After school. The owner, Mr. Langevin, looked like a nice man. He's just finished building a small three-story unit with four apartments. One for him and his wife on the top floor, one for his

daughter, one for his son, and a last one on the second floor we might be lucky to have."
"Did you see it?" Denise asked.
"Yes, three bedrooms, but only one bathroom."
"That will do." she said. "Are you in, François?"
"How much?"
"Three hundreds francs a month."
The bell rang. It was time for our class. Gaston had something like chemistry or physics, but it was later.
"I'll be here at two o'clock," Gaston said. "I'll wait for you, then we'll pay a visit to Mr. Langevin."

Denise and I left the cafeteria and joined Mr. Gouhaux as he walked into the classroom.
"How did you do on your assignment?" he asked.
"You tell me, sir. "I worked on the Nibelungen. Six pages, but I could fill up a whole book."
"I bet you could. The subject is endless. And interesting, isn't it?"
I nodded as Denise listened to our dialog on a theme she didn't know.
"What's the Nibel something," she inquired eyebrows raised.
"Nibelungen," I replied. "The men of the mist."
"I like to hear about that. Where did you find it?"
"Searching, sir. I've always been interested in the legend of the Nibelungen. Wagner had composed a masterpiece on the subject."
"And what about you, Denise?"
"I worked on the Trojan War, sir."
"Could be interesting too. Let's start the class and talk about this."
The amphitheater was already full when we arrived. Mr. Gouhaux had his reputation which attracted a lot of students in History. Geography was another world only attended by a fistful of people including Denise and myself. The reason I'd noticed was the

difference in the teaching. Geography is a fact. Nothing to embroider. History, on the other hand, had always been subjected to any improvisation and, I would say, improvement. One can tell the History of the world in one way and someone else would say the same thing with other words and more talent. That was what made the difference between Mr. Farelacci and Ms. Barbier. Mr. Gouhaux had as much talent as my High school teacher plus an unusual sense of humor that made his class attractive. Besides, the little weird farting noises he made with his hands as to punctuate a quotation or a special sentence, kept the students' attention.

"You had three options," Mr. Gouhaux said with his resonant and agreeable voice. He didn't need any amplifying devices to reach the upper row of the classroom. "First, you could have chosen the Trojan War, second, the Roman Empire, or, third, anything else you liked. How many of you have chosen the Trojan War?"

A dozen students or so raised their arms. "Good," the teacher said. "Did the Trojan Horse inspire you? How many have chosen the Roman Empire?"

Twenty hands went up.

"I can see that the History of Ancient Rome has attracted many of you. Probably atavism has something to do with the interest showed by the area population and its Italian roots. But it's all right. You had the choices and you have chosen. Now, who picked up the third option?"

I raised my hand, and I was the only one. "I've worked on the Nibelungen," I said and looked around. I saw most of my classmates asking the question I expected. "What in the world is that?" they whispered as if they were scared to look too stupid to ask aloud. Suddenly I wondered if it was a smart move from me to take such a risk. I'll be forced to talk about my essay or, if I were lucky, to read it aloud which would be easier.

"Come to the board, Mr. Borny, bring your copy and tell us what

you did find interesting on those demonic characters."
I walked to the board as if I was going to the guillotine. I hated having all those faces on my back some with an unpleasant smile on their lips. What am I doing here? I thought. Why didn't I shut my big mouth? I looked at Denise. She smiled then thumbed her nose. "That's not funny," I said aloud.
"Don't you worry," Mr. Borny, "she's next."
The smirk on Denise's face vanished instantly.
"So, what's your story?" Mr. Gouhaux asked then sat down on the edge of his desk, hands together making his usual little noises.
I shuffled a few pages nervously before I began to think what I was going to said next. Where do I start, I thought.
As if the teacher had read my mind, he said, "Why don't you start from the beginning?"
I closed my eyes for a few seconds trying to remember the first lines of my essay. Then I began with a quivering voice, a voice that became gradually stronger.

"In the late 1750's, a German priest, Father Schiller, made an astonishing discovery while traveling through Eastern Europe. He stopped accidentally in the tiny village of Mikulov where he found, in a disaffected and dilapidated church, the most extraordinary manuscript made by men. It was eight inches thick with a leather cover and golden illuminations. Three golden rings, ten inches in diameter, bound the manuscript. Inside was the most prestigious design a book had ever had. According to the date written on some pages the pieces of art, it dated from early twelfth century to late thirteen century. Monks and friars had composed the masterpiece. Some artists had signed their names and the dates they had completed their work."
"Did the work have a name or a title?" Mr. Gouhaux asked.
"Yes," I replied, "*Das Nibelungen Lied*. The Song of the

Nibelungen. The manuscript was stealthily brought by the priest to his hometown of Braulage, in what we call today East Germany."
"Hold on, François. Let's make it clear. The priest, Father Schiller I believe, found a manuscript in Moldavia that is nowadays Romania, and brought it to his country which is Germany. So, what did he do with it?"
I was surprised the teacher called me François in the classroom. He only called me by my first name in private. At school, he would call all his students by their last names always preceded by *monsieur*.
"He kept it religiously and, for a long time, secretly," I said coming back to the subject. "But after two hundred years one can still see the manuscript in the same little church it was brought in."
"Have you seen it?" someone asked.
"No, I've never been to Germany but I read a book translated from German and published in the mid-nineteenth century. Father Schiller wrote it a hundred years before, published in German in 1804, and translated in many languages much later. In his book, Father Schiller explained the legend of the Nibelungen, the men of the mist, who came from Iceland, and traveled all over Europe to settle on the slopes of Mount Hartz, near Braulage."
"So, what is the Nibelungen's legend?" Mr. Gouhaux asked.
"That started in the Yucatan Peninsula in Mexico in the late 11th century. The legend said that the Mayans worshipped a pagan deity; a blue donkey that was supposed to be misogynous. The women were kept away for the statue was lethal to them. In the case of adultery, which was common at the time, the woman was thrust against the statue. Within twenty-four hours the adulteress would expire."
"I wouldn't like to live in those times," someone said. I was almost sure it was Denise. The professor smiled. "Go ahead," he said looking at me, "interesting."
"The Mayas left Chichén Itza, the capital of the Yucatan peninsula in the 13th century when the King Humac Ceel burnt the city. They

stampeded off the country taking with them their devilish Blue Donkey and carried it as far as the Caribbean Islands. The heterodox belief of the Mayas spread among the Indian population of the West Indies like a fire in a thicket of dead trees. The Mayas stayed there two centuries. They were welcome by the Arawak and Caribbean Indians of the islands who were more than happy to share their hosts' knowledge and their modern civilization."

"Two centuries," the teacher said. "So, where did they go after that stay?"

"This is the best part, at least the incongruous part. They left the Caribbean, all of a sudden as if in hurry, as Christopher Colombus was preparing to land on what today is known as Hispaniola. Was it only a coincidence or could they have seen an ominous sign in the coming of the Spaniards? Those Mayas were educated, good astronomers as well as good architects and mathematicians. Besides they were astute astrologers. They could have foreseen the discovery of America and perhaps they didn't want to mingle with the incoming conquistadors. The fact is that they left for a long voyage towards Iceland. Of course, they didn't forget their Blue Donkey."

"And here come the Nibelungen, isn't it?" Mr. Gouhaux said.

"Yes, but it's more complicated than those simple words. The Mayas weren't greeted as well as in the Caribbean. The Icelanders care little for those short men, with slanted eyes, who looked like something they never saw before. Aesthetically unattractive and somehow frightful."

At that point I paused waiting for eventual questions. But the class was silent and, I had to say, looking very much interested.

"Father Schiller," I pursued, "wrote in his book that after a long sojourn in the cold island, those dwarves began to mingle up with the autochthon population. And the offsprings of that multi-racial mix happened to be the Nibelungen. A weird blend of Mayas and Arakwak Indians, Caribbean, Icelanders, and God knows what more. The amalgamation had produced a strange race of dwarf Indians with blond hair, blue eyes, dark completion and dwelling on gruesome matters."

"Strange features," Mr. Gouhaux said.

"Strange indeed, but also scary."

"Did they completely disappear from the Caribbean?" Mr. Gouhaux asked.

"Not totally. There are rumors that they found some traces of those dwarves in the forest in Central Haiti. But this is not confirmed."

"Did you make that up?" said a voice.

"Hardly. Legends like the Nibelungen are hard to die. But if I were you, I would take this story with circumspection. For me it has been fun to do the research, and if I don't quite take what I wrote as completely true, I think it's a curious story in many ways. Isn't it?"

I returned to my seat as my classmates applauded mockingly.

Next was the embarrassed Denise who came to the board with her copy about the Trojan War. She was pale, I recall, shaking, and seemingly ready to cry.

Much later she told me that she had felt as if she were naked. Of course she wasn't, but they all ogled at her as if she were. Her nice body outlined in a tight summer dress, and her beautiful face prompted bad thoughts from that bunch of perverts we had in the classroom.

However, she started her exposé with confidence and finished it, with a flourish of details, all within the half hour I left her before the end of the class. This time the whole classroom applauded. And it wasn't mockingly. But I always wondered, since that happened, if it were Denise's talent —and she undeniably had some— or her looks, and she certainly had good ones.

"We don't have much time left today," Mr. Gouhaux declared when Denise was through, "but none of you students are forgotten. You'll come to the pillory the next time."

Denise and I walked out of the classroom towards the cafeteria where Gaston awaited us. Mr. Gouhaux caught up with us, then sat at our table. "You made it up, didn't you, François?" he said laughing.
"Absolutely, Sir."

21

Mom was happy for my friends and me. "It's time for you to start living like a man, by yourself, and learn the unforeseen turn of events. You're nineteen and I know you can handle it. I mean life."

I wasn't so sure. Besides the two weeks I spent in Spain the previous year, I'd never been far from home and Mom was always there to put me on the right track.

"I'll help with your apartment," Mom kept on. "I don't have big needs now and I make enough money for you and Juliette. Besides, we still have some reserves from the sale of the barber shop."

I knew Mom didn't spend a penny of that money, but usually she didn't talk about it. Perhaps this reminded her of Dad.

"We start moving Saturday," I said. "Gaston and Denise are ready and excited."

"I'll take the day off," Mom declared peremptory as if she wouldn't take any refusal from me, "and we'll buy some furniture with the money we have saved."

Here we go, I thought, the infamous money of the sale is coming out from the dark, like a ghost. Mom finally opened her mind and the banking account.

"It's fine with me, but I also have some savings in my bank," I said proudly.

"Save it for Aline. Aren't you supposed to visit her in Spain next year?"

"I would hope so. I can't wait."

"Of course you can't.

* * *

It was Sunday afternoon in our new apartment. I was worn out and so were Gaston and Denise. The day before, Mom and I went to the *Galeries Lafayette*, the department store three blocks from home. I would have bought anything at first sight, but shopping for two hours to purchase a small bed, a table, a chest of drawers, and two chairs, was beyond my patience. Mom noticed my exasperation while she talked to the vendor at the Galeries. She frowned two or three times as to say, "Not a word François, I'll handle it." Actually she did well and even managed to scrap a few francs off the tag prices from the salesman.

Denise's father, Henri, had generously agreed to put his truck at our disposal, to pick up my furniture at the Galeries after he had loaded his daughter's possessions, to make a long circular journey to Grasse where we loaded Gaston's junk, and to help us unload and move the whole cargo on the second floor of the little building in Saint-Laurent. It was some Sunday for Henri, his only day off of the week. We bought him a pizza while unloading his truck, and he was satisfied with a glass of cheap wine we had bought for him. Good guy, this Henri.

Yet, we were infinitely happy, after all those peregrinations, to be at last in our own home.

Denise made short work of arranging the rooms, with good taste, I have to concede. She had brought some curtains and was already hanging them up. And we had to help her. "Why couldn't she wait the next day or the next week to do that?" I asked.

"You know women," Gaston said with a shrug, "they must do everything right away as if the world would end within minutes."

"I wouldn't have minded if I didn't have to help."

Denise didn't say a word as if she hadn't noticed our conversation. But she was through by six o'clock when she began to cook some

eggs and bacon for dinner. "Wow! That I like," I whispered.
"You see," Gaston said, "she's such a good girl. Thanks Denise."
She laughed as she set the table with her own tableware.
I picked up *Nice Matin*, the local newspaper, and sat down on the balcony overlooking the garden in the backyard. It was a nice day with the little warm breeze coming from the ocean bringing in the heady smell of lilac.
"Oh no!" I suddenly whined.
"What's wrong?" Denise asked as she served the dinner.
"Ms. Barbier, is not any longer Ms. Barbier. She's married a guy I never heard of save that he was her fiancé for a while."
"Who is Ms. Barbier?" Gaston asked.
"The most beautiful History teacher you can dream of. She was my teacher in high school. The whole school was in love with her. Teachers as well as students."
"That included you," Denise stated.
"Yes, including me. I know some of my former classmates who are going to mourn. Perhaps even commit suicide."
"But not you," the mischievous Denise uttered.
"No, not me. I'm now in love with the most attractive girl you would meet if you come with me to Spain."
"Aline?"
"Yes, Aline."
"I thought it was Denise." Gaston couldn't pass that one, of course.
"Denise is my second love," I retorted.
"I'm happy with that," Denise added as she came close to me and gave me a kiss on the lips.
"That's what I thought," Gaston said. "You got them all."
"No, not all, only two."
I remember, we laughed as Denise reminded us that the best dinner we'd ever had was ready. Bacon and eggs.

* * *

Early the next morning, we went all three of us to pay a first visit to Mr. Langevin, the landlord, and write him a check for the first month of rent. Usually, the rule was to put down a month value of rent for deposit as security. But Mr. Langevin waved the deposit and, with a smile, told us that the first month was a gift from him to three broke students. What a deal!
But it wasn't the last one. We had, on many occasions afterwards, the opportunity to appreciate Mr. Langevin gentleness and generosity. He always managed to make us happy and thankful with his kindness that became month after month as natural as the air we breathed. He always had something nice to say or to do.

When Mr. Langevin died many years later, all three of us, without consulting each other, attended the funeral. It was the first time in years that I met with Gaston and Denise. They were both happily married, and so was I. Gaston was still looking like a fifteen year old boy, though he was now a doctor, and Denise was as beautiful as ever. It seemed to me that she had gained one or two extra inches since college.
For a few hours we talked about our life in the second floor apartment in Saint-Laurent, our student years, and the good time we'd had together. We had spent four endless years together in this nice house.
The building hadn't changed but for a slight patina over all. Our apartment was still rented to students but from the university of Nice. Ardaillon, unfortunately, had disappeared from the beach and with it the students of Saint-Laurent. But Nice was a few minutes away by train and students were coming to Saint-Laurent to escape the now turbulent city.
In the same site where Ardaillon was standing for so many years,

high standard apartment buildings had risen above the ocean. Even *The Fisherman* restaurant, where Denise used to work in her college years, had vanished completely.

That was sad but life continued as if nothing bad had ever happened in the world.

* * *

It was now May. The university was closing the following week for summer vacation, and one could tell the general jubilation of the students by the turmoil on the campus. Seniors were certainly the happiest. They were through after four years and, I presumed, ready for the real life, their diplomas, whatever they were made of, under their armpits. Denise, Gaston and I weren't ready yet, but the first year at Ardaillon had been a success for all three of us.

We had decided to keep the apartment even though it wouldn't be much used for the duration of the summer. I was going to Spain, probably for a month, or maybe longer; Denise would spend some time with her family in Menton before going to Italy, and Gaston would certainly go to Paris as he had planned for a while. Good luck to him.

22

Aline was waiting at the Chamartin train station in Madrid. She wore a pink summer dress with a red belt that made her waist really remarkable, Italian sandals, a chiffon scarf, and a hibiscus flower in her hair. Prettier than ever. I almost jumped off the compartment through the window as soon as I caught sight of her.

I'd written two or three weeks before telling her the exact time I would arrive in the Spanish capital. Which was presumptuous from my part. Trains in Spain never reach any destination on time.

I climbed down the train and ran to her as she ran towards me.
"I've almost forgotten how good you looked," I said after I kissed her with all my heart.
"I missed you. It's been such a long year," she said tears in her eyes.

I kissed her again and again as we walked out of the railroad station. People watched us with a mixture of annoyance and disgust.
"In Spain, they don't like couples kissing on the streets," Aline said laughing.
"Who cares? I'm not going to give up kisses when I have them free. In Spain or in any other countries."

She still had her blue convertible Renault parked just in front of the main entrance next to a no-parking sign. I pointed at it, but she didn't seem worried.
"I've had a *CD* status for a few months now," she said with a shrug.
"Diplomatic Corps," I translated.
"Yes. No policemen would write a ticket to a nice young lady who

wears such a sticker on her car."

"Daddy, right?"

"Nope. My job at the embassy. I rose to the rank of press secretary. A diplomatic function, that is."

"You didn't write anything to me about that."

"I didn't write to you to brag about my social status," she said suddenly serious and gentle. "I write to you because I love you, and I want to keep you close to me. At least in my mind. I don't want you to forget me while you are mixed up with young beautiful female students. I wrote you every day since you left last year. Did you notice?"

Of course, I did. There were days where I had three or four letters. And days without.

"I couldn't wait to see you again," she said.

"You knew I'd be back. I wrote to you, if not every day, as often as I could. Remember, I'm still a stupid student at Ardaillon."

"Yeah, yeah! And what about that apartment in Saint Laurent? Who is this girl, Denise? Huh!"

"Oh, nobody. Ugly as sin. Gaston takes care of her."

"I don't believe she's hideous. I can't picture you mingled with unattractive women. So, don't lie to me." She laughed, but I suspected she was serious.

"All right. The truth is Denise is a beautiful girl, nice too, and cute. She has eyes almost as beautiful as yours, but blue. And you know I prefer green eyes. Only thing, she's three or four inches taller than me. She has to bend over to kiss me."

"She kisses you?" Aline yelled.

That was my turn to laugh. Yes she did, I thought, but I didn't tell.

We reached *Calle Cervantes* and the Filomena Hotel around noon. Too early for lunch in Spain, but I could wait.

"Filomena is impatient to see you," Aline said. "I talked to her yesterday. She said she has prepared her best room for you."

We got out of the Renault and walked to the entrance as Filomena ran to meet us at the door. She was in tears when she reached us and elated like a child who met with his fairy godmother. Her hug almost shocked me, but she ignored Aline. Filomena grabbed my hand and dragged me to the counter as Aline followed.

"I've prepared the best room in the hotel, all by myself. I wasn't sure you were coming this year, and when Aline told me that, yes you'll be here today, I was so happy." Then, she realized that she didn't pay attention to Aline. She turned all of a sudden, stammered excuses. Then she kissed her.

"My God," I said, "if I knew how I would be welcomed I would have come much earlier in the year."

"You are quite welcome, my dear François. Everybody will be here tomorrow night to greet you. You remember Maria Teresa, my daughter?"

"How can I forget the good time we had at Chinchón at her wedding, and the food, and the sangria, and the songs. Yes indeed, I remember her and her husband Leonardo. What about José and Jacqueline?"

"They're here since last week. You know they got married?"

"No, I didn't."

"In Paris, the week before Christmas. I went for the wedding. It was so cold over there, with snow and rain, and freezing wind."

"And stupid Parisians," I added. "Christmas is not the best time to go to Paris. It's better to go to the Canary Islands."

"It's where they went for two weeks. Now they're in Madrid. They can't wait to see you, they told me."

We climbed to the second floor to my room. It wasn't the same as last year. This one was much larger and in the corner of the building which gave me two windows overlooking *Calles Cervantes* and *San Augustin*.

The room smelled a mix of lavender and Fly-Tox, an odor I recall from the previous year. A large bouquet of yellow daffodils was in a blue vase on the coffee table beside a bottle of champagne Dom Perignon 1938, in a bucket filled with ice, and two flutes.

"This is your welcome," Filomena said cheerfully.

How did she know I loved Dom Perignon? I'm not a fan of any alcoholic beverage, but the Perignon had always been my weakness. Fortunately, this champagne is so expensive that you cannot get addicted to it. Unless you're a millionaire, of course. And I wasn't.

"There are only two glasses," I said eyebrows raised.

"That's for you and Aline," Filomena said. I brought that bottle when I went to Paris for José's wedding, and I saved it for you."

"We need another glass for you, Filomena," Aline said. "We won't drink without you."

She smiled at Aline's remark, her eyes a little wet, turned around and said, "I'll be right back."

"I believe she has lost some weight," I said, "hasn't she?"

"Yes indeed. Her triple chin has reduced now to two and a half."

We laughed as the Spaniard returned to the room. We were shameless to make fun of such a good human being.

"Now I can open the bottle," I said as I grabbed the Dom Perignon. I poured into the glasses and offered one to the ladies. "*Salut,*" I said raising my flute.

As Aline looked over the room sipping her champagne she said, "It's a nice place Filomena has saved for you."

"Thank you, Filomena," I said, "but your philanthropy won't ever get you rich."

"I am rich," she said with a twinkle in her eyes. "Didn't you know?" Then she laughed with her crystalline soprano voice.

Maybe she was lying, but I didn't care. Later I heard that Filomena owned several businesses in Madrid and even in Barcelona and in Seville. She was indeed a rich and extremely nice lady.

"I have to go," Aline informed me. "We have a press conference at three. I'll be here around six. It will be almost time for the paseo. You must be tired, François. Take a nap unless Filomena wants to take care of you while you're waiting for me." She kissed me, kissed the Spaniard, and walked out waiving her hand and smiling. She stopped at the door and said, "Oh, I forgot. Tomorrow is my first day on vacation. One month, one entire month. We'll have plenty to do. I've already made a list of what we're going to do."
She disappeared in the staircase.

* * *

I slept almost the whole afternoon lying on the bed, still dressed in my travel clothes. It took a few minutes to realize where I was. Yes, that was Spain with its olive oil smell and the daytime silence of the streets. In no time the traffic would build up and it would be impossible to cross any street without being run over.
I had a shower and it seemed that even the water smelled of olive oil.
I went down to the minuscule lobby where I sat waiting for Aline. Filomena stepped in a few seconds after me smiling. "Are you hungry?"
"I'm starving," I answered. "I haven't had a real meal since I left Nice."
"I could prepare something to kill your hunger, but I guess you and Aline are dining out."
"Probably. I don't know her intentions yet."
"I understand she lives near La Puerta del Sol."
"Yes, but I don't know where exactly. She found that apartment after I returned home, last summer. Most likely when she had this terrific promotion."
"What promotion?"

Definitively Filomena was a woman. Inquisitive like the whole Inquisition.

"She's press secretary at the embassy."

"Wow! I didn't know. This is a serious occasion for celebration. I still have some Dom Perignon in my cellar."

Celebration must be Filomena's middle name. She could find an excuse for festivities even at a funeral. Eating and, mostly, drinking took a large part of her life. That's the way she was and, heck, it was her life after all.

"We'll celebrate," I said, "when your entire family will be here. Is that a deal?"

"Deal. Now, I don't know about Aline's new apartment, I wonder how big it is."

"I'll let you know as soon as I visit it."

"My idea is why don't you live with her while you're in Madrid. She must have enough room for both of you."

Damn Filomena. She was intruding in our life but the idea didn't even cross her mind. "I am an old fashion idiot," I said.

"It's not that I want to get rid of you. Oh no, God. I would be the happiest woman if you stayed here year around."

Aline arrived just in time to save me. I was not going to repeat the conversation with the Spaniard.

"What are you up to tonight?" Filomena asked after I kissed Aline.

"First a good dinner," Aline answered. "In all probability at *El Bodegon Logroñes*. It will be sort of an anniversary. That's the first restaurant François and I had dinner last year."

"That's a nice thought," Filomena said. "Logroñes is a renowned restaurant."

"François loved the *Calamares a la tinta*." She winced in disgust, turned around and kissed the fat lady. "We're gone now."

The *Bodegon* was still there with the same terrace adorned with

small Spanish flags, the same menu, and the same smell of olive oil. Rosita, the waitress we'd met the previous year, was as pretty and unmarried as before. Aline had remarked about that too. She looked at me and asked, "Did you notice that Rosita is still single and as gorgeous as ever?"
"No, I didn't," I lied. "How do you know?"
"What? That she's lovely and unmarried? Look at her finger. No ring. A Spanish married woman would die rather than not wearing her wedding ring. As for the good-looking, I trust your taste."
She smiled and I began to think that Aline might be a little jealous.
Of course I glanced at Rosita when I stepped in following Aline, but I'm sure no one had noticed that. And certainly not Rosita who paid not much attention to us. I'm an expert in prying stealthily. When I first saw Aline, that night on the *paseo del Prado*, no one had remarked that I'd been scanning everything on her. Her face, her legs, her waist, and the rest as well. I could tell how tall she was, what was her weight, the color of her eyes —that's the first thing I saw— the color of her hair, and the perfect row of white teeth when she smiled. I could have told what size of shoes she wore and the color of the handbag she carried that day. All this within thirty seconds. I was already in love, and at that time, I thought, hopelessly.
We were seated on the terrace among a dozen other patrons prattling on. Rosita came to our table smiling and asking what would we like to have. I decided, though I had said I would never renew the experience, that I'd try again those ugly *Calamares a la tinta*.
"But we'll have first the *Cochinillo asado*," Aline said, "with a half bottle of *vino tinto*, red wine. "With the Calamares a la tinta, we'll have half bottle of white wine."
"I thought you didn't want to try the calamares," I said a little surprised.
"I'm also courageous, you know. The bold gets fortune, they say. And then, I want to accompany you in your act of bravery."

The suckling pig was delicious with those little roast potatoes basted with its juice. We didn't talk much during the feast. When the calamares arrived we averted our gaze from the black thing, and began to talk to forget our boldness and avoid a sight we didn't rate highly. But, as in my first experience, the calamares happened to be delicious.

"Next time we'll try octopus," Aline said and laughed.

"No we won't."

"Yet, it's a delicate meal."

"Have you tried it?"

"No, but I heard. Dad says it's a good thing to try any new recipe. You like it, you eat it, you don't like it, you throw it away. I read a book titled *The World At Lunch*. Stunning. You wouldn't believe what people eat on earth."

"What, for instance?"

"Termites."

"Termites?" I yelled. Oops! Sorry. Everyone in the restaurant stared at me. "This is crazy. Only anteaters eat that stuff."

"And humans too. I met, not long ago, a doctor settled in Central Africa. Chad to be precise. Fort-Lamy, the capital where he lives, is a small flat city, dry and very much hot during a few months of the year, and cool the rest of the time. Around the town, one can see thousands of huge termite hills. Once a year it rains nonstop for a month. After the flooding, the temperature takes a dive of about thirty degrees. That's when the insects swarm to create new colonies and new mounds. At that time, the natives net the termites by the thousands, pluck their wings and throw them into a frying pan. The doctor said he had tried them and swore that they were delicious."

"Yeah, let's give all the termites of the world to your dear doctor. I'm not sure now I want to finish my calamares a la tinta."

"You want to hear some more?"

"Nope. My stomach is now upside down and it's going to take a moment before it finds its balance."

"I'll give you the book."
"No, thanks. I'll pass."
Aline paid the check and we got out. The evening was fresh and the streets crowded. It was true that it was only eleven P.M. The night was still young.
"Do you want to see my new home?" Aline asked looking at me with the corner of her eyes. I'll fix some coffee. I have ice cream too."
I wasn't sure I wanted to see the apartment, but I could hardly turn her down. "Let's go."
We found the Renault in the parking lot behind the restaurant. We got in and Aline turned the ignition without looking at me.
Plaza Del Sol was illuminated *a giorno* when we passed through. People were everywhere, mostly on the asphalt as if cars didn't exist. Aline lived two blocks away, on Calle del Carmen, a short street between Callao and Gran Via. She found a parking spot not far from her building. It was a nice construction probably not older than twenty or twenty-five years which was almost brand new by Madrid standards.
The apartment was on the third floor and no elevator. We climbed the steep stairs without a word and found ourselves in front of a door marked number 312. I never forgot the 312.
We entered into a mini vestibule with mirrors on the walls, shut the door and stepped into a large den with a superb marble floor.
"That looks very nice," I said a little befuddled. This was luxury, I thought. A Persian carpet —I'm sure it was Persian— laid thick almost from wall to wall uncovering only a fistful of black tiles. Dad must have helped greatly. The furniture was pricey, no doubt, and so were the paintings on the walls, the curtains on the windows, and the appliances in the kitchen.
The bedroom was almost as large as the den and handsomely furnished. There was a vast four-poster bed surrounded by a light transparent muslin veil. That was the first time I saw a bed topped

with a canopy that wasn't on a magazine. More paintings on the walls, more expensive artifacts everywhere and more signs of opulence.

"You like it?" Aline asked staring at me a little anxious.

"Do I like it? Why don't you ask me if I like the air I breathe? I love it. I have to concede that it's a little too much for me. If one day you come to Nice, you will understand what I'm talking about."

I didn't remember had seen such a jewel box anywhere close to my house.

We walked out of the bedroom holding each other's hand. "I'll make some coffee," Aline said then smiled. "You're sure you like it?"

"Yes, I'm sure. This is gorgeous. I've never seen such splendor in real life. Only in movies. American movies, of course."

She smiled a little relaxed. "I bought everything from an American lady. She was supposed to remain in Spain much longer but she had been recalled without delay to the States. She's a writer at the Washington Post and very happy to find a buyer so quickly. For me it was a great bargain. Dad helped me, of course. I couldn't afford those beauties with my salary or my savings. But I love it. If one day I have to leave Spain, I will take everything with me, no matter where I go."

Maybe to Nice, I dreamed.

I was speechless in front of those marvels. "I'd like some coffee," I finally said just to hide my embarrassment. "With cream please."

We sat down on the sofa sipping our coffee. Aline opened a drawer and pulled out a folded sheet of paper. "This is a list of what we could do while on vacation. I'd like you to read it and tell me if you agree. We have a car —I brought it to the mechanic for a checkup— and we have money."

I read the list aloud and said, "It's going to take six months if you want to do everything on this paper."

"Probably. So we do what we can, enjoy the month-long vacation, and return to Madrid in time for me to resume work and for you to return to Nice and to college. Is that all right with you?"

"It is except that, depending on what we intend to do, I might not have enough money."

"I have," she said peremptory. She got on her feet, walked to the kitchen, and returned to the den with two bowls of ice cream.

"Do you want to stay here tonight?" she asked staring at her bowl. "You can sleep on the sofa," she quickly added. "Or do you want to return to the hotel?"

"Here it is fine. Filomena is going to wonder what I'm doing."

"She'll figure it out. We'll have the *desayuno*, breakfast, at her hotel, and then we can round the city and stop whenever we feel. Tomorrow night we have dinner at the hotel, remember? José and Jacqueline will be there, and so will be Maria Teresa and her husband."

"Leonardo, yes. Filomena has waited so long to have us together that we can't refuse her the pleasure."

"Then, day after tomorrow we can leave Madrid towards northeast to Saragossa, then east to Barcelona. With no rush and no obligation. Is that all right with you?"

"Just fine."

* * *

The evening was agreeable. Filomena had set her apartment as for a *fiesta* with a huge table right in the middle of her dining-room, a lot of flowers, a record-player with a stack of records three feet high, and three bottles of Dom Perignon in as many different ice buckets. Madalena, the hotel chambermaid, covered the service. As soon as Filomena entered the room, Madalena began to pour wine.

José and Jacqueline, our two newlywed Parisians, were already in the place when Aline and I arrived. We were kissing each other when Maria Teresa and Leonardo stepped in. More kisses and more hugs. We were happy to meet again with the two couples whose faces exuded nonequivocating radiated happiness. Jacqueline had gained a little weight, but this didn't take anything from her beauty, and her spirit remained as joyous as before.

Maria Teresa had gained a lot of weight but this was normal since she was six months pregnant.

The mood was great and when Filomena began to sing all the misery in the world was forgotten. We didn't need any record player or any other kind of music. Filomena provided all. We had wine, then some more wine, and champagne, and enough Jerez to get the whole Spanish Guardia Civil drunk. And the food was great. No calamares a la tinta, and no roasted suckling pig, but a mixture of the best Spain can offer. I asked Filomena the names of all the dishes she had served. But she was incapable to recognize her own cooking and, if she accidentally did, she could only mumble the words. Madalena came to her rescue.

"These," she said, "are *ángulas* and I noticed that you like them."

"Ángulas? Of course, I should have recognized these. Actually they are good. Perhaps a little spicy for me. What are they?"

"Baby eels. They are macerated raw with olive oil, bay leaves, salt and pepper, and chili. Very hot chili. You eat those ángulas with a wooden fork."

"Oh! I wondered why we had a wooden fork next to our plate. I understand now. No one wants to use a silver fork. It might melt in this sauce. And what is this?" I pointed to the leftover in the kettle.

"This is the *Pote Gallego*. We also call it *Fabada*," Madalena pursued. "Made of white beans, cabbage and pork."

I wrote down all those names and the ingredients. "Are you going to open a Spanish restaurant?" Aline said laughing.

"No, but remember, my mother is a cook and interested in any foreign recipe. Besides, I want to be able to recognize the food if I come across something like that. And these, of course, are crabs," I said turning to Madalena.

"*Si, Señor.* We call that *Centollos* and they are prepared with hot sauce."

"I noticed that. My tongue has doubled in volume since I started eating those damn things." I've spoken the last words in French to Aline. I didn't want Madalena to feel bad with my profanity.

"This must be accompanied with a very good *Turis* white wine," Madalena continued.

"The wine was nice indeed," I said. "Where does it come from?"

"From the region of Valencia, from the vineyard of Villar del Arzobispo. Did you read the label?"

"Only the percentage of alcohol. 15 percent seems to me a little high, isn't it?"

"Jerez is higher, but did you notice the year?"

"No, why?"

"1918. It's the year Filomena's son Mariano was born. She bought a truckload at that time. Each year, at Mariano's anniversary, she would open a bottle. The poet Garcia Lorca used to love the wine."

"And she kept on even after his death." I said.

"Yes. But today isn't Mariano's birthday. She brought that wine for you. Take it as a great honor. I don't recall she has ever done that for anyone."

"I'm flattered but she didn't have to. Did you know Mariano?"

"Yes, I was working for Filomena for sometime when the boy was born. He was an adorable kid. When they found his body near the museum, she was so devastated that I thought she would commit suicide. I didn't leave the hotel for the following three months, checking on her almost every minute. That's when she began to drink heavily. José and Maria Teresa were some reason for her to live. But, still, she's not what she's been."

"Why do you think she likes us so much?"

"She likes you because of your look almost like a twin brother to Mariano. Same hair, same nose—"

"Hum!"

"Same eyes. In another words, same general appearance. Ask her to show you a picture of her son. You would be surprised."

There was a long pause. I was thinking of Mariano. That guy had no luck. Dying at eighteen years of age must not be fun.

I walked to the table hand in hand with Aline. She didn't say a word, just listened to the sad story.

I turned to Madalena. "And finally," I said showing some leftovers, "I know that is chicken cooked in a crust. Very nice too."

"That's why we also have red wine to go with the dinner. It comes from the Monterrey Valley, Ribeiro de Avia's vineyard. Strong wine. Can't drink much unless your name is Filomena."

"I've noticed the high level of alcohol. Not for me. Any particular year?"

"No. Only the *Turis* is a 1918 vintage."

"What else is really Spanish? As a dish I mean."

"You should try the *criadillas*. Very special, and very good too."

"What is it?"

"Bull's testicles. They are fried with flour and eggs. Try it."

When Aline realized what the criadillas were, she burst into an inextinguishable laughter.

"Yes sure," I said laughing in communion. "Do you like them?" I asked Madalena.

"I've loved criadillas since I was ten."

"You started young."

"There is no age for that."

"Well, you're a woman. You must know."

"What does that have to do with my loving criadillas?"

Madalena shrugged and walked away smiling certain that she had pulled a trick on us with the criadillas, but couldn't figure out why we all laughed. "I'll serve the champagne now, she said."

José, Jacqueline, Maria Teresa and Leonardo joined us in the laugh but I doubted they knew what we were talking about. Aline's laughter has always been candid and infectious.

After dinner, and when Filomena woke up from her drunkard's nap, we all went for a stroll on the Paseo del Prado in the coolness of the night. We walked aimlessly amid a much alive crowd, until I almost fell asleep at two in the morning, Aline's arm hooked on mine. I heard one day, during World War II, that German soldiers could sleep standing. Like horses. I would rather say like mules but this is my personal opinion and no one has to share it. Well, that night I had an inclination to believe the saying for I, myself, had fallen asleep walking.

"We have to go back to the hotel," I said when I woke up, "tomorrow will be a long day if we want to reach Barcelona before dark."

We returned to the hotel and I walked Aline to her car. "I'll be waiting for you in the morning," I said as she climbed into the Renault and I gave her a last kiss.

23

We had lowered the top of the Renault and put our small luggage on the back seats. Filomena was standing at the door, a handkerchief in her hand, and tears in her eyes. "Come back safe," she said. "I'll miss you."

We took off around ten o'clock waving goodbye to our friend before we headed towards the Castilian countryside and Saragossa, our first stop before a more serious route. Barcelona was our first planned stopover but we probably wouldn't reach the Catalonian city on the first leg. Didn't matter anyway. We were in no hurry.

"You still don't have a driving license, do you?"

"Yes I do. I've anticipated your asking me."

"Fantastic. We might go farther if we take the wheel in turn."

"Whenever you feel tired, I'll take over."

She looked at me, smiled and laid her hand on my knee.

* * *

What happened to the countryside? I thought. I had been dozing for the past hours and I woke up as we passed through Guadalajara. On the right hand side I stared at an imposing structure but had no idea what it was.

"That's the Palace of the Duke of Infantado," Aline said when she caught my glimpse at the castle. "Or what remains of the palace. Bombs had destroyed it almost in its entirety during the civil war. They tried to fix it but I believe it's beyond repair."

"How do you know all that? Have you visited Guadalajara

before?"

"No, but I read as much as I could on Spanish history. Our king Francis I, when made prisoner by Emperor Charles V in 1525 at the battle of Pavis, in Italy, was brought to Spain to be jailed in Madrid. The retinue stopped here and the French king was received with great pomp. Emperor Charles was a bad camper that day."

"I remember I've read something on that about Francis I," I said. I looked around then I said, "I would like to stop for some coffee, then I can replace you at the wheel."

We found a small cafeteria on the main avenue and parked the car right in front. It was nice inside. Very much different from the pitiful state of the town where shambles were still about everywhere since the war. Everything was brand new in the little café. Mirrors all over the walls, modern appliances, a counter with glass windows that couldn't be older than a few weeks, and tables covered with fine linen and each decorated with a bouquet of artificial flowers. In a corner of the counter was an Italian coffee maker, the first I ever saw. We ordered two *cafés con leche*, picked up two churros on the counter, and sat at one of the tables.

"Long way from Nice," I said thoughtful. "I'm here, in Spain, in a very unattractive city, with the most beautiful woman in the world, miles away from my home, and enjoying it."

She smiled, and I could tell that her glistening eyes looked at me with tenderness. She didn't say the word but I could tell.

"Yes, me too," I whispered simply. How we understood each other with a sole stare.

The expresso was good, perhaps a little strong for my French taste. A few patrons walked in and out while we were sipping our coffee, and every time a customer left, the three waiters chanted in unison, *Gracias*, in two distinctive syllables —gra...cias— in a tune that resembled an E-Flat. It was melodic, cute, seemingly spontaneous, and certainly a little more obsequious that it should be. I gave Aline a questioning eye. "That's the way they thank the customers for being here," she said. "They are trained for that."

We got up, thanked the singing waiters, and walked out on the E-Flat note. The heat slapped us on the face after the coolness of the cafeteria. Aline handed me the keys and I sat behind the wheel. "Let's take off towards Saragossa," she yelled in happiness extending her hands above her head as people turned their glance to us smiling.

"Shouldn't be a long way," I said.

"No, but we might have to spend the night there. The highways are presently in construction in the entire country, so we could face slow traffic and bad path. The government has taken the bull by the horns —that is what they say— to improve the road network in big need. In a few years it will be all right. In the meantime we'll have to do with what we have."

"I'm in no hurry and, as you say, there's nothing we can do."

We kept silent for a little while. Aline watched the scenery which wasn't that scenic. Bare countryside with occasional rivers or streams, two or three thickets of stunted trees, and a few villages crushed in the heat that had already passed the one hundred degrees level. Poverty seemed to be present everywhere, at least in the villages we'd come across so far. Another pause as I let my mind wander. I thought of the attractive woman next to me, how I met her in an extraordinary fate that had one chance out of a million to be repeated. I pondered the idea and it made its way to my mouth.

"We had known each other for two weeks last year," I said keeping my gaze on the road. "Then we wrote letters for the last ten months—"

"I still have your letters."

"What do you want to do with them? Publish them?" I said laughing.

"No, but I read them over and over, and it seems that, while I read, you were next to me."

"It must be boring. The same letters over and over." She slapped me on the cheek, then leaned and gave me a kiss.

"We have learned a lot about each other. You know what my mom does, and that my father forgot that he had a wife and two children. I know your father is an Attaché at the French embassy in Madrid. What about your mother or brothers and sisters?"

"No brothers and no sisters. And no mother. Well, kind of."

"Kind of what?"

"I have a stepmother. Mom left us, when I was five years old. We lived in Casablanca, Morocco, at the time—"

"Casablanca? What were you doing in Morocco?"

"I was born in Casablanca.."

"What? I'm in love with an Arab and I didn't know." I laughed so hard that I had to stop on the shoulder of the road. "Casablanca! I repeated. Good Lord. How long did you live in that desert?"

"Morocco is one of the most modern countries in the world, my dear," she said obviously a little upset. "Of course there is a desert. Half of Africa is a desert. Well, a good portion of it anyway. But I was born and lived until two years ago in a very modern city, with modern building, large avenues criss-crossed by the latest models of American cars."

"I was just kidding you, my love. So, your mom left you."

"Mom was born in Marseille like my father. They met there, got married and move to Morocco where Dad was appointed Counselor at the governmental *Résidence Générale* in Rabat. The following year, the French Government opened a representation in Casablanca where Dad was sent as a director and where I was born."

"How exotic! Don't you miss Morocco?"

"I like Madrid and Spain, and my job. However, I enjoy returning to Casablanca now and then."

"Do you remember the life with your mother?"

"Not really. Mom was a professional singer when Dad met her.

She had always bragged about being a child prodigy. But it's true. At ten years of age she was singing with the professionals at the Alcazar Theatre in Marseille. This is probably what she missed when she married my father. She quit the family life to resume her career. Dad was devastated as I remember, but he remarried a few years later when I was twelve. He wed a true duchess. Don't laugh. It's true. Her name: Suzanne Chauveau de Belrance. And probably something more. But she wasn't interested in being of a duke's descent, and her two sons didn't care either. But her brother did assert his rights to the title and was called Sir Chauveau de Belrance until he passed away. His wife is still identified as Madame de Belrance."

"Does she really care?"

"Sure she does. She even had her stationery printed up with a ducal crown."

"You have two stepbrothers, you said."

"Yes, Bernard older than me, and Gerard younger. Fondeville their last name. My stepmother was married with Fondeville with whom she had two sons."

"Where are they?"

"One in Paris studying architecture and the youngest one living in Marseille with his aunt —the duke's wife— and studying nothing. But Gérard is smart and will find his way through life."

"In the last minutes I've learned more about you than in ten months of correspondence. You're full of little mysteries."

"Not anymore, am I?"

"My life looks rather dull in comparison. No duke in my family, no commercial Attaché in any embassy, and any stepbrothers or sisters. Mom never remarried. An experience, she says, she's not willing to repeat. I can't blame her, but I miss my father."

* * *

Not much traffic late in the afternoon. I could drive sometimes up to fifty miles an hour. In the rearview mirror I watched the sun setting behind the hills. Darkness couldn't be long to drop in the countryside, but we weren't far from our first stop in Saragossa.

"This is the Ebro River," Aline said with a sigh of relief. "We're a bridge away from stopping for the night."

I turned the lights on as we passed the *Puente Piedra* Bridge that spanned across the Ebro. Dusk fell slowly on the city as we reached the left bank and the first lights appeared.

"I believe it's a relatively new city," I said. "It was rebuilt last century after the independence war against Napoléon. The city was almost entirely destroyed by the emperor, his brother Joseph and their army of over a hundred thousand soldiers. Bad memories for the Spaniards who finally got rid of Joseph. If I remember correctly it was in 1814. Five years after the French invaded Spain to install Joseph on the Spanish throne."

"Well, the History student has done it again," Aline said. "Thanks for the class."

"You're quite welcome. I've got some more. I'll save it for the next class."

"I can hardly wait."

We stopped right after the bridge in front of the Cathedral *de la Seo*. We had driven about 160 miles from Madrid on not-so-good roads at an average of forty miles an hour. We got out of the car to bring the circulation back to our legs. The square de la Seo was illuminated with streetlights all around the well-maintained garden.

Turning our back from the cathedral, we perceived, across Don Jaime I Avenue, the elongated square del Pilar and the massive basilica of Nuestra Senora whose central illuminated cupola reflected in the waters of the Ebro River.

"Let's walk to the basilica," Aline proposed. "It's good for our legs. Besides, we have to buy a guide with the map of the city and look for a hotel."

We brought back the top of the Renault to its closed position, locked the car and walked hand in hand across Don Jaime I Avenue. Before we got to the basilica we found on the left hand side, a small souvenirs shop with its lights on and a handful of people inside. "We should find a map there," I said as if I had discovered a gold mine.

Two minutes later we were studying the guide sitting on a public bench of the square.

"We're here," Aline said after she oriented the map. "On the last page is the list of the hotels. The closest from here seems to be the Hotel of Castile, *Santa Isabel* Street. It's here, a few blocks away. Let's go back to the car and look for the hotel."

The traffic started to get heavier with the crowd on the streets as it is usual when night falls on a Spanish town.

We turned around the square at *la Seo*, got on Don Jaime I Avenue, got lost and mixed up on a one-way street, had to drive a few more blocks, took a right turn at *Mendez Nuñez* and another right turn at *Alfonso I*. Three blocks down the street we found Santa Isabel and the Hotel de Castile. Aline let go a big audible sigh. "Here we go finally," she said obviously relieved. "Our first night together on vacation has begun."

* * *

We woke up with the sound of tolling bell at six in the morning. Matins seemed to be earlier here. A song came to my mind right away: *Frère Jacques*, a Middle Ages tune that every children learns in the first grade in France and probably everywhere else in the world.

But it wasn't the last bells we would hear in Spain. Not that morning and not any morning that we spent there. For the next hour all of the city's churches vied to win the contest of who was going to awaken more people. And that morning serenade lasted our whole month of vacation. Never got used to the gracious chimes at six in the morning. Aline didn't seem to be bothered. Of course, she was used to the morning awakening since she lived in Madrid for the past three years. Madrid has its share of bells.

It was close to eight o'clock the following night when we arrived at the Hotel of Castile. Aline insisted on a room with two beds. The concierge was somehow befuddled though he didn't say a word. For me it was a sort of disappointment, but I kept mum too.

The dining room was just opening with a gang of waiters graciously whirling around the table that reminded us how hungry we were. A smell of food drifted into the lobby as we filled up the hotel registration cards. A young guy, not older than thirteen or fourteen, helped us to carry our luggage.

"Let's go eat," Aline said after she dropped her small handbag. "No time now to open the suitcases. Just let's go."

Down again to the lobby, then to the restaurant, we sat near a window so we could enjoy the vision of the crowd moving on the street.

"Same crowd everywhere," Aline said smiling. "You'll see the same spectacle wherever we stop, but only in the evening and late into the night."

"I believe I'll never get tired of it," I said. "We should have that in France."

"You mean the *paseo* habit?"

"Yes. We do have something equivalent in Nice but only in summer on the promenade des Anglais. And most of the walkers are foreigners. At Mardi Gras we have similar walking but that stops as soon as the parade is over. Sometimes it is only nine or ten P.M. Too bad."

"Let's eat and we'll join them."

We ate so rapidly that we didn't even notice what the dinner was composed of. Could have been the hunger or the hurry to get on the street. We walked out and found ourselves mingled with a small throng.

It was around ten when we reached Don Jaime I Avenue. The real crowd started there. It was almost impossible to move surrounded by compact groups of people, except to follow the flow. No way to steer in any direction. "Just let it go," said Aline.

There were predominantly young couples, laughing and yelling at each other in an incredibly sympathetic atmosphere. People smiled at us as if we were regulars on the paseo.

On the pavement, it was difficult for the cars to drive through, but no one seemed to care. Pedestrians or motorists.

"Everyone seems to enjoy the nocturnal promenade, don't they?" I said.

"Typical Spanish tradition. El paseo is their best moment of the day. They don't need a date, they don't need an appointment to see a friend or to meet with someone. They know that in taking a walk on the avenue, they will encounter anyone they want to."

"I remember my first trip to Madrid," I said, "where I encountered who I wanted. I didn't have to look for a long time. Actually I wasn't looking. Or was I?"

Aline smiled. "I remember," she said, "a certain French guy who didn't want to intrude. So I had to introduce myself, at the risk of intruding, if I wanted to have a chance to meet you."

"I could have missed you," I whispered. "It would have been a shame. But my angel was with me that night. One day I'll talk to you about my guardian angel. He has been good to me my whole life on unnumbered occasions."

"I want you to tell me about your guardian angel."

"Someday. I promise."

We let the human current carry us amid cheerful people as we kept hand in hand afraid to lose each other. A young couple stopped smiling in front of us. More likely pushed against us. "I heard you," said a very pretty girl. "You're French, aren't you?"

"Only by accident," I answered. "We could have been Hondurans or Czechoslovakian."

She laughed. "Yes, sure. Is that so visible?" I said.

"At least audible," the man said in French.

"And you are Spanish," Aline said.

"Of course. Not much opportunity to see foreigners in our country. People are scared to come to Spain. Perhaps it's our bad reputation since Franco is in power."

"I don't believe that," Aline explained. "World War II has just ended only a little over three years ago. There is not much stability in Europe yet. You, Spaniards, didn't participate in the last conflict, but you had your share of misery."

"We were too young to remember," the girl said with a shrug as if she were sorry to have missed the civil clash. "Of course, we know about it now. We're History and Archaeology students at the university of Saragossa. Actually we are from Barcelona."

"What are you doing here?" Aline asked. "I heard Barcelona has one of the best universities in Spain."

"That's right. My name is Juan de la Fuente," the young man said with a broad smile, "and this is Amelia Delmonte."

"I'm François Borny and this is Aline Delheuil. We're spending some time in Spain for two main reasons. Aline works for the French embassy in Madrid, and, as far as I'm concerned, I want to learn some Spanish before I return to the university in Nice. That's where I'm from."

"We are in Saragossa because we convinced our respective parents that its university is better for what we're studying," Amelia said.

"Actually, the truth is to get away from them," Juan added laughing. "And our parents aren't even aware that we know each other." He chuckled as if it were a good joke.

"But today has been our last day at school," Amelia uttered with a sad smile. "We have to return to Barcelona for the duration of the summer vacation. School resumes only in October."

"Barcelona. That is where we are heading," Aline said. "We'll probably spend another day here and then we'll dart towards Catalunya. For how long? We just don't know."

"Perhaps we could ride the train together tomorrow," Amelia proposed arching her eyebrows with the question."

"We have a car," Aline said. "You are welcome to join us if you want to. We'll be leaving day after tomorrow in the morning."

"That would be fantastic," rejoiced Amelia. "Where are you staying in Saragossa?"

"At the Hotel of Castile."

"Santa Isabel Street," Juan announced, "a few blocks away from here."

The crowd was much thinner when we reached the end of the paseo. We found ourselves Plaza d'España surprised to be so deep in the center of the city. But the company was friendly and enjoyable and we didn't see the time flying. We spoke Spanish most of the time though our new friends would have liked to speak more French.

They walked us to the hotel as my eyes began to give up and midnight chimed somewhere in one of the multiple belfries of the town. The interminable road from Madrid had worn me out and I assumed Aline too. But she kept talking to our friends half in Spanish, half in French. It was obvious Aline liked them. I would have liked them too and even more if they had let me go to bed.

They accompanied us into the lobby where Amelia slumped onto a seat next to the restaurant as if she didn't intend to leave us. "What do you want to do tomorrow?" she asked like if our future were definitely bound to theirs.

Actually, I thought it is.

"Walk around the city and visit what is worth to be visited," Aline responded. "No special plans, but we might as well do that since we're here anyway."
"I'll buy lunch tomorrow," Juan said, "with the money we'll save from the train fare. I know the perfect restaurant for four young crazy guys. You will eat things you probably never had before."
"Don't bet on it," Aline said. "You wouldn't believe what François can eat. Like calamares a la tinta."
"Did you really try that?" Amelia asked surprised. "French people are not supposed to eat that. At least, did you like it?"
"Well, yes I tried, and yes I liked it."
"So, you would eat anything else," Juan figured out.
"Don't push too hard," I said. "I won't try again those baby eels in hot sauce. How do you call that?"
"*Ángulas*," Juan said laughing. "But they are not baby eels. They are larvae. You tried them and probably like their taste."
"Hum!....Yes, until I knew what they were."
"It's all in the head," Amelia said.
"Well, would you eat termites?" I asked insidiously.
"Noooo!" both cried out simultaneously.
"Yet it's a delicate dish in Central Africa," I said with a mocking glance in Aline's direction. "Experts say that nothing is better. But it's all in the head, isn't it?"
"All right, all right," Juan said. "We've got the message. I won't try to hoax you into any sort of mysterious dish."
"I will make sure first to know exactly what it is," I said and we all laughed.

* * *

It was one o'clock in the morning when I turned the lights off. Aline was already into her dreams of which, I hoped, I belonged.

Three minutes later, at least it seemed like, the bells of Santa Isabel Church tolled. Someone had brought them into the room. Had to be or the chime wouldn't have been so loud.

Aline opened an eye, smiled at me and said, "I'm hungry."

"Well, so much for the hunger," I said. "Nothing is open in the middle of the night here."

"What time is it?"

"Six. You'll have to wait for breakfast."

"I know," she lamented. "That's the terrible thing when you live in Spain. You can have dinner at midnight, but not breakfast at six in the morning."

The restaurant opened the door about nine. We were first to sit down while two ladies, half asleep, tried desperately to finish setting the tables for breakfast. A nice smell of fresh coffee lingered from the kitchen towards the lobby.

One of the waitresses brought some doughnuts still warm, then poured some coffee in two huge bowls. Aline had already started to eat without a word. She was really hungry. I watched her with the corner of one eye and smiled. She looked so pretty in the morning even stuffing her mouth with *churros*. She managed to smile at me her mouth full. Her green eyes were greener with the sunlight coming through the window. "What?" she said.

"Nothing. I'm just looking at the most beautiful woman in the world."

"I think you already said that," she replied mouth still full.

Juan and Amelia appeared at the restaurant door smiling and waving at us. They sat at our table after Amelia had first kissed Aline.

"How was your night?" Juan asked looking more at Aline than at me.

"Too short," I complained. "Only in Spain you have two-hour

night. In my civilized country we have regular eight-hour sleep."

"At least," added Aline.

"Do churches ever close for holidays or vacations or something?" I asked with the most outraged look I could display.

Juan laughed. "No," he said, churches in Spain are sacred—"

"And numerous," I cut in.

"You have one just at the corner of Santa Isabel, twenty yards away."

"You're wrong. That church was in my room this morning, and don't say I'm lying."

Juan started a long laughter that he communicated to us. "Wait till you're in Barcelona. The cathedral has the biggest bell in Spain."

"Can you find us a small village in the surroundings without any church."

"No, there is none," Amelia said. "Sometimes a village is only composed of one church. People, living in isolated shacks, come from as far as several miles as soon as the bells toll. There is nothing around. Just a tiny church."

"Yes, but those people, who come to that church don't have any where they live. Right?"

"Right, no churches where they live."

"So, find me such a place."

"You won't like it. Even pigs and dogs flee those houses. Believe me, better listen to the bells."

"All right," I said. "Let's go visit some churches and put some dynamite inside the bells."

We walked out towards the parking place where we had left the Renault. We lowered the top and all four of us climbed briskly into the car. The weather was gorgeous, not yet hot which it would turn out to be later in the afternoon.

"Where do we start?" Aline asked looking at Juan.

"Perhaps the *Aljaferia*. It's not far from here and I believe quite interesting. It's a nine-century old Moorish palace. The catholic kings used it as their palace before the Inquisition took over. Inquisition, weird organization. Religious but not so charitable. People were burnt at the stake for heresy on behalf of God. The Pope Gregory IX was the first to institute the damn association." He turned to Aline. "Sorry," he said, "but let's forget the Inquisition and enjoy the visit."

We spent the day driving from one side of the town to another, visiting both cathedrals and the *Lonja*, the trade center of Saragossa. We saw masterpieces of architecture, some of the finest representations of the Spanish architectonics.

We crossed over the Ebro River on the road to Madrid on Juan's indications and stopped at a small restaurant apparently frequented by students. It was noisy, darkened by cigarette smoke, but apparently fun and pleasant.

That reminded me of the *Fisherman* restaurant in Saint-Laurent with the same odors of fish and grilled meat.

Juan and Amelia shook hands, a lot of hands as Aline and I were seated in the middle of a cloud of smoke.

"Can we have dinner outside?" I begged Juan when he was through with his handshakes. "I rather die of natural causes."

"Sure. I was going to propose the terrace near the river. I can't stand smoking either," he said with a wince.

Dinner was excellent but I didn't ask what *Ternasco* and *Chilidrón* were. It looked like some kind of grilled meat with a hot sauce made of tomatoes, peppers and chili. Hot but good. We had some heavy red wine from *Cariñera*, a region not far from Saragossa that produced the high-alcohol vino.

We were back to the hotel around eight, tired but happy with our day. A nice shower, a change of clothes and we were ready to walk back to the paseo. Our two Spanish friends joined us in the lobby about nine o'clock.

"We are going to visit Barcelona for a few days," Aline said when Amelia asked her what our plans were. "Then we'll head south to Valencia, and if we think we have time, Seville and Grenada. All will depend on the time we spend in each of those cities. Then, of course back to Madrid and work for me, and France and the university for François. Until next year."

She smiled holding my hand, then kissed me gently on the cheek.

"To next year," I said, "but we aren't there yet."

24

The train at Chamartin station in Madrid left around ten o'clock in the morning. Aline was there on the platform like a lost soul, crying all the tears of her body. She hadn't said a word since I got onto the train, and showed my intense face at the window.

"This past month has been the best time I ever had in my life," I said with a smile trying to control the tremor that shook my back.

"You don't fool me," she finally mumbled. "You are as sad as I am."

"Much more," I said. "You stay in this beautiful country and I have to return to Saint-Laurent—"

"And to your friends.... To Denise," she added after a short hesitation.

"I love you," I said as she cried not even trying to hold her tears.

"I love you too." The train began to take off on the narrow track, as Aline tried to keep up with the speed, running next the car. She finally stopped waving her hand as her image faded away like a mirage. "To next year, my love" I said to myself knowing that she couldn't hear me.

* * *

Mom was at the station in Nice. I had called her a few days before at the *Restaurant de la Gare* to tell her when I would arrive home.

But what surprised me quite a bit was the presence of Denise. What in the world was she doing with Mom? Of course they knew each other since I moved to Saint-Laurent with my two friends, but this didn't explain why Denise was there. And what about Gaston?

"He is still in Grasse," Denise informed me when I asked.

"What are you doing here in the station?"

"I thought you would be pleased to see me. Aren't you?"

"Sure. Just surprised." I kissed Mom and, of course I had to peck Denise's cheek. I couldn't have been as rude as to ignore her.

"Denise came to see me at the restaurant," Mom said, "and asked when you were arriving."

"How was that long vacation?" Denise inquired looking a little annoyed. "How's Aline?"

"Great, we had a wonderful time. What about you?"

"I went to Italy with my parents as planned. Boring, but couldn't help it."

We walked out of the train station and headed home two blocks away. Denise didn't look like giving up. She followed Mom and me, which I thought was a little disturbing. I would have liked to stay alone with my mother but I couldn't decently get rid of my roommate. Mom seemed to like Denise. They had their arms hooked to each other as I followed, dragging my suitcase.

"Juliette should come home tonight," Mom said. "She hasn't seen you for a while."

"How is she doing in her job?"

"Very nicely. She has no problem for her future. She turns seventeen next week."

"Are you sure? Seventeen. How old am I?"

"Close to twenty," she murmured with a smile. "That reminds me how old I am."

"You will never be old, Mom."

Denise had been to the apartment in Saint-Laurent, she said. She cleaned up a little to prepare for our second year at Ardaillon. Everything was all right. She had talked to Gaston on the phone since she returned from Italy.

It appeared that they were ready and even eager to start school. And I was not. Spain had taken a toll on my life. Aline's company had been so exciting for the duration of that wonderful vacation that I wasn't sure I could cope without her. For a month we'd never parted. She was there when I awakened and when I went to bed. Most of the time in two different rooms, but I knew she was on the other side of the wall. Now, dreams had faded away and I was back to reality.

* * *

We had left Saragossa early the second morning in company of Amelia and Juan, two superb human beings who had taken the life from the right side without worrying about any possible accidental occurrence. They took their existence at ease letting things happen at will. And they were obviously in love, holding hands, staring at each other, and kissing constantly. They offered to the world their beautiful straightforward faces. No dissembling, underhand or disingenuous looks. As Aline had said to me, "What you see is what you get."

We sometimes switched place in the car. If I was driving, Juan sat on the front seat leaving the two ladies on the back. And if Aline drove, we, the boys, sat behind.

We had stopped around noon for a quick snack and a visit to the bathroom. It was hot, well over ninety, but the breeze, blowing on the convertible due to the speed, made us feel like in a mountain resort. I was most of the time in the driver's seat with the two women chatting non-stop in the back.

Barcelona looked right away a huge but pleasant town. "It's the second largest city after Madrid," Juan said proudly. "Capital of Catalunya and the most important port in Spain."

The route N11, that entered the city from the west, was obstructed by a series of road works in the last kilometers. The traffic was heavy and slow. "Looks like Madrid," Aline said. She was driving, nicely relaxed, following Juan's directions on how to slide easily into the city avoiding the bottlenecks on the way.

"You see on the left hand side the hill of the Tibidabo." Juan said. "It overlooks Barcelona from the west. That's a must to visit. Interesting."

We found ourselves General Franco Avenue without any problems not really knowing how we got there. "You turn left on *Las Glorias* Square to *Meridiana* Avenue," Juan said. "The first street on the right is *Guipùzcoa* Street. That's where Amelia lives. We better drop her before her parents call the *Guardia Civil* and Franco's Secret Police."

It was a nice two-story house in the back of a huge front yard delicately manicured. Flowers everywhere arranged artistically with greenery around a fountain surmounted with two winged cherubs each holding a lyre.

I didn't believe Amelia's parents had to stand in line at the welfare building to receive government aid for poverty. Aline looked at the house filled with wonderment.

"That's the house I want when I get married," she said after she stopped the car at the curb.

"You better start looking for a rich man," I replied. She turned round and slapped me. I watched the impact of my words on her face and was already sorry. She smiled and said, "I would live in a log cabin if it's with you and if it's all you can offer me."

"I'll buy you that house," I said kissing her hands. "I promise."

We all got out the car and Amelia picked up her suitcase. "I believe you had better come in with me to defend my hopeless case. Dad must be worried not seeing me yet."

We walked to the house through a wide driveway as a servant opened the French door before we reached it. "Your parents are desperate," the man said. Then he added, "Good afternoon, Amelia, how was your trip."

Amelia laughed giving the servant her luggage. "Well, thank you, Francisco. Where is Dad?"

"With the señora, climbing the walls in the drawing room. They're waiting for you."

We entered a large vestibule through the French door, and then walked into a huge drawing room almost entirely covered with carpets. Paintings were hung on the walls along with a few tapestries representing hunting scenes.

A couple got up as we entered the room. They were handsome, classy, and probably in their mid-forties.

"You're late, Amelia," the woman said apparently upset before she kissed her daughter.

"My parents," Amelia said with a wry smile turning towards us. "These are my friends Aline and François, they are French, and Juan, a classmate at Saragossa University."

"Please to meet you," the lady said, and I could tell she wasn't. She had looked at me as if I were a thing of another world. Or, perhaps, she didn't like my being French. Amelia's father walked to us smiling. He was tall and slim, with a mane of gray hair falling on the back of his head, very blue eyes on a face that had seen a lot of sun lately. He looked like a seafarer, I thought.

"*Vous êtes les bienvenus dans ma demeure*," he said in a perfect French shaking our hands. "This is my wife, Rosalia. I am Don Ricardo Burgos Delmonte, waiting impatiently for that little girl who gives me a lot of trouble." There was a pause while he kept his smile and said, "Not really, but I'd better keep an eye on that beautiful young lady." He trudged to his daughter, and she cuddled in his arms. "Good to see you, Dad."

"Please have a seat." Señor Delmonte said. "Or perhaps you rather sit outside. Francisco will serve us some refreshments."

The outside was a carbon copy of Eden with no snake and no apple tree. God must have presided over the building and decoration of this heaven. A multitude of flowers of all kinds, trees unknown to common mortals, plants and shrubs artistically trimmed and pruned, all set out around a swimming pool just a little larger than a soccer field.

We all sat on garden armchairs covered with thick cushions as I watched Aline agape staring marveled at the backyard.

Francisco, the servant who welcomed us when we arrived, appeared from nowhere bringing soft drinks conscious that our young age didn't allow us to drink any alcoholic beverages. The domestic poured a scotch for both parents then disappeared through the vegetation without a word.

"So, you are French?" Ricardo said turning his gaze towards Aline. I have the impression that he liked my girlfriend. As I liked her too I didn't appreciate the sudden interest he showed to my señorita.

"*We* are French," I replied so the señor noticed that I was there too.

He smiled to acknowledge the message, and then turned to Juan. "And you are my daughter's classmate, Juan. How long have you known each other?"

The Inquisition wasn't dead, I thought. Tomas de Torquemada was still alive and well. I expected Juan to be smart in his answer. He was. "A few months," he lied, "since we have both enrolled in Archaeology class. We found out that we were from Barcelona and we sympathized. She's an admirable young lady."

"I couldn't agree more," Señor Ricardo admitted, "and I want to keep her that way."

I loved Juan's answer but not quite Señor Ricardo's. The last part of his sentence was somehow offensive to my friend. But Juan smiled without a word.

Anyway, I had an inside laughter for I knew for a fact that Juan met Amelia in high school, years ago, here in Barcelona. At the time they had already planned to go to Saragossa University just to get away from that guy and his wife sitting in front of me with, what seemed to be, a little condescendence.

"You're from Barcelona too," said the lady of the house speaking for the first time since our introduction. She looked a little surprised as if being from the city she lived in was an honor reserved only to a few elite groups. And obviously Juan didn't look as if he belonged to that class of citizens.

"Yes, Señora. I live on Jaime I Street where I was born twenty years ago."

"Oh! Pretty quiet street near the *Ayuntamiento*, isn't it?"

"Yes, Madame, the City Hall. My father works there."

"Oh! What does he do?"

"He's the Mayor of Barcelona."

Gadaboom! I thought, here's the bomb, right on the mouth. I loved it. That stuck-up lady thought she was the queen bee, and here she was talking to Barcelona's number one citizen's son. I knew that was coming up, of course, and it came right on time in the right place. We all knew Juan was the Mayor's son since we had a lot of time to talk about ourselves during the interminable trip from Saragossa.

It was a sudden and brutal change in the couple's attitude. Señor Ricardo got swiftly on his feet. He approached Juan, a smile as wide as the Panama Canal on his face and his hand extended like a blessing. "As I said before, you are welcome in my modest home." He shook the young man's hand with effusion.

Yes, right, a modest home, I thought. That the kind of adjective I like for a home that size. But all the bragging was gone. Señor Delmonte was another mortal, just like us. Weird how two simple words had changed the atmosphere: Mayor's son.

Señora Rosalia got up, hooked her arm into Juan's and we walked together like a bunch of friends through the garden. "Let me show you our house, Juan. So you are Señor Gustavo de la Fuente's son. It's an honor for us to have you here."

"It's a pleasure for me to meet with Amelia's parents."

We strolled around the swimming pool watching the admirable vegetation, stopping time to time to listen to Rosalia telling us about certain flowers or shrubs, giving scientific names as if we cared, before she showed us the way through her plantation.

At the east end of the garden Rosalia led us to a greenhouse. "This is my pride," she said opening the door. Inside an explosion of colors hit us with surprise. I don't know much about botany but I could recognize orchids. There were hundreds of all shapes and colors along with roses and other unidentified flowers. "I spend most of my time here," Mrs. Delmonte whispered as if she didn't want to wake up the flora.

This woman, I thought, needed to get a little more attention from her family, not only satisfaction from a beautiful greenhouse. Perhaps more hugs and kisses from her husband. She's making up for what she doesn't have at home, coming here and spending hours talking to her flowers. Money, she's got aplenty. But what about love and interest? She was a beautiful but sad lady.

We walked out, Aline holding my hand. The little breeze, coming I believe from the Pyrenees Mountains, refreshed the air deliciously with all the scents it could carry down the valley.

Francisco was cleaning the mess we had left with our drinks then asked if we would like some more.

"I believe we have to go," Juan said. "It was a pleasure to meet you, Señor and Señora—"

"No, no," Ricardo cut him. "You're not leaving so early. You are my guests for diner tonight, my friends."

"So, we were his friends now," I told Aline in a whisper.

"Be nice," she murmured.

"Sometimes I can't help it."

"And you may as well stay for the night," Amelia's father

continued. "I know your French companions have nowhere to go so far. Am I right?"

Amelia jumped into the dialog with excitement. "Oh, please," she begged, "it would be so much fun. I know François and Aline have no room reservation for tonight, have you?"

"Well," Aline started with a glance in my direction. "No, we have nothing yet. What do you think, François, and you, Juan?"

"I have to call my father," Juan said seemingly annoyed but, I was sure, thrilled in his inside. "He's expecting me today. I assume he won't be too happy knowing I'm here in Barcelona, a few minutes away from home, and delaying my visit. May I use your telephone, Señor?"

Ricardo showed him the telephone on a console next to the vestibule.

"I'm glad you will stay tonight," Don Ricardo said. "We have a lot of rooms on the second floor. Francisco will show you the way. Besides, Rosalia and I have a surprise for you tomorrow."

We heard a vague murmur coming from Juan talking on the telephone. He was smiling when he returned to us. "It's all right," he said. "Dad asked me to salute you, Señor, and you Señora."

"How nice it is from his part," Rosalia uttered all smile. "Return the salutation when you'll see him."

Francisco stepped in, silent and efficacious, from nowhere, like a ghost. That man appeared and disappeared suddenly and always at the right moment. "Francisco, can you get our friends' luggage?" He turned to Aline. "Would you like to put your car in the garage. There is a lot of room there."

"Yes, sure, it would be nice."

Aline walked out following Francisco. He showed her the garage whose door was already open. Aline unlocked the trunk showing three pieces of luggage.

Without a word, Francisco picked them up and Aline drove the car into the garage next to what looked like a brand new Mercedes-Benz. She walked back to the house behind the servant who had waited for her in front of the French door.

25

Denise had finally decided to leave. She got on her feet, kissed Mom, kissed me, and walked to the door. While I cleaned my suitcase of dirty laundry, she had some tea with Mom. "I'll see you on the fifteenth at school," she said, "unless you come earlier to our apartment. It's ready. I'll be there tomorrow probably with Gaston who decided to spend some time in Saint-Laurent as a springboard to the second year college. I'll resume my work tomorrow night at the *Fisherman*."

"I walk you to the station," I proposed. She smiled but something was wrong in her smile. I'd find out when I joined my friends in Saint-Laurent.

I ran back home where Mom was already cooking dinner. Always doing something. "I think you've been a little rude to Denise," she said. "She is a nice young lady and a good friend of yours, isn't she?"

"She sure is and if I was rude, I'll apologize tomorrow." I knew I had been. "But I would have liked to be with you and no one disturbing our privacy."

"You'd better apologize. Ist das klar?"

Here we go again, I thought but didn't dare to say a word. Mom, speaking German again, wasn't in a good mood. We hadn't seen a Kraut since the end of the war, four years ago. I thought she had forgotten the words. Evidently not.

"So, how was your trip?" she continued, and she was smiling now.

"Fantastic. A month of dreams, discovering new places in the country, meeting new people, and loving everything in sight. I wrote to you from Barcelona where we spent a few days invited by the

Burgos Delmonte."

"The owner of the *Banco de Aragon?*"

"That's the one. Good people, him, his wife, and their daughter, Amelia. Perhaps a little weird but very easy to frequent. For a while, that is. They have too much money and they show it. A little disturbing."

"What was the surprise you wrote about?" Mom asked. You said that the next morning Mr. Delmonte promised you a surprise."

* * *

It was a surprise. The next day we left the house early in the morning, all six of us. We had spent the night at the Delmontes' mansion after they offered us a great dinner. We all had our own bedrooms on the second floor.

Later that night, I believe Juan had stealthily visited Amelia though her room was on the far end of the first floor. How did he manage to overpass in silence the parents' room? I have no idea for I heard him. But I'll found out before we leave Barcelona. As if it were my business.

At six o'clock, after an early breakfast, we climbed into Ricardo's Mercedes, headed towards the port and stopped on the waterfront. We had passed through the deserted *Ramblas* towards Colombus' statue, took a left turn and found ourselves in a parking spot near the sea.

I looked at Aline; she looked at me, and then shrugged. In front of us we could see a marina with a flotilla of pleasure boats of all sizes. The closest to the Mercedes was a superb two-masted sailing vessel with her sails properly furled. A man was on board apparently working somehow. I read the name on the bow: *Buenaventura.* No need for a translator to know what that meant.

The man on the deck waved his hand at Señor Delmonte then walked to the stern where he unhooked a chain opening the accommodation bridge.

"*Buenos Dias*, Don Ricardo, he said taking off his sailor hat." He turned to Rosalia and Amelia, "Señora, Señorita."

"Buenos dias, Domingo," Rosalia said with a tight smile.

Ricardo motioned everyone to join him on the deck. Aline looked at me and shook her head. "No way I'm stepping on this floating device," she said as she turned a little pale.

"Why? You don't like boats?"

"Not that one. I don't mind a steamship like the three-hundred-and-fifty foot *SS Ville de Marseille*, but not a ten foot boat."

"This boat is a ketch, my love. You see, she has two masts and she's at least a sixty-foot beauty. I never had before the opportunity to sail. Not a ten-foot, not a twenty-foot, and certainly not a sixty-foot boat."

"You go. I'll wait for you right here."

"No, if you don't go I don't go."

Señor Ricardo Delmonte climbed down the accommodation ladder and walked to us. Juan was already on the boat and so were Amelia and Rosalia.

"What's the matter?" Don Ricardo asked looking at Aline.

"That was your surprise?" she asked sobs in her voice.

"Yes, she is a wonderful vessel, isn't she? Lots of fun to sail. What's wrong?"

"I don't like small boats. I'm afraid of the water when it's too close to me and too deep."

"You don't have to go to the water. We'll all stay all on board, I promise."

"And if I fall over board?" After a few seconds she whimpered, "I can't swim."

"You can't?" I asked stunned. "You where born in Casablanca, a half a mile away from the ocean."

"The ocean was a remote sight. Never been to it. My stepmother, the duchess, hates the ocean and she managed to make everyone in the family hate it."

"I'll teach you how to swim. Maybe in Señor Delmonte's swimming pool. I bet you it won't take more than thirty minutes. Deal?"

Aline looked at me, tears in her eyes. "I'm so sorry, but I'm so frightened by the ocean."

"All right," I said. "Here's what we are going to do. You climb onto this damn boat," I winked at Ricardo, "you put on a life jacket, I'm sure Señor Delmonte has a few, you give me your hand and we sail off. All right?"

She winced staring at the *Buenaventura*, then looked at Juan and Amelia, both smiling and waving at her, and we walked towards the boat. On the accommodation bridge she tried not to look down at the glaucous water of the port. Finally she stepped on the wooden deck as Amelia, Juan, Rosalia and Ricardo applauded.

Two minutes later, the señor presented a yellow life jacket to Aline who shrugged in it quickly. She felt more secure, she said though she still had an ashen-face.

"We'll be out of the port in no time," Ricardo said after he had put on his head a captain's hat. That's where he got his tan, I thought. He must spend long hours on his *Buenaventura*.

"Domingo," he yelled to the man who welcomed us on board, "let's sail off."

"Si, Señor." The engine was on, purring gently without much noise. But the sails remained furled until we got out of the port.

And then, it was another situation. The sails were unfurled within seconds and, with the help of the backwind, suddenly tilted the *Buenaventura* on the starboard side. The list, as far as I can tell, was close to thirty degrees. Aline yelled her fright as if we were going to capsize.

But nothing happened. The boat, once on her position, remained stable. No false moves, no jerking and no tremor. The vessel held superbly despite the swell and the strength of the wind.

My stomach went up to my throat for the first minutes. Then went back where it belonged. I could imagine the scary effect of the tilt on Aline. She didn't let my hand go. She was sitting next to me and I could feel her tremor. "We'll be all right," I said fighting my own fear to appear as the courageous man I was supposed to be. "Look how smooth it is. The boat is still on the water."

Little by little Aline's face regained its natural color and, miracle, she even let my hand go. She smiled for the first time since we arrived at the quayside.

"How do you feel?" Señor Delmonte asked with a smile.

"I think I'm going to like it," Aline said. "Give me a moment."

"I'm sure you will. Everybody likes it if it's done the right way with the right boat. This is a sixty-five footer with all the equipment a vessel of this size needs. She can sail sixteen knots an hour. Which means around thirty kilometers."

"More than Aline's car," I said. I didn't move quickly enough to avoid Aline's slap. "Just kidding."

"We're going to round Cape Tortosa in about three hours," Delmonte proposed cheerfully. We'll cast anchor somewhere in a little cove I know, have a good dinner while in the calm waters, and return to Barcelona before dark. What about that?"

We all applauded. Even Aline. Within thirty minutes she had changed her mind about swimming and the ocean depth.

* * *

"That was your first sailing," Mom said. "Were you scared? I would have been."

"You can't swim either. I thought you were the only person alive I knew who couldn't swim. I met the second one in Spain. But that didn't last long. Aline learn how to survive in the water within a few hours. After that first lesson it had been almost impossible to get her out of Ricardo's swimming pool. Now she can outswim me anytime."

"So, were you frightened when you all went out to sea?"

"I was terrified but I had to hide my fear to everyone, and mostly to Aline. When the boat took her list just out of the port, I thought that we were going to capsize. And the look of the swell didn't reassure me. For my first sailing I would have liked a quieter ocean. But it lasted only a few minutes. After that I could move on the boat as if I were born there."

I thought for a moment of the sailing to Cape Tortosa. As it was downwind Ricardo pulled the spinnaker from the hold and, with the help of Rosalia and Domingo, hoisted it. Within seconds the beautiful sail deployed giving three or four extra knots to the *Buenaventura's* speed.

"But the sailing back to Barcelona was something else."

"How so?" Mom asked as she went back and forth to the kitchen dragging behind her the delicious odor of her cooking.

"We had hugged the coast at Cape Tortosa before Don Ricardo tacked briskly to face land right on the calm waters of the cove. Less than a furlong away was a sandy beach crowded with a million people. While we had lunch on the foredeck we watched small boats navigating around us. People on board waved their hands and yelled probably, I imagine, amazed by the beauty of Señor Delmonte's superb craft."

I recalled the moment. It was nice to look like a rich man on board of a magnificent cruiser, probably envied by the jolly boat sailors admiring our prosperity. It's not mine, I wanted to say, but didn't.

"Then, it was time to sail back home," I continued. "I mean Ricardo's home. That was when things turned to be sour. Starting there, right at the tip of the cape, it seemed that the situation had become serious and was even worsening."

Ricardo and Rosalia had pulled the spinnaker down when we cast anchor facing the beach before lunch, folded it meticulously and Domingo took it down to the hold. "We won't need this on our way back," Ricardo had said. "No spinnaker into the wind."

I wondered why. Some time later I understood how sails worked, and spinnakers have only one function: speed up the boat, but downwind.

"Ricardo didn't make any more jokes, nor did he offer any drinks as he had done on our way to Tortosa. Now no more questions of small talk, or doing anything but keeping all his attention to the sailing. Rosalia appeared to be an excellent assistant. She knew what to do and when to do it. She was the perfect complement to Ricardo's work on board."

Within minutes, the wind had increased drastically. From a mere twelve to fifteen knots coming from the rear that we could barely feel, to a little terrifying thirty knots riding into it. The swell of three to four feet in the morning had changed to a ten foot. Typical of the Mediterranean Sea. In a moment we couldn't see the land. I looked at Aline but she seemed to be comfortable. Just holding the rail behind her and beautiful as a figurehead. She had kept all the day her yellow life jacket without a complaint.

The list at the time was close to forty-five degrees, I guessed. Frightening, but then, the boat keeping a constant trim, everyone sat down, calm and apparently relaxed after Don Ricardo and Domingo had snugged down.

Mom had set the table while listening to me. The dinner was ready and a terrific smell of I didn't know what came from the kitchen straight to the dining room. It was nice to be home, but I missed Aline and her smile, her omnipresence, and her exceptional attitude. It would be one year before I returned to Spain and I didn't know how I was going to cope with my solitude.

But first things first, as Mom always said. College for the second year and God will provide the rest.

26

We were exhausted when we reached Ricardo's mansion. But it was a good fatigue, as my mother would have said. I was familiar with that kind of weariness after a day at the beach or a day in the mountains that top Nice and its surroundings. We would get home hungry, played out, but ready to go to the bed, have a good sleep, and start over the next day.

I thought of the brutal introduction to seafaring that Aline and I had experienced. However, we had done pretty nicely, I believed. My green-eyed darling had loved the initiation as much as I did. And maybe a little more. That was the kind of adventure I was ready to live again any time and anywhere. Aline's fear of the ocean had faded away within minutes, and now she was thrilled at the idea that we might sail again.

"Any time you want," Señor Delmonte said. "Next time we would go north close to the French border to Cape Creus. Good place for fishing. Do you like fishing, Aline?"

"I never tried," Aline replied, "but I'm ready."

"Or perhaps, we could sail to Majorca. Why not? It's only nine to ten hours sailing with a good breeze, and the island is so beautiful. There are a lot of little coves around the island where we can cast anchor and spend the night on board. We could also go on land and visit Palma de Majorca where good food is a tradition."

I could tell Aline was all ears. She watched Don Ricardo and listened to what he had to say about these trips. I knew she was ready for another experience. It didn't matter where and, as we had plenty of time, why not to Majorca.

"But then" Ricardo kept on, "you have to stay a few more days with us to have time to enjoy the sailing."

His offer sounded good. Too good to be from the heart. I wondered why he was so nice to us. Or was it to Juan de la Fuente, the mayor's son, that all this kindness was intended for. And what was Señor Delmonte's idea? Was he up to something? We shall see. Or maybe not.

However, Aline and I had benefited from the situation. What a shame, but for a few days we had the feeling that we were living the life of the rich and famous. We would wake up and be off that dream as quickly as we went in.

"I'm sorry," Juan said, "but I have to go home. Father would be in a bad mood for a long time if I stay in your home more than is appropriate. I'm afraid I have to call him."

"Please, you know where the telephone is," Señor Delmonte said. "Say hello to your parents."

Juan walked to the telephone. We heard a muffled murmur then he hung up and joined us. "Father is coming to pick me up," he said. "He'll be here in thirty minutes."

"We're happy and honored. We didn't expect the visit of the mayor," Rosalia said. "Meanwhile, Francisco will serve some drinks."

"Buenas noches, Señor Alcalde, Don Ricardo said with his natural smile. "Welcome to my home. It has been a while."

"Since the last election," Señor Gustavo de la Fuente replied with the same smile. "But it's always a pleasure. I can tell my son likes your company. I understand why," the mayor added with a look at Amelia who blushed like a red peony.

The mayor was very impressive. Taller than Don Ricardo he was much heavier. Not quite fat but on the borderline. No hair on his head save for a dark fringe that let a round tanned cranium. A large moustache covers his whole lip right to the nose. His voice was that of a politician, sounding melodious and agreeable. He was affable, classy in his manners, and very friendly when he stepped into the drawing room at Ricardo's mansion.

Don Ricardo introduced us as two French people and his daughter Amelia as Juan's classmate in Saragossa. The mayor hugged his son briefly, and then turned to Rosalia and Ricardo extending his hand.

"Please have a seat, Señor Alcalde," Rosalia said after the mayor bent over her hand for a ceremonial *baise-main*.

"Why does everyone call him Alcalde?" I whispered to Aline.

"That means mayor."

"Stupid of me, I should have guessed."

"I heard you had a nice trip to Cape Tortosa," de la Fuente said. "Juan enjoyed it tremendously. I wish I could take some time off and enjoy a little sailing. But my small jolly boat wouldn't take me to Tortosa."

"Any time, Señor Alcalde, just let me know. We'll set sail to anywhere it pleases you. We were planning a trip to Palma de Majorca if my guests decided to stay a few more days in Barcelona."

"Majorca?" Gustavo de la Fuente said thoughtful. "It's been a while since the last time I set foot on the island. I love Palma. I might give it a thought and let you know. You really tempt me."

"Would be my pleasure, Alcalde."

"Your mother would like to see you sometime before school resumes," de la Fuente said turning to Juan. Then he smiled.

"I'll be going with you tonight, Father."

"That's good, son, that's good."

I had a glance at Amelia. She was sad to know that her lover wouldn't be with her tonight. Aline looked at me then shrugged.

Francisco came in with a tray of bottles and glasses and laid everything on the coffee table. "I'll do the service," Ricardo said. "Thank you Francisco."

The servant disappeared sliding on the garden tiles without a word.

A real spook.

"I'll be presiding at the bullfights tomorrow afternoon at the *Monumental Plaza*," the mayor said. "You're all welcomed to join me. It will be only *novilleros*." He turned to Aline and me and explained, "Young toreros with young bulls. They are not yet known but they are fun to watch. They show more courage, I would say craziness, than they should."

"We'll be honored," Ricardo said as he poured some scotch in three glasses. "Sangria for you?" he asked turning to Aline.

"That would be fine."

We all drank in silence for a few minutes, then the Alcalde said, "Señor Delmonte, I would like to have a chat with you in my office. Any time you can waste an hour. Or we might have lunch some time next week."

"Sure. Is Tuesday too late?"

"That's fine. It's no rush. I only need some advice from a financier friend." Then he got on his feet. "I am very sorry but we have to go. I'll send someone to pick you up tomorrow around four in the afternoon. I'll be waiting for you in the presidential box at the plaza."

Juan was already standing. He saluted the señora, then shook hands with Don Ricardo thanking him for the excellent time we had spent together. He walked to Aline, hugged her and kissed her on both cheeks.

I believe he did this little ceremony to have an excuse to kiss Amelia. He walked to her, hugged and kissed her on the cheeks while Señor Delmonte smiled. I'd bet he knew better.

We walked the mayor and his son to the curb where a limousine awaited them. Juan turned around when the chauffeur opened the car door and waved at us. *Asta mañana*! He cried before he disappeared into the car behind his father.

* * *

"Did you like the bullfight?" Mom asked with a wince on her face. She was sitting across the table from me as I enjoyed my first meal without olive oil.

"Not really," I replied. "Too bloody for me. They say the *toro* has a chance against the torero. I don't believe so. A very small number of bulls have ever escaped death for killing the matador. Some had the luck to walk alive if the matador failed to present a good show. The president of the *corrida* — the bullfight— waves a green handkerchief which disgraces the torero who would have a hard time returning to the ring in the near future."

"If that was the only bullfight you have seen, you haven't learned a lot about," Mom said.

"I wouldn't have probably understood much of it if I had gone to the bullring by myself. I was lucky to have a friend like Juan who is an aficionado first class. He knows everything about toreros and bulls. He explained to Aline and me what was what and who was who. Like veronica passes, muletas work, estocada, picador and banderillas. All the terminology you have to master, I believe, if you want to enjoy the corrida. I didn't master anything, so I didn't enjoy. I don't think I would ever go back to a ring again, and I am sure Aline won't return. She had missed three quarters of the fight when she turned around and closed her eyes to avoid watching the bull being massacred."

"How is she?"

"As adorable as ever. She is the nicest lady I've met in my life, Mom. I can't wait till next year."

"For now, studies, that's what counts. Right?"

"Right," I said and smiled. "Three more years. Still a long way to go. Tomorrow I'll be in Saint-Laurent-du-Var. Need some fresh clothes, new bedsheets and pillows."

"I have it all prepared for you," Mom said with a look at me, a gentle look with her beautiful green eyes.

"I knew that." I got up, walked to my mother and hugged her as tight as I could.

* * *

Denise and Gaston were finishing their lunch when I arrived at our apartment around one o'clock. A bottle of wine, half full, lay on the table next to two glasses half empty.

"Are you drinking my personal wine reserve?" I asked before I even said good afternoon.

Denise got up, opened her arms and hugged me. "Good afternoon to you too," she said. "Welcome back, horrible jet setter. Your mother told me how you spent your time with Spanish millionaires cruising all over the Mediterranean."

"At the risk of repeating myself, I would say one more time, women talk too much."

"Even your Mom?"

"That includes Mom, yes. What I wrote her was for her own benefit. Not for my second best girlfriend. I wrote to you, didn't I?"

"Yes, to Gaston also telling us how much you love Spain. But no details." She laughed, then let me go though not before she kissed me on the lips. "You are going to tell us who that millionaire friend of yours was? And the mayor of Barcelona. Wow! Where did you meet those guys?"

"That's a long story, but I promise to do my best. I'll tell you all about the extraordinary vacation I had in Spain with Aline."

"Yeah, yeah!" Denise said with tight lips. "Aline. You already said that. We're waiting."

* * *

Late in the afternoon, the first buildings of Palma de Majorca loomed in front of us as we approached the port, all sails furled safe the jib that allowed us to coast along almost in a slow motion.

"We'll have a slip here for tonight," said Don Ricardo as he handed me a field glass. "Look at the people on the *Paseo Maritimo*. On the right hand side you can see the cathedral. A beautiful piece of art."

I watched the land. In front of me walkers ambled lazily preparing for the evening paseo.

We kept silent for a while admiring the scenery and breathing the multitude of odors coming from the hills.

"I have called the Port Captain from Barcelona and made a slip reservation for tonight. Tomorrow we'll look around the island for a small cove, shielded from the northern wind, where we'll cast anchor for a few days." He turned to the Alcalde and asked, "Is it all right with you, Señor de la Fuente?"

"That's perfect. After such a nice crossing from Barcelona, a little rest would be welcomed. Then, I invite you all to *Sóler Es Port*. We'll have a room and a good dinner there."

The restaurant *Sóler Es Port* is a huge fifteenth-century manor admirably maintained. The courtyard is a vast circle, beautifully flowered and manicured, at the center of which a huge fountain sprayed water that changed color every thirty seconds.

Tables had been arranged outdoors around the fountain and under the stately trees that probably had been planted there when the building of the manor had begun.

But the dining room itself had been installed in an old mill with a very large olive press in the center. No more olive oil came out of it but the impressive machinery reminded the patrons that Spain was and still is a large producer of that damn oil I'll never get used to.

We had a nice crossing from Barcelona with most of the time

Rosalia at the helm. Don Ricardo got busy with Domingo taking care of everything else on the yacht. Sails, winches, rigging, and mostly, feeding us with a huge en-cas Francisco had prepared in Barcelona. Señor Delmonte was also in charge of the drinks. At noon he opened a bottle of sparkling wine from San Saturdi de Noya, a vineyard near Barcelona, and said laughing, "That's our national champagne, almost as good as Dom Perignon."
Yeah, right, I thought. But it was good enough served on the yacht.
In the afternoon Aline laid down on the foredeck where she fell asleep. Spanish champagne had its toll on her. When she woke up, late that afternoon, she had the color of a roasted hazelnut. Two more days of such a treatment and I would have an African as a girlfriend. Aline, I found out later, never got burnt red. Just darkened up.
I recalled the American friend I'd met years ago on the beach in Nice. His name was Jimmy Gunn and I remembered he looked like a cooked shrimp after a moment in the sun. No, not Aline.

We had left Barcelona around seven in the morning with gorgeous weather and a little breeze from northwest that couldn't be more than five knots. Just enough to give some life to the sails as the ocean joined the party as beautiful and flat as a pond. No tilt on the *Buenaventura* whatsoever. Rosalia was the skipper all day long and enjoying it. A real seafarer greatly fitted to the ocean work, and, besides, extremely attractive in her red and black swimming suit.
Don Gustavo de la Fuente, the Honorable Mayor, showed up with his wife and his son Juan as the Delmontes prepared the boat with the help of Domingo, the sailor.
The Alcalde's wife stood barely five feet, skinny and bony, her eyes a little bulging, and sad like funeral lamentations. She didn't talk much and smiled even less. What three opposite characters were the lady, her husband and her son. She was clad in black with a long dress wrapping her narrow shoulders and her flat chest. I couldn't picture,

even with great effort, the mayor in a bed with his wife. A bulking, energetic city administrator with a woman who must have been dead for decades. She reminded me of a story I've read about zombies in Haiti. Maybe she was one of them.

We greeted each other, Aline and I happy to see Juan again after those two morose days filled with Amelia's despair.

* * *

"How is this young lady, Amelia I mean?" Denise enquired perfidiously. "Your third best girlfriend, isn't she?"

I laughed. Denise could see or imagine a lot of inexistent things mostly lust. "Just a friend," I said. "She's crazy in love with Juan, and I'm crazy in love with Aline—"

"And me," she cut.

I laughed thinking of that evening we spent with the Delmontes.

"After Juan departed with his father from Don Ricardo's mansion after the sailing spree to Tortosa, Aline and I had a pleasant evening at the Delmontes' with a sumptuous dinner served by Francisco next to the swimming pool. Ricardo and Rosalia showed the best part of themselves, their education, their general knowledge of the world and the unconditional love they had for Spain. They knew every part of the country from the inside as well as from the outside. They spent, they said, a lot of time circumnavigating the peninsula, which explained their tan and their healthy looks. They liked to talk about their peregrinations and we took a great pleasure in listening to them. Amelia was silent and obviously cheerless. She already missed Juan."

Denise and Gaston listened to me without a word, drinking their wine.

"Then," I continued, "we returned to our respective rooms on the second floor. It was around midnight and Aline and I were tired. It had been a long day, but we didn't complain.

"The next morning we decided with Aline to spend some time visiting Barcelona. We knew nothing about the city besides what we had seen driving across to Amelia's home.

"We strolled all around town, going from Plaza de Catalunya to Christopher Colombus statue, near the port, then walked back to the Barrio Chino, one of the weird areas in town. We were told that the Barrio was much more fun by night. We'll try next time.

"We stopped on the *Ramblas* for a glass of *orchata de chufa*, made of I don't know what, but cold and delicious when you are thirsty. Close to noon we sat at a café terrace at the Ramblas de la Flores and had a glass of draft beer and a dish of fried calamares, those little ugly things I began to be used to."

* * *

The memories came back to me as if I had just left Aline. It was a full day, I thought. We were worn out but it was a nice fatigue. The sun was darting its rays through the foliage of the trees. Aline exposed her face to it, eyes closed, a smile on her lips, really enjoying the moment. Her pretty face had started to tan during the last cruise to Tortosa. Now she looked more like a real Bedouin coming out from the desert of Casablanca. A gorgeous Arab, I had to concede, but an Arab I was in love with.

Aline seldom let my hand go. Sometimes remaining silent as to take pleasure of the time we were together, but still smiling at me, sometimes talking non-stop like a radio DJ. All that mattered was to be together anywhere. And this was a place we loved to be together.

It had been awhile —almost three days— since we could talk to each other without anyone around. We loved Juan and Amelia, and their parents, but I believed it was somehow impossible to get rid of them, even for a few hours. We had nothing to offer but our presence and our occasional smile. So, why were they trying so hard to keep us close to them? We loved their company. They were nice to us, funny, educated and evidently great human beings. But, Aline and I were never so happy than when we were together by ourselves. In this particular period of the year —vacation time— we knew it would last a month. Some time in the future, I wasn't sure when, we'd make it last much, much longer.

Darkness would hit Barcelona within an hour and Aline suggested to return to Don Ricardo's home without using the car headlights. It would be hard enough to find our way in the daylight. We walked back to Plaza de Catalunya, where we had left the car with its top still down.

We did find our way. The Delmontes relaxed by the swimming pool, a drink in their hands. Amelia ran to Aline and kissed her. She asked how was our day. Here it was boring, she complained whispering the last words.

Señor Delmonte got on his feet, walked to us, shook my hand and hugged Aline. Yeah, why not, I thought. Rosalia approached, hugged me and kissed Aline. Wow! That was friendly. As soon as we sat down, Francisco materialized with sangria and two glasses. It was nice to sit in the freshness of the backyard. There was a little wind from the nearby Pyrenean Mountains slightly undulating the surface of the swimming pool. In a distance an owl hooted then took off in the air.

"Calm evening," Rosalia said when we stepped in the garden. "We love being here in spring and summer times when the weather is clement. It happens also in winter when the wind blows from the south with a perfumed warmth."

"We would love it too," I said staring at the sky. "I believe anyone would like it."

"You're welcomed any time you want to come. You don't even have to announce your visit. Just show up, and if we're not here, we're not far."

That was a nice offer, I thought. Aline looked at me and smiled. I know she would be ready to accept the invitation.

* * *

We had accepted Don Ricardo's offer to join them for a trip to Majorca. Juan had called Amelia to say that his father had decided to take some days off and sail with us. Amelia was in high spirits. One could tell by the drastic change in her behavior. She switched instantly from almost despair to euphoria. What does love make, I thought.

There was a pause of a minute or so. Don Ricardo broke the silence looking at Aline. "Is that your car?" he asked nodding towards the garage.

"Yes. I've had it for three years but it's a 1938 Renault. It has been taken care of, I assume, for it works very nicely."

"I saw you have a CD plate. Do you belong to any diplomatic representation in Spain?"

"Yes, sure. I couldn't have such a plate if I didn't. The French Diplomatic Corps in Madrid."

"Very interesting," Rosalia said, "but I think it's late. We better go to bed. We have an early awakening tomorrow if we want to spend the night in Palma de Majorca."

We got up, everyone kissed or shook hands to everyone, and said goodnight.

27

At seven A.M. Gaston, Denise and I walked through the gate at Ardaillon. It seemed an eternity since I crossed the campus in the company of my two friends. I believed the trip to Spain had elongated the last summer break. A month, wandering with Aline in one of the most interesting countries in the world, had made my brain forget how long I'd been away.

The crowd in the campus, on this first day, had grown stronger since last year. It was perhaps only a feeling, but the university appeared to have enrolled a lot more students.

For us it was the second year and, as we walked into the library filled with freshmen, we had the impression to have known everything in that school for a decade. We were the old guys and those poor trembling freshmen were as stupid as we had been a year ago.

We walked to the amphitheater talking loud as if the school was ours, showing off as veterans of World War I, staring at the new trembling students, then patting some of them patronizing. "Don't worry, pal, it's not as terrible as it looks," I said. "We know. We have been there."

Denise had taken my arm, smiling around when we entered the campus. That was what old students were supposed to do. Always a girlfriend hanging on one's arm. The fact that Denise was four inches taller than me didn't annoy her. Just me.

We went to the cafeteria where Denise bought some coffee and croissants. A few students there surrounded Mr. Gouhaux, our History teacher. When he caught sight of us he got on his feet and walked in our direction a cup of coffee in his hand.

He first hugged Denise —he liked her too— then shook our hands. "Nice to see you again" he said. "Last year's experience didn't prevent you for coming back. Well, I'm glad you opted for a second year."
"We have already opted for the next two as well," Denise said.
"We'll be in your class, Sir," I said.
"Happy to hear that. We have the fifteenth century in this year's program. Hope you'll like it.
We sat down drinking our coffee but Mr. Gouhaux remained standing. "I've got to go. It's my turn to welcome the freshmen at the amphitheater," he said. "Want to join me?"
"Yes, why not," Denise said, "Though we've been there already once. But it can't hurt."
We all walked to the amphitheater holding our cups of coffee watching the young students pale and forlorn in the crowd.
Mr. Gouhaux trudged to the lectern, hands together, making his usual farting noises and smiling as if he were happy to be there. At least he looked happy. I thought he might be.
Behind him were three teachers I knew from last year. I'd forgotten their names except for Professor Schwartz who had made last year's inaugural speech. He looked as miserable as he ever looked with his long hair and his aquiline nose that seemed to have grown a little longer.
Gaston nudged his elbow in my ribs, almost fracturing two or three of them, and said, "Remember him?"
"Who? Schwartz? Yes, I remember. He's one of the best teachers here at Ardaillon."
"He looks worse than last year," Gaston added.
Denise leaned over me and asked, "What are you two talking about. Complotting or something?"
"Always curious," I said with a smirk. "This is men talk," I lied.
"Men? I don't see any around here." Then she laughed. Loud enough to make everyone turn their glance to her. "Sorry," she said

embarrassed. "Won't do it again."

The first day of school went easy like always. The hard work would start just the next morning.

At two thirty in the afternoon I left Denise and Gaston to join the printing shop that hired me back for the part time job I had for the past two years. Roger, the old fat engraver was still there not willing to retire though he was sixty-five. His voice was as beautiful as ever and his songs the same melodies he had been singing probably since his childhood.

I was always happy to go to work, meet with my friends in the department but also with the pressmen, the bindery people and the office personnel. It was a nice place to work though I wouldn't have liked to make a career in the printing business. But for my years at the university, it had been fine and helpful.

I usually went home —about a mile away— around ten o'clock and joined Denise and Gaston who were working on their assignments due the next day.

Photoengraving implied the use of powdered bitumen and resin that flew in a constant cloud in the engraving department. Those powders stuck to every part of the body. Hair, face, hands, neck are unprotected from the sticky material. I would get home and slip into the shower to scrub the undesirable products for half an hour.

Then, I would eat something beautiful Denise had prepared, work for an hour or so on my next assignment, then go to bed and fall asleep within seconds.

We were already deep into studies at Ardaillon. Not much time for anything but work. Work at school, then work at the shop and, back to our apartment, homework.

Gaston was the lucky one. He didn't have to work besides school, his father helping him nicely. But he helped at home cooking sometimes and even cleaning up our mess. I meant my mess for Denise was a perfect house lady keeping our common room always in good order. My bedroom, as I didn't spend a lot of time there, was in general, in good shape. I surprised Denise a few times picking up my laundry, emptying my trash basket and even passing a quick rag on my furniture. She was a great young woman, but still four inches taller than me. No hope for me to catch up with her.

That Friday night I got home later than usual. We had been busy at the shop and Roger was sick. No songs that night. I couldn't believe how sad the department was without Roger. No one talked or laughed. We did our job, a little more than our usual share to make up for our singer.

It was past midnight when I reached the apartment. Gaston and Denise were already asleep, I thought perhaps together. No, not Denise and Gaston. They didn't match, though they were very good friends. Or maybe because *they* were friends.

I went straight to the shower, then to bed. Homework would wait until Saturday.

* * *

I wasn't sure first. Was I awake or was it a dream. No, it was not. Denise just slid into my bed. A single bed doesn't give much room for two. I could smell her delicate perfume and feel her breath on my neck her chest against my back. I was awake then. Really awake. Couldn't help but turn to face Denise.

It was late the next morning when I awoke, and I already regretted what I did. I could hear some noise coming from the kitchen or the dining room. I didn't want to get up; I didn't want to face anyone. What I'd done was beyond insanity. I should have gotten up, gotten angry, and walked out of my room.

Instead I was ashamed to confess that I enjoyed the night more than I thought I would. I was not really surprised by Denis's behavior though I never expected that it would go that far.

I thought of Aline. Writing to me every day crying her love for me and I, stupid asshole, I deceived the only love I had ever had. That was a dirty trick from Denise but I should have been strong enough to put an end to any attempt or idea before it started.

I got up trembling, picked up a sheet of paper and an envelope and began to write. I couldn't keep it to myself. I had to puke it out, to cry it to Aline. It would be, perhaps, the end of our love, and it would be all my fault. I was so sorry, but as Mom used to say, sorry might not count.

An hour later I walked out of my room. Gaston was working on one of his assignments and Denise cooking something on the stove. They both looked at me, Denise smiling happy to be alive and well, and Gaston arching his eyebrows in a mute question.

I didn't say a word, went to the door and walked out without a backward glance, straight to the post office.

28

I've tried to avoid any contact with Denise though it was almost impossible. We attended the same classes and lived in the same apartment. I thought about breaking the deal with Gaston and her but I hadn't the courage to leave them alone to pay for the rent. It could have been a little too much for them.

Denise had tried a few times to start a conversation but I always managed to go out or away without a word.

It was Sunday and I decided to visit with Mom. I hadn't seen her for the past two or three weeks. I had just called the restaurant a few times saying that everything was all right.

Now it had been a change in my life and I hated it. Mom would help, I was sure.

I met Mom in the stairs leading to the second floor of the apartment building. She just arrived from the grocery store, her hands full of all kinds of bags.

"Haven't seen you for awhile," she said with reproach.

"I know, Mom. I've been busy with school and with my night job."

"Obviously not enough to prevent you to fool around with Denise."

I looked at her befuddled, not sure how she knew already what had happened. I followed her in the apartment trying to avoid her glance. I finally said, "That's why I came to see you."

"I know, stupid you." She dropped her grocery bags in the kitchen and returned to the dining room.

"So, what's wrong with you?"
"She tricked me, Mom, but I blame nobody but me."
"Are you going to tell Aline?"
"I already did. It could be the end of our relationship."
"If she loves you it will be the end of nothing. It's good you told her. Now wait and see, but don't get too hard on yourself."

I didn't have to wait too long. The following Friday, a week after my foolishness, Aline showed up in Saint-Laurent. She didn't say she was coming. Just showed up.

The weather was horrible with a heavy storm that hit the Riviera.

When I came home after work that evening she was in the apartment talking to Gaston. They had introduced themselves and Gaston let her in. Denise wasn't there yet, still working at the *Fisherman* late as usual on Friday.

Aline got up, smiled at me, a tight smile I noticed, then we hugged. No kisses, not much talking, not much smiling. "What are you doing here?" I asked my heart pounding in my chest. I was happy to see her. That meant that she was open to an explanation. I didn't know what to tell her, what to add to the words of apology I wrote a week ago.

"Before I have any final thought," she said, "I want to be sure that everything is not definitely broken between us. I took three days off at the embassy, flew this morning to Nice and spent half a day looking for you. I must be back on Wednesday. Just enough time to see you and, perhaps, to kiss you goodbye."

She smiled. "It will be up to you."

Gaston had disappeared in his room. A few minutes later Denise walked in. She looked at me then at Aline a smile in her face. "That must be Aline, I suppose," she said a little contrite.

"I am and you are Denise, of course. I won't say I am glad to meet you."

"I understand. Is there a way I can fix what I broke," Denise said with tears in her eyes. "I am so sorry and I would like you to believe me. Nothing is like it was anymore. We were three friends and I destroyed that. Should I leave Saint-Laurent and the university and return to Menton?"

"I don't think it will be necessary," I said. "I have my share of fault. If some one has to give up the apartment it would be me. I'd missed the good time and the fun we had coming back from school or from work, and I would like to have that life again. I don't know if it's possible."

"I'm ready to forget the whole mess and return to Madrid my heart in peace if I can be sure this won't happen again."

"It won't," I said pitiful.

"It won't," Denise repeated crying. She walked to Aline and opened her arms. Aline disappeared in Denise's six-foot frame. They both cried and I almost did.

"I hated you when I heard your name for the first time," Denise said with a broken voice. "I knew François was in love with you. I thought I could monopolize him and make change his mind. I was, and still am, in love since the first day I met him at the amphitheater. I had hoped he wouldn't return to Spain."

Her voice broke and sobs choked her. "I wanted him for me, and the other night, I'd drank perhaps a little more wine I'm used to. That gave me the stupid courage to join him in his bed. I thought, stupid me, that I had vanquished, that I finally had what I was dreaming."

Aline patted her head. It was almost funny to see a five-foot little lady comforting a giant. "I am very sorry for you. I just wish you a happy future but I would have to repeat, without François."

"I probably wasn't thinking that night. If François believes that he can make it as it was before without a thought in the back of his mind, I would be the happiest girl in the house."

That was the end of an incident that wouldn't repeat itself.

* * *

Aline left Nice early on Tuesday morning. I skipped the first hour at the university knowing that I would be in time for Mr. Gouhaux's History class.

Aline and I had left the apartment of Saint-Laurent after we kissed Denise. There was no room for Aline to sleep so we walked out and went to the taxi stand a block away and rode it to Nice.

I woke up Mom at one in the morning and introduced her to Aline. Mom was gracious as if she had known my girlfriend forever. If she had been surprised at this wee hour visit, she didn't show it.

She brewed some coffee, pulled a cake from the refrigerator and we talked to almost four o'clock.

One could tell that the two women got along nicely. They liked each other and could have talked endlessly if I had listened to Mom.

"I think we should have a little rest," I suggested.

Mom got up, apologized and said, "I am so happy to have met you, I could talk the whole day. But you must be tired after such a long trip and —she looked at me with an evil eye— after that clarification. You can sleep in Juliette's room. She won't be here today but she will tomorrow and Sunday. I'm glad you can meet her for your first trip to Nice."

We woke up around noon with a smell of fresh coffee and toasted bread. Mom had always been the world champion for toasting bread.

It was a delicious French breakfast at noon. Juliette arrived at that time and I introduced her to Aline.

We spent the afternoon wandering on the *Promenade des Anglais*, Juliette, Aline and I. The Promenade was a little deserted after summer vacation. The weather was gorgeous following the heavy rain of the previous night. The ocean remained a little agitated as after a storm, but the wind had gone somewhere else.

When we returned home, Aline was in good spirit and Mom had

cooked one of her secret dishes.

Sunday morning I took Aline, Juliette and Mom for a tour around the city, up the hill, to Vallauris where Picasso had just open a workshop. The village was, as usual, crowded. Vallauris is a charming little town composed solely of shops, souvenirs, pottery, clothes and restaurants. In another word a village for tourists. The season had ended in September, but people kept visiting the city all yearlong.

Aline had enjoyed the visit and when she left she was in better humor than when she came. Her smile had returned to her face as her green eyes had regained their vivacity. One thing was sure: we were made for each other regardless of the accident on the road. When she walked to board the plane at the airport, she kissed me. At that moment she had whispered, "I want to be the future Mrs. Borny."

She walked to the gate, waved her boarding pass, smiled, and then disappeared into the corridor leading to the plane.

29

I went back to Spain after my second year in college. That was my third trip to that beautiful country of which it seemed I couldn't get enough. With Aline I spent another month wandering around Spain, starting by Saragossa where we met again with Amelia and Juan who were finishing their four years of university. They had graduated in archaeology with the hope to go somewhere around the world searching for signs of the past. Egypt was their choice but first they wanted to get married. The parents had agreed, of course. What a better fish to catch on either side.

We had stopped for a day in Barcelona. Our first visit, naturally, was with our friends, the Delmontes. Ricardo and Rosalia hadn't changed a bit. They still looked terrific with their tanned faces and their slim bodies.

Their smile had become a friendlier one. We could feel that their greeting was sincere unlike the first time we'd met. But this was the past forgotten for a long time. After our first sailing we were certain that we had found real friends.

They were happy to see us and invited Aline and me to a short sailing around Barcelona. It was a nice thought but we declined for we wanted to visit Valencia, which we missed the previous year, having much to do with Palma de Majorca where we shamefully spent two weeks. Señor Gustavo de la Fuente, the mayor, had to return to his *Ayuntamiento* —the City Hall— and picked up a plane after a week of euphoria in the island.

What a good time we had there! I recalled. Don Ricardo rented a car and we went off for a tour of the island. The food was terrific and the nights of a world class. We didn't return to the yacht for two weeks, spending the time on land. Two weeks is barely enough to visit Palma de Majorca.

It was a memorable vacation time. I don't believe Aline nor I will ever forget that year.

The following wasn't bad either. I turned twenty years of age and Juliette almost eighteen. She was a beautiful lady, now in possession of her trade. No more boarding school, no more training class. She made good money and lived with Mom in the same damn apartment building where I saw her for the first time.

* * *

Then came the year I was so desperate to see: 1952. Four years had flown away so quickly, I couldn't believe we were there. May came with the last exam at the university. I was exhausted. My brain was like a sponge, a squeezed one, but in a few days it would be over. Gaston, Denise and myself will part, abandoning the apartment General de Gaulle Avenue in Saint-Laurent-du-Var. Mr. Langevin, the landowner, and his wife had prepared a little goodbye party, which was thoughtful. Four years in the same apartment with the same neighbors had begot some friendship between the Langevins and us. We'd miss the place and, perhaps, the whole thing: college, *The Fisherman* restaurant, the cafeteria, and an all our friends and all our teachers.

The next morning we kissed each other goodbye and left Mr. Langevin and his family as tears welled up in everybody's eyes.

Gaston rode the bus to Grasse and Denise and I picked up a train to Nice and Menton.

In the car we didn't say much. It was a day we all waited for, and now it was over and it was sad. Sad for we parted after four years of

friendship, of fun and, of course, of worries. We overcame the latter with bonhomie and patience.
"What are you going to do now that you're a 1952 graduate?" Denise asked without looking at me.
"I guess I'm going to Spain at least for six months. I want to master the language, the History and the culture. Perhaps enroll for a time in the Madrid University. What about you?"
"Get married, I guess, and then look for a job. I'm twenty-two. I should have kids by now."
"You'll find a good man, Denise. You are a terrific woman. Beautiful, smart with a college education and so caring. You won't have any problem finding the right guy at the right time. I would like you to invite me at your wedding. I might return the favor."
Denise got married at the end of the year and I was invited along with Aline and Gaston to the wedding. I was back home from Spain after a six month-sojourn in Madrid and, I believed, with a new and improved Spanish. I was ready for a teaching job. I had the choice: Spanish or History.
I was already an old graduate from college —six months— but I recalled the party Mom gave to my friends and me to celebrate our diplomas. I asked Gaston what he was up to after college. "I'm not finished yet," he said and a smile lighted up his childish face. "I'm going to Montpellier, to medical school. I think I would like to be a doctor."
"I'm sure you'll make a terrific one. You are a very bright young man and you are my friend."

* * *

Aline made a special trip for the graduation party. Denise was there and so were Gaston, Juliette, and our old friend: Alphonse Renard, my Dad's companion in the mountains during World War II.

We hadn't seen him but only a few times since the memorable day, three years after the war, when Alphonse and Dad reminisced about some events that happened in the mountains in the company of friends within the Résistance. How they had killed that German officer in the middle of a freezing night in Nice and how three of their friends had been tortured and killed in retaliation.

But this time Dad wasn't there to listen or share the memories. Dad was in Paris where he had hidden for a few years. He never wrote to me again and I thought I liked it that way. The last letter was a lament about his life with us. I believed we were the ones who should have complained. This belonged to the past for Mom, Juliette and me.

The celebration dinner took place, as usual, with success. Mom had cooked my favorite *coq-au-vin* and baked a royal dessert: *baba-au-rhum*, a round cake soused with a little rum, and a *clafouti* that is a kind of cherry pie originated in Brittany.

After a few glasses of wine Alphonse was inexhaustible. Memories from the war came back to him and he was ready to talk about them. War had ended seven years before so it wasn't any longer dangerous to talk about friends involved in the struggle and even give their names.

Alphonse had truly enjoyed Mom's cooking. He always had. We talked about the good time when Dad was here, when we would go fishing or swimming, when Mom would prepare a picnic and we headed to the beach or the mountains.

Alphonse had joined us often. He never got married, had an occasional girlfriend whom he always introduced to Mom and Dad. Then he would show up on Sunday invited by Dad and he would be alone. Or with another girlfriend.

But he liked the mountains more than the beach. As Mom and Juliette preferred the heights of Nice and the surroundings we would go for some fresh air amid the pines of the forest. I loved the smell of pine trees, and even today, when I find myself in a cluster of those trees I look for the unmistakable smell.

"With your Dad," Alphonse said, "we have covered kilometers of tracks, roads, trails and paths in those mountains we used to know like the back of our hands. Forests are thick up there between Sospel and Lantosque. Besides, the main roads that link both villages are composed of an infinity of paths and trails. But they are in the wilderness and the access of either of the two villages is not easy. They are separated by only twenty kilometers, but twenty kilometers of bushes, brambles, rocks, boulders difficult to climb, and paths only used by the deers and the rabbits. Your father and I became very much used to that kind of climbing. We had a group during the war, a few of them old enough to be grandfathers. Most of them couldn't move very well in those steep slopes. So, your Dad and I would volunteer for the liaisons between our people scattered in the mountains between Pugets-Théniers, Saint Sauveur, Sospel and Lantosque."

Aline was holding my hand, listening to the raconteur that was Alphonse. He had the tempo of a good storyteller. He knew when to stop in the middle of an anecdote to give a little suspense effect, have a gulp of wine, then restart with a new intonation and a new tempo. We were all ears in the silence of the room.

"One advantage of being in that part of the hills was the fact that the roads were so narrow that we could trap the Germans and block them in the middle of nowhere. Tanks had difficulties crossing the narrow and weak bridges which threatened to collapse anytime people would sneeze a little too hard."

"Besides, we could see the Germans coming up the mountains. By the time they reached Sospel or Lantosque, we had vanished into thin air. We had been moving many times from one point to another one, and sometimes it wasn't just a picnic. Most of the moves were made by night, in the rain or under a snowstorm with no light we couldn't turn on, of course. Other times it was under German or Italian fire, from the ground as well as from the air. Some of our friends couldn't make it, too old or too sick, and preferred giving up and surrender to be taken away by the enemy. I recall some of them we never saw again. It was the price of our stupid game."

Mom got up to pour some wine into the glasses. Alphonse was a little red, but it could be from excitement. His diction remained loud and clear.

"One night we had decided to put some animation in Menton," he continued. "The road down from Sospel ends there after a few dozen of hairpin bends very difficult to master. But near the little city the road becomes wider and straighter."

"What kind of animation did you get?" I dared to ask cutting Alphonse's story.

He smiled with a pleasant smile and his little glassy eyes looked around as if my interruption had created a fatidic gap. "We just wanted to play the cat and mouse game with the Germans and the Italians. We had a car, a black Citroën front-wheel drive, very good for the mountains and the hairpins. Five people in it, two Americans who spoke fairly good French, Harris and José a Mexican guy, with guts big like that, Paul Blanchard, a teacher who got caught by the Germans in Marseille but managed to escape, Pierre Borny, your father, François, and myself at the wheel.

"At two in the morning, we left the car in a dark, narrow street, not too far from the road to Sospel, and walked furtively avoiding the German and Italian patrols. The Americans carried the explosives. They knew how to use them. They had been parachuted two weeks before with all kinds of equipment. Two radio-transmitter-receivers SCR300, beautiful M16 automatic rifles we never had before, a few cases of ammunition, and a lot of explosives. They were ready to blow up the whole country if there were any Germans. And Krauts there were aplenty.

"We kept walking through the back streets, listening for any suspicious sounds of German boots on the cobblestones. There wasn't much light, and it was good for us. No one on the streets for it was curfew time and, besides crazy people like us, the population preferred to stay home at dark.

"We reached the ocean thirty minutes later. The surf was heavy that night so we didn't care about making some noise. Moored at a long pier were two Italian corvettes pitching heavily in the swell. A sailor was on the pier walking back and forth carrying a submachine gun on his shoulder.

"We had to get rid of the poor guy for what we intended to do. José volunteered. Harry said he was a knife artist. That reminded me of that German officer in Nice. I hated knives but we had to do it.

"José crawled —I never understood how he did— like a snake on top of the boulders, his dagger in his hand. For a few minutes we could only hear the waves breaking on the sand beach. A patrol car passed by while we were waiting for an action from José.

"We didn't see anything, didn't hear the slightest noise, but the Italian was down on the pier the knife through his throat. José must have been thirty feet from the sentry. He got up quickly, ran to the sailor, retrieved his dagger and hurried back to us. That was easy, I thought. How is he, I asked? *Como una enchilada*, flat, I remember him saying with a chuckle.

"Harry got on his feet, picking up his haversack and asked his countryman: are you coming? José had smiled showing, in the feeble glow of the ocean, a row of white teeth like a wolverine. I thought he was scary. They walked bent to the first corvette, jumped on in total silence. A minute later they climbed down on the pier and hopped on the second boat.

"Less than three minutes later they were back chuckling. We can go now, Harry had said."

Alphonse emptied his glass in one gulp and Mom got up to pour some more wine. I wondered how he was going to return home after the amount of wine he had drank that day. But somehow he managed and a few months passed before we saw him again with a new girlfriend.

"We returned cautiously to the Citroën still hidden in the dark," Alphonse pursued. "We climbed into it and waited. It was not too long after that we heard a terrible but enjoyable explosion followed by another one almost simultaneously. That was two corvettes into the drink.

"We didn't waste anytime rushing up the road to Sospel. We knew that Gestapo cars were going to show up from everywhere like mushrooms in the springtime. Two command-cars were already on our tail two hundred yards behind us. But Citroën manufactured a good car. That front-wheel-drive could beat any other car in the mountains. The Gestapo understood that long ago. Citroëns were the only car they used to track fugitives.

"We negotiated the first bend of the road at high speed before we reached the first bridge. We stopped two hundred yards farther, parked the car on the shoulder, and Harry and José ran to a nearby bush. We waited, watching the command-cars puffing up the hill. When the first one reached the bridge we heard the third explosion of the night. It was enough. The Germans wouldn't go farther until they repaired the road infrastructure, which was in a very bad shape. But for the night they had lost two corvettes and a command-car including all the personnel.

"A moment later, from the Sospel Pass we could see behind us a huge flame glowing in the night and, in the other direction, the quiet village that seemed to waken. Now was the hard part. We couldn't, of course, just drive down hill to Sospel with the Citroën. The small garrison of the village had begun to move in the direction of the pass.

"We engaged in a narrow track that rounded the mountain to prevent any attempt from the Germans to block us. The trail wasn't much larger than the car and on one side it was a six hundred-foot drop into a deep precipice that ended where a little creek meandered. No pavement but dirt and slippery mud. I couldn't drive faster than five kilometers an hour. The important thing was to get away from the main road before the Germans arrived from the village.

"We hid the car in a dilapidated farm at the bottom of the valley when we finally arrived unhurt at five in the morning. It was still a long way to Lantosque but the Germans and the Italians wouldn't follow us where we were going."

"How was it up the mountains?" I asked.

There was no answer. I looked at Alphonse then smiled. He had fallen asleep between two sentences. His chin resting on the chest, he breathed slowly with a little snoring. "Well," I said, "we might have the answer next time."

"But, maybe not," Mom said and, with a little pause, she added, "You have a letter from America." Then she smiled.

"America? I don't know anyone in America," I said surprised. "Who wants to write to me?"

"Think again, Son."

Juliette was watching me with a glow in her eyes wide open. She knew something I didn't. Mom handed me the letter. I recognized the American stamp before I read the return address. "Damn," I said.

"Watch your language, Son. There are nice ladies here."

"My Goodness," I said with a startle of shock. "My God, that's impossible. I thought he was dead. I read aloud: Jimmy Gunn, Atlanta, Georgia."

"Okay, Okay," Juliette cried desperate, "open it."

My hands were trembling when I unsealed the letter. I looked at Aline. "I never told you about my friend Jimmy. He had disappeared from our lives before World War II ended. I thought he must have been killed somewhere in the battle of the Bulge where I last heard from him, and I forgot about my friend. That was eight years ago."

"What does he say?" Juliette asked febrile.

I read the first lines in silence. *Dear François, Dear Juliette, and Dear Ophelia*:

He saw Mom a few times and he remembered her first name though no one called her Ophelia anymore. I had almost forgotten it. How did he do that? Much later I found out that Americans have a gift for remembering first names.

"Come on, come on," Juliette yelled. "Read aloud."

I started over but this time for everyone to hear.

Dear François, Dear Julia, and Dear Ophelia.

It was eight years ago, I remember, I saw you for the last time in your beautiful city of Nice. I finished the war with another wound. Nothing new, is it? We met when I was first wounded. I believed at the time, and I still believe, that it was a good omen. I made a friend, then I met with a nice family in a country where I knew no one.

You might think that I've forgotten you. That didn't just happen. I was repatriated after the battle of the Bulge with a scare in my back that almost matched the one I have on my chest. You remember, François?

"I remember," I said. "He was laying on the pebbles at the beach, stripped to the waist, and almost burnt to the bones. He had a large scar cutting his narrow torso and was eating a huge sandwich of which he offered me a portion. I remember his blue eyes and his little blond mustache, and his smile."

I kept on reading.

I stayed six months in Atlanta Veterans Hospital with a few visits from my family and friends but not able to move much. At the time, I thought of you all wondering if you were still going to the beach and

if Mom was still cooking that delicious Canard a l'Orange she someday had cooked for me.
  Then I went back to school. At Georgia State University. Us, veterans, can benefit from a government special aid to complete our education at no cost. Besides, a nice allocation was given to whom wanted to restart school. I jumped at the opportunity and here I am with a bachelor degree in Finances as if I needed that to manage my one hundred and thirty dollars the government allowed me for service rendered during World War II.
  That was nice. I had a degree and now a good job in a big company in Atlanta. I've been working there for the past two years which means that I am entitled to two weeks vacation.

  My idea is to spend those two weeks in Nice if that's possible without creating any untimely inconvenience in your life.
  I would like to see you all if this letter reaches you. You might have moved since the last time I saw you. I hope not.

  I'm waiting for an answer before I make my mind on where to go for Christmas. I'll be off three days before Christmas to three days after New Year.

  Thinking of you.

  Jimmy Gunn.
  "Wow! That's some surprise," I said. Juliette was on my back trying to read the letter faster than I did.
  "Give me this," she said snatching the letter from my hands. "I'll answer our friend."
  "I thought he was my friend," I replied laughing.
  She shrugged and walked away with the missive. She knew enough English to write a fairly decent letter.

"Now, we have another surprise," Mom said. "Not good this one." She handed me a letter with the official tricolor seal of the army. "They didn't forget you, Son. You are still a French citizen and your provisional exemption has ended."

I opened the summon and read that I had to report to the Gendarmerie within six months after my graduation. Then, I'll be routed, like a package, to any regiments in France or overseas. "I do that," I said with a look at Aline.

She smiled at me, then said, "A year and a half, right?"

"I believe it's what it is. Two years ago it was only twelve months. We can't have it both ways. Secure my exemption for college and get the twelve months I could have if I went to the army instead of school. Well, let's look at the bright side. I'll be twenty-four, just in time to enter the real life."

Aline smiled but it was a sad grin. "I can wait," she said. "There's nothing we can do."

"Right." I stared at Mom for a few seconds. She was smiling too. She shrugged and said, "We'll manage without you, but come back quickly. Aline and I won't wait for ever."

Alphonse got suddenly out of his ethylic nap, looked around and said, "I think it's time for me to go." He got up, wobbled towards the door, then changed his mind and came back to kiss Mom without a word.

"We'll see you next time," she said. "Bring some more memories. We love your story-teller side."

He smiled, pointed his finger at me, but didn't say anything. He disappeared through the door in the middle afternoon sun. "He's never out of stories," I said. "I love listening to Alphonse. He's got some memories I'm never too tired to hear about."

30

It was a gorgeous day when the Pan Am flight 308 from Paris landed on the runway that edged the Mediterranean with only two hours delay.

Mom, Juliette and I were waiting on the terrace of the airport for almost three hours but not getting bored for a minute. We had watched the numerous planes landing and taking off which we didn't have very often the opportunity to see.

The DC8 of Pam Am graciously touched the Tarmac. "Here he is," Juliette said springing to her feet. "Do you think we're going to recognize him?"

"We might not," Mom said. "It's been a long time."

"I will, no matter what," I said. "I cannot forget his childish face with his blond mustache and his straw hair—"

"And his smile," Juliette added. "That couldn't have changed."

My sister looked like she was still in love with Jimmy. She might have forgotten him during the eight-year gap, but Jimmy's letter had brought back nice memories to her. And she couldn't wait to see our friend.

Mom was first to recognize him when he stepped out of the plane and climbed down the ladder. We could see him on the Tarmac walking at a slow pace towards the airport, his overcoat hanging on his left arm, and carrying a small piece of luggage in his right hand.

Jimmy Gunn had enormously changed if he was the passenger Mom identified. He was a huge guy topping six-foot plus and probably weighing over two hundred pounds. We couldn't see from the terrace if his eyes were blues and if his hair and mustache were blond. We rushed down to the lobby and waited in front of the arrival terminal.

Mom had good eyes. It was Jimmy with his smile and his blue eyes. He identified us right away. At least I believed he recognized Mom and her big nose. She hadn't changed a lot since the war, but we had, Juliette and I. We trudged in his direction, but before we had time to make a move towards our friend, Juliette had run and was already in his arms.

Jimmy was twenty-seven, I was twenty-two and Juliette almost twenty. Mom smiled at the sight. "I think she likes Jimmy," I said thoughtful.

"I think she likes him a lot. Hum!"

Finally our friend joined us as we waited for Juliette to let us welcome him. "What did you do with your life to have changed so much," I asked. "You were barely taller than I was when we met first, and now you must top me half a foot."

"Yes, my mother also said so. I guess I got taller and heavier as I grew older. My Dad is a big man too. And what about you. You have gained some weight and some height. And Juliette is a beautiful woman today. She was a child when I saw her last time."

I could see a smile of delight on Juliette's face. She was indeed a beautiful lady. Tall for a woman, though not as tall as Mom. She was full of life with an obvious desire to go far on her track. Mom always said that she would be a great, successful lady.

"I received your letter, Juliette, and I was happy when I did. I wasn't sure you had received mine. I appreciated your picture too. It was nice of you."

"What?" I said, "a picture. You didn't say you would send him a picture." Then I laughed.

Juliette blushed and turned to Mom. "Let's go home," she said a little embarrassed, but not much.

"I have a reservation at the *Hotel Negresco*. You must know where it is."

"Everyone knows where the Negresco is," I replied. "It's the best hotel in town. On the Promenade with an uninterrupted view on the *Baie des Anges*, the Bay of the Angels, and the Mediterranean. We rode a taxi to the hotel and helped Jimmy with his check in. We let him go up to his room and waited for him in the lobby.

Then we strolled along the Promenade under a magnificent blue sky and a pleasant little warm breeze that blew up to Avenue de la Victoire towards rue Mirabeau where our apartment building was still standing.

"It's a nice weather for December," Jimmy said. "Is that usual to have such a sunshine at Christmas time?"

"Pretty much," I said. "This is the *Côte d'Azur*, the French Riviera. That's why we have so many tourists at this time of the year."

"I want to see the beach where I met you, François."

"That's easy," I said pointing to the pebble beach. "That's where we met, eight years ago. Now, I'll show you exactly where, though you might remember."

We walked another two hundred yards or so. There was a flight of steps going down to the ocean. "That's it," Jimmy said. "I remember. That was the place where I lay down to burn my skin off on my first day out of the hospital. That's where I met you."

"Right. I saw you broiling like a stone crab and I thought you would have a bad night that day.

"Bad is an understatement. I had the most atrocious night of my life. But that never happened again."

"I'm cooking a Canard à l'Orange today," Mom said. "It should be almost ready when we get home."

"I remember that too. Canard à l'Orange is what you cooked when you invited me the first time."

"And I believe you liked it," Mom added.

"I loved it. You can find that kind of cooking only in a handful of restaurants in America. But I didn't find any in Atlanta."

We crossed over the Promenade, walked through Massena Square to reach Avenue de la Victoire. Rue Mirabeau was a few blocks away.

"Here we are," I said when we arrived at home, "the Cour des Miracles hasn't changed much. Same messy building, same sloppy courtyard, other kids on it but same kind."

"I recall the street, the building—"

"And the mess?" Juliette asked.

Jimmy smiled when my sister took his hand in a peremptory way as to say, "This is mine," though she didn't say a word.

We climbed up to the second floor and Mom ran straight to the kitchen. A marvelous smell slapped us right on the face, a smell of the Canard à l'Orange simmering now for over four hours. "The best cuisine," Mom said, "is slow cooking. I started this animal in the morning around six."

The table was set before we left home to the airport and the apartment looked almost nice with a lot of flowers Mom and Juliette had put everywhere. Nice is a city where flowers can be bought fresh and cheap almost everywhere.

Jimmy had brought the little briefcase he carried when he got off the plane. He sat on the sofa, the open briefcase on his lap and started pulling little packs wrapped with ribbons. He picked a square box and handed it to Mom. "It's a souvenir from Georgia," Jimmy said. "Hope you like it." It was a silk scarf with a map printed in color showing the main cities with their landmarks neatly designed.

"Here is where I live," my friend said pointing at Atlanta. It's a beautiful city, huge with modern buildings and numerous monuments from the Civil War."

"When we were wondering what happened to you during the war and we had no news, I tried to remember where you were from. I couldn't."

"When I left Georgia to go to war I was living in Carrollton where

I was born. It's a little city west of Atlanta. When I returned home from war I didn't waste my time in Carrollton. I enrolled in Georgia State University and since my graduation I live in Atlanta where I work for a large insurance company. I know you have finished college, Juliette told me. What are you going to do now?"

"Go to the army. It's time for me though I don't like it. But eighteen months is not a long time."

"Much less than my time," Jimmy said.

"I spent the last six months in Spain improving my Spanish. When I return from the army I'll go back to Madrid and bring my girlfriend with me. I'm going to marry her, Jimmy. She's a marvelous lady."

He kept pulling some little packages from his briefcase. He gave me one about ten inches square. It was heavy. I opened it uncovering a beautiful enamel dish with gold rim and a delicate painting representing two officers. I looked at Jimmy as he smiled. "Those two men are heroes in the south. They are two confederate leaders: Jefferson Davis and Robert E. Lee. This same picture is carved on the granite of Stone Mountain, north of Atlanta. Gutzon Borglum, an American sculptor commissioned by the state, started the carving in 1917 and was replaced in 1925 by another American artist, Henri Lukeman who couldn't finish the job for lack of money. But one of those days the job will be done."

I looked at the plate. "It's handsome," I said, "but your confederates lost the war, didn't they?"

"Yeah, but they are still loved in the south."

Juliette was waiting. She knew something was coming. In fact it happened to be a small box with a nice tricolor ribbon. "Open it," Jimmy said. "I'm sure you'll like it."

It was a golden medallion with a chain that probably could have been used to anchor the Bismarck. Juliette stayed agape for a minute. She couldn't take her eyes from the jewel. "It must weigh at list ten pounds," she finally managed to say with tears in her eyes. Jimmy smiled then got up. He walked to my sister and help her put on the medallion.

"You will have to walk bent over," I said. "Yet, what a marvelous thought."

Lunch was great as was the Canard à l'Orange. There wasn't much talk but Jimmy and Juliette communicated surreptitiously during the entire meal.

I opened a bottle of Dom Perignon to enjoy with the huge cherry pie Mom had baked while we were eating the canard. It turned out to be a little euphoric after the second bottle of champagne.

"Let's have a walk to help the digestion," I proposed. Mom was already in the kitchen busy with the dishes. "You go without me," she said. "I've too much to do here."

It was still nice outside the building. We strolled gently down Avenue de la Victoire to the Promenade des Anglais. Juliette hadn't let Jimmy's hand go for a second.

The breeze had calmed a little but the temperature remained around seventy-five degrees, which was remarkable for December, even by Riviera standards.

We had walked several miles westward. Almost to Saint-Laurent. Night had fallen already when we retraced our steps. We reached the Negresco about nine o'clock. Jimmy had to be exhausted with the time difference between Atlanta and Nice. He must have been awake for over twenty-four hours.

"I think we are going to let you have a good night sleep," Juliette said. "We'll be home anytime you want to come. Unless you want me to pick you up in the morning."

"That's would be fantastic," Jimmy replied. "I would like to visit Monaco. I didn't last time and I don't want to miss it this time. You both can come with me."

"I believe you'll feel better without me," I said with a smile. "You and Juliette go. Have a good time."

"Can you pick me up at nine?" Jimmy asked Juliette.

"Yes, sure," she said. She got close to our friend and kissed him on both cheeks. "We had a very good day and we are glad you came."

"The pleasure is all mine." I shook his hand and we walked away. Jimmy stayed a moment at the door waving every time we turned round.

"It was indeed a very nice day. Let's go home."

The ocean shimmered under a radiant moon.

31

We accompanied Jimmy back to the airport on January 5th. Two weeks of good time for him, for Mom, for me and, mostly for Juliette who had enjoyed Jimmy's visit tremendously. Mom had proposed to cook every day for our American friend but Jimmy had turned down her offer and, instead invited us every night to different restaurants. At noon Jimmy and Juliette would disappeared to returned home around seven P.M. just in time to get dressed and try another eatery.

On the eve of Jimmy Gunn's departure for the States we had a nice dinner at the *Hôtel de Paris* in Monte-Carlo, one of the most renowned restaurants in France, though Monte-Carlo is not France but part of the Principality of Monaco.

At the end of the evening Jimmy turned toward me with a smile as large as the English Channel. He held Juliette's hand, looked at Mom, then came back to me. "François," he said, "You are the man of the house since you all are orphans from your father. So, what I have to say will be said to you in the manner an American knows how. I want to marry Juliette.... Of course, if she wants me."

Juliette let out a little shriek as if she were surprised. She didn't fool anyone. The cry is fake, I thought. She knew very well what to expect from Jimmy. Or she was stupid. And Juliette was anything but stupid. Mom had a glance in my direction. We exchanged conspiring looks and smiled. We had seen that coming with hurricane force. That was not a surprise. Not for Mom, nor for me.

"You told me," I said looking at Jimmy Gunn. "Now you ask her."

Juliette jumped on her feet and cried, "Yes, yes, yes," before I had even finished the sentence.

"Well," I said, "that's an agreement of sort." Jimmy got up, fished a little box in his pocket and kneed. "Juliette, do you accept to be my wife?" he muttered opening the small case displaying a beautiful ring not as big as my car's spare tire, but it was pretty close. Mom rushed to Jimmy and hugged him. "I'm proud to have a son like you, Jimmy," she said with a torrent of tears coming down her cheeks. "You're welcomed at the Bornys' residence."

Yeah! I thought, Bornys' residence. Rue Mirabeau, the Court des Miracles.

That night Mom and I returned home hand in hand and when I looked at her I believed it was the first time in a long while that I saw happiness in her face.

"First step to the Americas," I said dreaming.

"What do you mean, first step?"

"Juliette is going to Georgia. Who is going to follow her?"

"Only God knows, my son."

* * *

Jimmy's letter arrived home a week or so after his departure. It was a large envelope heavier than usual for a love letter, but it contained a whole stack of printed material including an application for a residential visa to the United States. One form was filled up by Jimmy Gunn to be presented to the US Consulate in Nice along with about two thousand other forms Juliette would have to fill in.

Since my sister was exhilarated by the idea to marry Jimmy and immigrate to the United States, she didn't waste any time to fill up those questionnaires.

There was also a letter with the forms, of course, which Juliette read eagerly. "Jimmy is coming to Nice in July," Juliette said. "He asks me to make the arrangements for the wedding. Mom," she yelled, "this is true. He believes the application for the visa will be granted by that time. He talks about a honeymoon in Italy. Wow! Mom, I'm going to be an American."

I went in the army a week later to comply with the end of the provisional exemption of which I was the beneficiary. It was January 1953 and I knew I would be there until July 1954. Eighteen long months I couldn't avoid.

I joined Marseille's Fort Saint-Jean where my military future would be decided. After three days in the barracks, the draftees were packed by the thousands and sailed to Algeria on the *SS Ville d'Oran*. If it wasn't for leaving Mom alone I could have enjoyed very much the trip. Algeria was unknown to me, except for what I've learned in school. The discovery of a new country roused my curiosity. In spite of the common idea we had in France about Algeria, I knew that camels and dromedaries didn't wander on the streets like Brahman cows in New Delhi.

We found out that Algiers was a beautiful and modern city built on the slopes of a hill that overlooked the harbor.

It was cold, though I would have thought that Africa was always hot. But Algiers isn't really Africa. Not the one we imagine, the one that looks like Tarzan's jungle. North Africa is a modern country with buildings that could be found anywhere in the world, large avenues and well-maintained public parks.

Perhaps the only difference with a French city would be the inhabitants, a large majority being Arabs and dressed differently. The smell is also different but it isn't disagreeable. It's an odor of food cooked on the streets like *merguezes* (small sausages no one wants to know what's in them) *rates farcies* (stuffed pork spleens, stuffed with what?), *brochettes* (lamb kebabs) and small fish grilled over a makeshift outdoor cooking unit.

Yes, I know, this food sounds terrible, but if you have a little courage, —I had only a whit— and you want to singularize yourself among your friends, you try it. You'll find out that this strange looking food is delicious.

There is a little city east of Algiers named Fort-de-l'Eau. The building had started the previous century on the waterfront and the little village had become a very pleasant and prosperous city. On the main street facing the ocean, is a succession of cafés where one can eat the aforementioned food with no restrictions. With a few friends, during our military service, we would pick up a bus in Algiers at the *Place des Trois Horloges*, the Three Clocks Square, and ride —about forty-five minutes— to the seaside-charming town. For a few francs we could eat those merguezes, rates, kebabs and fish and drink an *anisette* or two, and return to the barracks around ten PM with our stomach full and our face burnt with sun.

* * *

Juliette and Jimmy got married on July 30th at the cathedral Saint Charles in Nice where, years ago, I was an insolent altar boy with my friend Sylvain Bénichou.

I still thought of Sylvain from time to time and what it may have happened to him. I remember the wee hours of the morning, Christmas Day 1943; the Gestapo took him away with his parents never to return home. I knew I wouldn't see him again and I felt sorry for my best friend.

The wedding reception was held at the Hôtel Negresco where the newlyweds would spend the night before leaving for Rome the next day.

They reappeared a week later with hours of memories from Naples, Capri, Venise and Rome. We spent a few hours on rue Mirabeau listening to them bragging about their trip and the delight they had felt during their sojourn in Italy.

And then, it was over. The wedding, the reception, the trip to Italy, and the flight to Atlanta. Mom and I remained alone in our *Court des Miracles* rue Mirabeau sad from being deprived of Juliette, but happy for her to have found the most adorable man on earth.

We sat, Mom and I, around the dining table and talked for a while about our lives, Juliette's success in hers, Jimmy Gunn's promise to marry my sister, which he kept, and also, reluctantly, of my father who had missed the best part of my life: high school and college graduations, Juliette's wedding and expatriation, and meeting my friend Jimmy Gunn.

Mom wasn't willing to talk about Dad so she changed the subject asking about my last trip. "You didn't say much about your last sojourn in Spain," she said matter-of-factly. "You didn't spend quite a month this time. Did you enjoy it as much as in the past ones?"

"I sure did. We didn't move much except when we went to Barcelona to pay a visit to the Delmontes. Same welcome as usual. Don Ricardo and Rosalia seemed to be happy with their lives. We were again invited to a trip to Palma but Aline wanted to return to Madrid and spend some time with her parents who would soon retire from the diplomatic business. And spend their time traveling around the world.

"What about Juan and Amelia?"

"We heard about them from the Delmontes. They had found a job with an English archaeological company for researches in Iraq. They had what they wanted. They got married with the blessing of both families and flew the next day to Baghdad."

"You say you met Aline's parents."

"Yes, finally. Charming people, mostly Armand Delheuil, her father. He's got the same green eyes and speaks at a fast rate with a cute drawl from Marseille where he was born and raised. We spent a whole day together in their house near the train station Chamartin where the duchess cooked an excellent *paella valenciana*.

Aline's father and his wife Suzanne, had a very interesting life within his diplomatic occupation. Traveling many places in the world from Casablanca, where Aline was born, to Madrid passing through Madagascar, Egypt and some other places whose names I forgot.

Meanwhile, Aline was in a boarding school in Casablanca until she graduated and found a job at the French embassy in Madrid."

"Did you visit with Filomena?"

"Of course. I couldn't go to Madrid and ignore the charitable lady. The nice *señora* was still there holding her business as usual. Not making money, I believe. But obviously she could afford with the help of her other businesses and, I assume, she didn't give a damn."

"Your mouth, Son."

I smiled. Mom couldn't stand any deviation from the fine language. She had not much education but she made up her lack of knowledge with a profound respect for other people.

"My Parisians friends, Robert Valois and André Delatour," I continued, "were again shamelessly taking advantage of the marvelous Filomena."

"That would be your last trip to Spain for a while, now."

"That was the last one before I'm through with the army. Then, we'll see."

When Aline accompanied me to the train she stood on the platform with watery eyes but without a word. I looked at her knowing that for the next two years or so we wouldn't see each other. I was going to miss her.

"When the train got off, while I remained silent at the window, she yelled all of a sudden, "You want me to ask my Dad if I can marry you?"

"What did you say?" Mom asked knowing the answer.

"I yelled in return, 'yes, yes' as I waved my hand and Aline

disappeared in the haze of the train station."
"For now you finish what you have to," Mom said.
"Well, my leave of absence is over. Tomorrow I'll be back in Algiers.

The next day I flew back for another year that was waiting for me in the barracks. It was still boring but the Saturday nights in Fort-de-l'Eau brought enough exhilarating entertainment and fun to forget the drill sergeant, the guard duty, the morning bugle, and the horrid food.

A few weeks later Mom received pictures of Juliette and Jimmy's arrival. They were welcomed in Jimmy's own house where a reception was held by his family and friends.

The house was a two-story built in the middle of a wooded area in Marietta, north of Atlanta. Greenery and flowers and a small fountain with sparkling water surrounded the swimming pool.

When Mom sent me the pictures I looked at them and thought: that was the America I wanted to live in. The country I've been dreaming of since my childhood. I was right then, flowerbeds, and bushes, and trees everywhere with swimming pools surrounded by mansions, and riches showing ubiquitously unlike on rue Mirabeau and its Court des Miracles.

* * *

The military service hadn't ended but, fortunately, there was a break in the lengthy boredom. I was sent, along with two of my friends, to Casablanca for training at the bomb squad facility in the Moroccan city. That was a nice change for once.

We arrived in the morning after having traveled by train from Algiers for eighteen hours. We weren't in a hurry so we took it easy.

The training with bombs —fake of course— was fun, not exhausting, and certainly not dangerous. We didn't learn much, but it allowed us to spend some time visiting a very interesting city invaded with huge American cars and American tourists. We definitely learned a bit about the exotic town and we loved it.

Some time later when I watched the movie *Casablanca*, I couldn't help but laughed at all the wrong images Hollywood had made up showing a complete lack of knowledge of Moroccan people, soldiers' uniforms, and commissioner's costume.

And that movie, I recall, with Humphrey Bogart, Paul Henreid, and Ingrid Bergman, had been, and still is, a big hit all over the world despite the mistakes in it.

For instance, an ugly officer represents the Germans and his uniformed staff who couldn't organize anything but the arrest of French citizens in a nightclub owned by Bogart.

Well, during World War II there were no German military personnel in Morocco. Only a commission of German civil servants who tried hard to keep a low profile. Probably military officers headed those men but they kept themselves in the shadow until the landing of the Americans in December 1942 when they were arrested along with a few Nazi French militiamen.

At the end of the movie, when Paul Henreid and Ingrid Bergman fled, one can see their plane flying over the nightclub at about one hundred feet in altitude. Casablanca airport is several miles away from the city and it's unlikely that a plane had flown so low over a town of two million people.

There are more mistakes and I wondered why no one had tried to check them before the shooting of the movie.

But that's Hollywood, and they would say, who cares?

* * *

I returned home in July 1954 after an eighteen-month period that, somehow, wasn't that bad. We had visited two new countries, new for me and most of my friends, had a good time in Algiers where, of course, we had visited the Kasbah —a weird place— and many other sites we had no idea existed.

Mom was at the train station once again when I reached Nice. I had called her at the restaurant as soon as I disembarked from the *SS El Mansour*, another horrible ship, after a rather stormy crossing of the Mediterranean. Most of the passengers, a majority discharged soldiers, were seasick during the twenty-six hour crossing.

I still had the waves of the ocean in my legs when I set my feet on land at La Joliette, Marseille. Then I took a taxi to Saint-Charles train station and left the city at eleven o'clock in the morning still dizzy from the horrible swell.

It was nice to be home in spite of the usual brouhaha and the smell that drifted up from the courtyard. For the number of years I'd been living in this building I always had to deal with toddlers making everybody's life miserable. And they weren't, of course, the same, nor were the mothers, the dogs or the chickens.

"So," Mom said, "how was your crossing back home?"

"Besides the dozens of sick people amid the odor of vomit, it was all right. Nobody moved from the low deck until we entered the port of Marseille. I'm glad I'm here."

"What are your plans for the next days?"

"First I want to go to Spain. I promised Aline to visit with her as soon as I got out of the army."

"When would that be?"

"Tomorrow, if I can."

* * *

I had called Aline at the embassy from Nice. It took me an hour and a half to get the operator in Madrid, then half an hour to connect the embassy, and finally reached Aline's office around noon. She was out for lunch. I almost bit the telephone, but I calmed down and left a message with her secretary.

So she was at the Chamartin Station when I arrived late that evening. It had been over a year and a half since I met her last.

We rode directly to her apartment calle del Carmen near Plaza del Sol.

The first shock was the lack of furniture. Almost everything was gone. "Are you going broke," I asked a little befuddled.

She laughed. No, I'm not going broke. I'm going to France."

"What did you do with your possessions?"

"I sold most of them but what I could put in my luggage." She showed me the way to the bedroom. There were half a dozen of valises, suitcases, bags, all lined up on the floor of the room.

"What is this?" I said. "Are you really going somewhere?"

"You bet." She smiled at me and said, "I going to Nice with you as soon as you return home. I submitted my resignation two weeks ago knowing that you were coming to pick me up."

I was somewhat confused. I knew Aline wanted to come with me but that was a little sudden, even a little premature. "I'm the happiest man in the world," I said kissing her, "but I just got out of the army and I don't even have a job."

"I have one," she replied laughing. "I start my new job at the Social Security Office in Nice in two weeks. It's good to have an influential Dad."

As I already said this woman must be from Brittany, stubborn as she is. I was thinking about testing her will, then I gave up. "All right," I said almost reluctantly, "let's go to France."

"I sold my car to the new tenant of my apartment, a South African lady who works at her embassy. See, everything falls into the right place."

"Yeah, yeah," I said with a wince, but I was thrilled to have her in my hometown. I knew Mom liked her. "Alea jacta est, the die is cast," I said as if Latin had no secret for me. I just made an irrevocable decision for our future.

But I'm sure it was the right decision, and many years later I knew the decision was the very right one.

32

It was sad news on our arrival in Nice. The express train didn't stop everywhere, not like the Saint-Laurent-du-Var's that halted to disembark and embark short-route passengers. The express from Spain didn't even slow down when crossing the little town.

It was a weird impression of emptiness as I stared at the city when rolling by. It looked almost like a ghost town. The usual commotion of Saint-Laurent had disappeared. No one on the beach though it was September a time when students would invade the streets, the beach and, of course, the university.

When I reached Nice, the first thing that came to my mind was to call Mr. Langevin, my former landowner when I was a student with Gaston and Denise. "What happened to Saint-Laurent," I asked a little anxious. "I just returned from Spain and I wonder what's going on in your city."

"Not much," Mr. Langevin answered. "Only that they closed the university which means that we no longer have students in town. That makes for a vacuum-like swept village. For it's what it is; a deserted village with a little over one thousand inhabitants when we were used having twenty thousand people moving in the area."

"What is going to ensue?"

"Well, for one, most of the businesses are going to close for lack of customers. Then people will migrate to bigger towns. Nice, Cannes, Grasse and even Marseille."

"When did they decide to close the university?"

I couldn't help but think about the cute restaurant on the beach, The Fisherman, we used to go to with Gaston. Denise worked there her four years in college. We had been lucky of sort to have the possibility to finish our classes in time. This year's sophomores and juniors would have to go somewhere else. I wondered about the teachers, Mr. Gouhaux, Mr. Schwartz, and other wonderful professors who might find themselves without a job.

"So, your apartment is not rented for this year," I continued with an idea in the back of my head.

"No. Open as the first day you and your friends took it. How long it has been? Almost six years."

"Yes, almost. As for your apartment, I'm interested in it."

"I'll give you a large discount," Mr. Langevin said laughing.

"You're welcome, my friend."

This was a big step already. Now, let's think about more serious subjects.

* * *

Aline had spent the night in Juliette's room which Mom had arranged superbly since my sister left to the Americas.

At eight o'clock in the morning I decided to go to the printing shop where I had worked part-time for four years during my college studies. The army had kept me away from it so I didn't know if I eventually could get my job back on a full time basis. At least it would be a job, though I didn't plan to be a photoengraver all my life.

The supervisor was still a woman, though not the same I knew. Besides, there were a few changes in the shop, adjustments they usually call inevitable. New people, old ones retired like Roger, and changes in the technique. From letterpress process they were switching progressively to offset. Two quite different types of printing that hadn't much in common with the exception of camera work and the plate making, though the plates aren't engraved in offset. No more nitric acid, no more bitumen or resin, no more mounting the plates on plywood. Only negatives, or sometimes positives. Easy to handle on two large light tables that had taken almost the entire room in the former engraving department.

Two presses had disappeared and had been replaced with two splendid four-color Heidelbergs.

I was welcomed by the owner, an old man with a thick snow-white shock of hair and a bad limp of his left leg, whose name was Antoine Laubry. He was a gentle human being spending the end of his life hanging onto the shop he had created thirty years earlier. His wife, a cute little old lady with more wrinkles than a prune, was known to repeat that he would die in his office.

I don't know if it was where he died, but it was there that he greeted me with his usual smile and handshake. "So, you're out of that damn army," he had said laughing. "I've been lucky. Missed both wars with my bum leg. They didn't even want me in an office. Are you looking for a job?"

"I'm looking for a teaching job. I applied at the Nice High School but still waiting for an answer. The Nice Academy is not in hurry to find teachers without experience. Saint-Laurent University has closed recently and professors are scattered all over the place looking for a charge at any school."

"I heard about Saint-Laurent. It's a shame. Give me a little time," he continues after a short pause, "and I might have a job for you. But you would have to make some adjustments."

"I heard. From letterpress to offset. I'm open."

"Good, let me call you back."

On my way out from Mr. Laubry's office I stumbled across a customer name Henri Dunan who worked for a publishing company in Monaco. He was a young tall guy I never saw without a smile on his face. We shook hands and said hello. "I heard you're out of the army," he said. "What are you up to now?"

"Looking for a job. I believe I might find one here if Mr. Laubry

decided to teach me this thing they call offset."
"You don't know yet for sure, do you?"
"Not yet. He'll let me know. I hope he won't be too long."
"The company I work for is looking for a proofreader. Can you spell?"
"I believe so though I've no idea what the job consists of besides reading proof, of course. I can spell, but can I proofread?"
"Probably not. It's more difficult than it looks. But if you have the knowledge of the rules of grammar and if you can spell, you will make it. The most difficult part is to train your eyes. It takes a while and a lot of practice. You'll read a text ten times and every time you'll find mistakes. That's funny. Then, sometimes, you won't find any mistake after the third reading. I don't believe there is anyone who can find all the glitches on the first reading."
"I'll take my chances," I said shaking his hand and thanking him for the tip. "But first I want to tell Mr. Laubry that I might have found a job."
"Sure. The least you can do."
I walked back to Mr. Laubry's office who watched me coming in a little surprised. "What's wrong?"
"Just want to tell you that I think I found a job with *Perspectives Publishing*. I talked to Henri Dunan, he's here, and he offered me a proofreader job. I'm not sure I'm fit for that line of work, but I'll give it a try."
"I'm sure you'll do fine, François."

* * *

Aline and Mom decided to go shopping and then went to Saint-Laurent-du-Var, to visit with Mr. Langevin about the apartment we were supposed to rent. The end of July would be here in no time and Aline and I would be moving in our new home as soon as we could afford it.

In the mean time I went to Monaco for my first interview. I wasn't quite sure what this was about. I understood publishing for I'd worked in Mr. Laubry's printing shop during my college years and even if it was on a part time basis, I'd seen magazines, books, and newsletters besides all the material a printer is supposed to produce.

One of the most important customers they had at Laubry, was the company I was going to for my interview. Not really scared but shaking.

I had put on my best suit —the only one I had— got my hair cut for the second time in a week, and installed on my face, the best smile I could afford.

I rode the train to Monaco, which took about twenty minutes from Nice with two stopovers in Villefranche-sur-Mer and Beaulieu. From the train station I walked to the Condamine where *Perspectives Publishing* had their offices, just across the street from the salt-water Olympic swimming pool.

A young lady with a very mini-skirt greeted me, and I asked to speak to Mr. Henri Dunan who, the day before, suggested that I apply for the job. I understood that he was in charge of the company; at least it looked like it.

"You decided to try as a proofreader," Henri said extending his hand to greet me.

"Can't hurt," I said with a nervous chuckle.

"Let me introduce you to the big boss."

We stepped into a large office with nice paintings on the walls and a thick carpet on the floor. I didn't recognize any of the pictures but they looked like expensive ones. However not Goya or Velasquez, I thought.

"This is François Borny, I talked to you about. He's just through with the army, has a college degree or two and has been working at Laubry's on a part time basis for over four years. He's looking for a

teaching job unless we have a better offer here."
Wow! I thought. He did his homework. He knew me from the shop but I couldn't believe he knew that much about me.
"And this is Mr. Paul Dunan," Henri said with a smile. "My father."
My mouth fell agape for a few seconds. This young man seemed to run the company. I didn't realize Henri Dunan was related with the owner of the company. I didn't know he was the one who decided to hire me even before I came to Monte-Carlo.
"So he knows printing," Mr. Paul Dunan said.
"Hum!" I said. "Not sure about that."

* * *

After so many years I still remember that first interview.

It was indeed a large company, *Perspectives Publishing*, owned by a Parisian company whose Chairman of the Board and CEO was Mr. Paul Dunan. His son Henri being the Managing Editor for six publications the company issued every year. Those magazines were generally concerned about the Third World and mostly Africa.

And they had an opening in proofreading.

The Chairman looked like a nice person, short and bald and a little above the reasonable weight, smiling, and it was then that I noticed the resemblance between the two Dunans. Paul must be around fifty or fifty-five years old while his son had barely reached his low thirties.

Paul offered me a seat and asked his son to bring some coffee and assist in the interview.

He looked like the Greek legendary *Minotaur*, I thought. Minus the horns, of course. I had no idea why I thought about the Minotaur. Perhaps the large eyes slanted down the wrong way, his long eyelashes but also his long narrow visage that ended with a short goatee. I never thought at the time that I'd call him Minotaur for the next twenty-four years. The nickname stuck to him and even his son called him, a while later, Minotaur. That was funny.

His bullish face was red with wine but he had the infectious family smile that lasted the whole interview. He glanced at my diplomas still rolled in my hands but didn't even bother to have a glance at them.

"Where have you been working so far?" the Minotaur asked still smiling as Henri stepped in with two cups of coffee. One for the old man and one for me, the non-coffee drinker. Have to make the best of a bad offer. I drank the coffee trying not to wince.

"Nowhere, Sir," I said answering his question, "If it wasn't for the part time job at Laubry Printing shop. I returned from the army and from vacation in Spain after I got these," I said waving the diplomas. "Six months to improve my Spanish and, perhaps I thought, to find a nice señorita."

"Did you find any?"

"Yes, Sir, I did, but she is more French than Charles de Gaulle."

"Good for you," he said laughing.

"Yes, sure, I'm happy with that, but she threatens to return to Spain if I don't find a job," I lied.

"Well, I have a single question for you," he said. "Can you spell *spermatophyte?*"

"I sure can," I answered not being sure at all. I've never heard that word before and didn't even know the meaning.

"Yes," I repeated. "S-P-E-R-M-A-T-O-P-H-I-T-E." And I stopped breathing wondering if I did it right. Droplets of sweat had beaded up on my neck since I came to Monaco and now were trickling down my back. I felt like at the movies watching a thriller.

"Bravo," he said. "I didn't know how to spell it. I learned something today. You're hired. Start Monday the 1st."

"Thank you, sir," I said with a broken voice. "My señorita might linger a little longer."

He chuckled then said, "You might hate me for that after a while.

But remember, I've nothing to do with your girlfriend staying."

I never had to regret it. I worked for twenty-four years for the Minotaur until he died in 1978, and they tried to send me to the headquarters in Paris.

And I'm still married with the French señorita.

That night, when I got home I checked the word *spermatophyte*. I had spelled it wrong. It was a *Y* not an *I*. And I could swear the Minotaur knew that.

That was fall 1954, and I had my first serious job like a real man in real life.

A month later I married Aline. It was a Saturday, October 30, 1954. And we moved to Saint-Laurent-du-Var. A simple ceremony with Mom, Juliette who came from Atlanta, Denise and Gaston, my best man.

That same day, early in the morning somewhere in Algeria, around the department of Constantine, a shaky old bus was stopped at a crossing road. In the bus were about twenty passengers of whom two were French. It was a young couple from Marseille. They just had their first position as teachers in a small village a hundred kilometers south of Constantine.

Four men, in military fatigues, climbed into the bus carrying submachine guns. They were Algerians. They walked to the young couple and ordered them to get off the bus.

There was no reason for alarm, but the young lady grabbed her husband's hand. "That's all right," he said to encourage her.

They climbed down the vehicle and were unceremoniously pushed away. A few seconds later, the bus passengers could hear the staccato of the machine guns. It was with horror that they witnessed the assassination of the French couple.

A man got off the bus. He was an old Algerian in his traditional *djelaba*. He asked why they had shot those young people. "They came to teach your children," he said outraged. There was a new staccato and the old man was dead.

The Algerian War had begun on October 30th, 1954 to last another seven years.

33

The Minotaur called me in his office that Monday morning. One of the secretaries, Martine, the prettiest with the miniskirt, came to my office to summon me to the big chief.

It was always a pleasure to talk to the Minotaur. He was always courteous, smiling and always had something interesting to talk about.

"How long you have been here," he asked after he pointed to a leather armchair across his desk.

"Almost a year, Sir."

"That long already. It seems that Henri brought you here a few weeks ago. How do you like your job?"

"I love it, Sir. I read a lot of interesting well-written articles about those countries I barely know. Gabon, Cameroon, Chad, Congo, Kenya. And even Haiti. It's fascinating. And my proofreading is improving."

"Would you like to write something about Cameroon?"

"I would like to though I'm not sure I would know how or what. My knowledge on Cameroon is limited to what I read in those articles I proofread and to what I've learned in school. I don't believe it's enough to write anything on that country."

The Minotaur got up, walked around his desk and grabbed a stack of paper several inches thick and dropped the whole thing on my lap. "All right," he said, "here is a large documentation on Cameroon along with about fifty or sixty black and white pictures. You read it, find out if you like it, and write a ten/twelve-page article for next Monday. An article you will accompany with as many pictures as you want. Is that all right with you?"

I smiled. "I thank you, Sir, but I never thought you would offer me that line of work."

"You can refuse, of course. And, by the way, you can call me Minotaur," he said laughing.

I could fill the blood rushing to my face like a torrent of lava. "That's what everyone calls me, right?"

"I wouldn't know, Sir," I lied as Henri entered the room also laughing.

"Yes, he knows," Henri Dunan said with a wink at his father. "Everybody knows." And they both laughed in unison as I walked out without a back glance.

Around four in the afternoon the Minotaur opened my door a crack, showed his elongated face, and said, "Let's go to *Caesar's* and have a beer."

Mr. Caesar was the owner of a small café-bar on the pier facing the harbor, a bar well known by the aficionados of the Monaco Grand Prix for the race cars rush at a hundred miles an hour a few feet away. The inside café is small with only three tables, but the terrace is wide and well exposed to the sun and the breeze from the open sea.

With old Mr. Dunan we had quickly taken the habit of a break around four in the afternoon. About that time, the door of my office would open and the bullish face would show without a word. No matter how busy I was, no matter the emergency of whatever I was doing, the Minotaur never broke the rite. For years we have been enjoying the interruption. And even when he retired, years later, he would come from time to time, show his gentle face and out we were towards Caesar's.

That first day we were sitting peacefully on the terrace watching the passersby and enjoying the weather and the beer. "How's Aline?" he asked.

"Huge and exhausted. The baby is due early next month and she doesn't want to quit working."

"She will have to. Give her my regards."
"Thank you, Sir, I will."
Then we went back to work that had lasted long hours that day until late in the evening. I was working on that curious Cameroon reading and taking notes, hoping that my copy would be good enough for publication.

It was. The Minotaur and junior came to my office the next day. He handed the copy back to me and said, "That's good, François. It looked like you have spent half of your life in Africa."

"Thank you, Sir, I tried my best," I said as I took the article. I glanced at it shuffling the pages. There were very few corrections I knew were made by junior. But that was all right. I would have my first text published in our magazine *Perspectives*.

"Now," Young Dunan said, "You need to go there and find out if what you have written is correct."

They turned around and walked to the door. The Minotaur stopped there smiling and said, "It's correct, I know. Let's wait for the birth of the baby and then we'll prepare a nice trip for you."

I was thrilled though I didn't know what Aline might think about leaving her and the baby. Mom would be there, of course, but still I had a feeling that this wasn't going to be good news for Aline.

Well, I found out really quickly that Aline never interfered with my work. All her life she had supported and encouraged me to do the best in my job no matter what it took. In her selflessness she never complained for my late home coming, never a word of regret because it happened that I worked sometimes on Sundays or for taking so little time off. She was there when I needed her. She has been a wonderful wife for many years, and still is.

* * *

Summer was gone and with it those vacationers who believed they owned the French Riviera. If you happened to drive out of your city —for instance in Paris— don't expect motorists to be lenient, to forgive the way you drive. It's arduous to find one's way in the capital if you are not a native. If you had to take a right turn, you better be in the right lane. But most of the times you know you have to take the turn when it's too late. So you try again, have a second round, and perhaps a third one, and struggle to pass from the wrong lane to the right one. No one would give you the right of way. If they can run you off the road, they will. That's the way most people drive in France even if they don't admit it.

But, when Parisians are on vacation on the Riviera, they take a sadistic pleasure to drive at a speed never exceeding twenty miles an hour, no matter the mess they create behind them. The winding road from Monaco to Nice is a narrow one hugging the ocean. No one can pass any vehicle for the fifteen miles of the road. And that is the time chosen by the Parisians to drive fifteen miles an hour which enrages everybody else. If you are driving bumper to bumper for miles, you can bet a Parisian is leading the line.

* * *

It was the eighth day of November. Tuesday that was, and I just picked up Aline at work at three o'clock and we went to the beach to relax for a moment and have a quick swim. Not my wife though. She could barely move. With her round belly she looked like an inner tube escaped from an eighteen-wheeler. But her face was still pretty and her smile didn't reflect the discomfort she must have felt.

After she sat on the uneasy mix of pebbles and sand of the beach, she felt relaxed with no desire to change position or to move. Of course, she would have rolled the inclined slope of the shore to the ocean if I had let her, but I was there to prevent any intrepid ideas.

I finally decided to go for a short swim. No more than a quarter of

a mile, I promised.
Aline loved the ocean, and she's still a nut for the Mediterranean, or any ocean by the way. But that day she was pregnant up to her eyeballs, and pretty close to hatching like an egg in a brooder. What was she going to give me? No ultra sound at that time, no scientific way to explore my wife's womb.
She was tired after a whole day at work and when I stopped at her office she complained about her general state. "I don't understand," she had said, "why am I so exhausted."
"Look at your waist," I suggested. "Perhaps that would give you an idea." My wife is smart. She looked at her body, and suddenly said laughing, "Oh! I think I have an offspring developing."
"Well, now you know what I mean," I replied.

The sun was rapidly sliding down behind the hill and I couldn't help but think about the way it disappears in summertime at the west-end of the horizon, behind the ocean.
I always liked summer better if it weren't for the obnoxious Parisians on vacation.
Next time I come to that world of sorrow I want to be born in the Sahara. No trees, no water, no winters, and no Parisians. But what a great beach. Only sand.
Once I was done with my little swimming, I helped my wife to get laboriously on her feet. We shook off the sand we had amassed in our nostrils and our ears, and spit out of our mouths, and went home to watch the news on the TV.
We got home when the coolness of the night began to fall over Saint-Laurent-du-Var. I helped Aline climbing to the second floor, to lie down on the couch, and I began to prepare the dinner. I was good at it, but for those who have bad ideas, I say: not anymore. Don't ask me anything.
I had parked my car in the little garage I shared with Mr. Langevin

and his son. Two cars would park straight ahead, and the third one, slantwise which always blocked one of the other cars. But it was no problem. If the first to leave in the morning is obstructed, the obstructer would remove his vehicle, and that was it.

As I came early that evening I just park straight.

The problem occurred at three o'clock in the morning that Wednesday November 9, 1955. The egg was ready to hatch, and my first child was coming through.

I went down to the garage, and of course, my car was blocked. I couldn't decently wake my landlord though he wouldn't have minded, I'm sure. The other option was to move the blocker's car. Though it was a small one, a four-horse-powered Renault, the engine is mounted in the rear, which makes the weight reach three hundred pounds, or so I believed.

Aline was already in my car moaning. I had to move Mr. Langevin's car out of my way no matter what. I grabbed the rear bumper and, inch by inch, moved the Renault toward one side out of my way.

Where did I get that strength had always been a mystery to me. And how did my landlord manage to get out of the garage? I don't know, and never asked.

A few days later, when my wife had returned home from the hospital with the most beautiful baby girl I'd ever seen, I tried to push the Renault the way I did at three in the morning. That day I gathered all the strength I could, I was rested, calm and decided, but unable to move that stupid car a single eighth of an inch.

Some time later I learned that the rear of the Renault weighed close to five hundred pounds. Two hundred and twenty-five kilos. A world record for a car lifter. A record for me anyway.

And the baby girl's name was Susanne. No Z. When I registered her at the City hall in Nice, I asked for *Susan* the American way. I thought the clerk would have jumped over her counter and slapped me. "No can do," she almost yelled. "Suzanne in French, that's all I can accept. So, it was Susanne for she misspelled it. And it was still not French. It takes a Z in my country. I thought for a second. The clerk refused *Susan*, accepted *Suzanne*, but scribed *Susanne*. She had to be an illiterate communist. I was laughing when I read the birth certificate. Then I had a back glance to the uneducated clerk, thumbed my nose, and stuck out my tongue.

34

After a week off from *Perspectives Publishing*, I returned to the office where the Dunans seemed to be desperate to see me. "Where have you been?" the elder said laughing knowing very well where I had been. He handed me a huge wrapped box, shook my hand and asked, "How's the girl?"

"She's beautiful," I said enthusiastic, then thanked him.

That was nice. I didn't know they would have thought about a baby gift, but they did.

"What's the news?" I asked not being sure I wanted to know.

"Here the last issue of *Perspectives*," Henri said handing the magazine.

On the front cover a picture I had selected of a semi-desert North-Cameroon with a herd of elephants in the foreground, and a few giraffes grazing on acacia trees in the background.

I loved that picture. This was the idea I had of Africa; desert, six-foot termite mounds, acacias, giraffes and elephants. Tarzan must not be far away.

"You like the cover?" the elder asked.

"Yes I do."

"You'll like the text too. We added a few more pictures than you had chosen. I hope you don't mind."

How could I mind? I was the proud writer of an article that was actually published. That was a first for me and, hopefully, it won't be the last.

"We're preparing the next issue which would be focused on the International Tourist Convention in Lagos, Nigeria," Henri said.

"Would you like to go?"

"I sure would like to. What would be the assignment?"

"A report on the convention. It will last about a week, so you'd have a lot to say about it. You'll be met by our photographer from Cameroon, Georges Martial."

"He who shot all those beautiful pictures of Cameroon?"

"That's the one. We had a reservation at the Ikoyi Palace Hotel in Lagos. It's the best you can have there. Martial will join you the next day coming from Duala on a Cameroon Airline flight. Pick him up at the airport. He doesn't speak English and would probably have some trouble there." He handed me a picture of himself with an older short man. "That's what he looks like. He's from Marseille but lives in Cameroon since the beginning of the Stone Age. You want to take the picture with you?"

"I'll be fine. I have a good photographic memory though I can't remember names. But Georges will be easy to remember."

"You're leaving a week from Monday at noon. You need some shots; cholera, smallpox, and yellow fever. Start today taking some quinine. This is very important. Try to remember that. About a week or two before and two weeks after you're back. Bring me your passport. We'll take care of the visa."

* * *

Mom came home on Sunday ready to spend as much time as it needed, which meant as long as I would be away.

Aline had prepared my suitcase, my passport, my vaccination certificates, and my quinine. For the whole week I was in a constant feverish state at the thought that, for the first time, I was going to fly over half of the African continent. I already had a flight to Algiers, but this was a short one.

I couldn't wait for the day of my departure. And now that I was almost there, I began to panic. I had a mix feeling of excitement and fear. The unknown had attracted me for a long time but the question now was: What was Africa like? Black Africa that is. I knew *Alger la Blanche* —Algiers the White— and Casablanca without Humphrey, but where I was going now was real Africa. I was flying to the unknown Nigeria. What did that country look like? How were the people there? And other questions I would have the answer only there.

I shook myself out of this childish worry. I can handle that, I forced my mind to believe.

Monday morning was a rainy day. Mom and Aline accompanied me at the airport with little Susanne.

"It's the first time I'll be flying for over eight hours," I said pathetic.

"You'll be fine," Mom said with a smirk. "You're a big boy now."

"Yes sure." I felt my knees playing castanets on a fast tempo. "I should have thought twice about this trip before I committed myself to the Dunans. Now I'm not sure I want to do this."

"Don't be ridiculous," Aline said. "This is the best promotion you could have. What does your business card say? Hum! Read again. Managing editor, right?"

"Yes, yes, I know. I'll be fine," I said after a short silence.

They called my Pan Am flight to Lagos. I kissed Aline, Susanne and Mom and walked towards the Immigration and Custom services. I turned round before I went through the gate and waved a shaky hand to my dear ones. It will be about two weeks before I'm back. I already missed them.

The plane to Lagos had a stopover in Dakar, Senegal, where it disembarked a few passengers and loaded some others. A huge young man got in the plane there and sat next to me. Before he opened his mouth I knew he was American. Probably the way he was dressed,

perhaps his rubicund face, and his red hair, or perhaps his jovial laugh when he addressed the flight attendant before he got into the plane.
I was right. "I'm Jack Mallburn," he said with a smile, extending his hand.
"I'm François Borny," I replied trying to match the smile.
"French, huh?"
"Sorry."
"Je parle Français," he said with a funny accent. He reminded me of my brother-in-law, Jimmy Gunn. "This plane goes to Lagos and Leopoldville, the former Belgium Congo," he continued. "Where do you stop?"
"Lagos," I replied. "I'm not going farther."
"You have made the right decision. You don't want to go to Congo. The political situation over there isn't very clear with all those greedy leaders. You probably heard of Tschombe, Kasavubu, Lumumba and other Mobutu. They're all trying to get the biggest piece of pie they can get. It's no good to be there presently."
"I heard of them. It's not very appealing."
"I'm staying at the Ikoyi Hotel in Lagos. That's the only one you can sleep in bed without too much worry. If you don't look too closely."
"That's where I'm staying," I said.
"What do you sell?"
"Nothing. I have a report to write on the Tourism Convention that will begin Thursday. I'm a publisher in Monaco."
"What do you publish?"
"A magazine, *Perspectives*, six times a year. And what do you sell?"
"Champagne," he said laughing. "A lot of it. Nigerians drink champagne like you drink water."
"What kind of champagne?"
"Any kind. American, Russian, Spanish and even Mexican."

"I didn't know champagne existed outside of France. What you're selling is sparkling wine."

"Right, but no one knows the difference. I mean, no one in Nigeria. But I sell also very nice champagne; Dom Perignon, by the thousands of cases. Do you know that brand?"

"I'm French," I said with a chuckle. "That's what we call real champagne."

"I am under contract with the Moët & Chandon champagne maker for the exclusive sale in Nigeria. Do you know that you can buy Dom Perignon cheaper in Lagos than in France? No kidding. So far there are no taxes in Nigeria for imported wine. That might change any time. And when that happens, I would have to look for another customer somewhere else in the world. Maybe Papua."

The flight attendant brought our lunch and asked what we would like to drink. "Champagne," Jack asked with a candid smile.

A minute later the attendant brought a half bottle of California champagne. She uncorked it and poured some into two plastic goblets.

"You see what I mean," I said with a wince. "I do not want to try this beverage. Not in a plastic goblet. Champagne is a distinguished wine, very proud and very sophisticated. It must be drunk chilly and in crystal flutes. The label on that bottle says *champagne* which is a very illegal term, according to the international rules of commerce. The word is a brand name coming from the region of Champagne, northeast of Paris and nowhere else. No other wines may use that name. But no one pays attention to those delicate rules."

Jack drank some of the wine, snapped his tongue and said, "Not bad for a California champagne."

"That's what you said two minutes ago," I remarked. "No one knows the difference and certainly not the Nigerians."

"Those Nigerians," Jack continued, "drink champagne at any hour of the day. In the States we drink beer or coffee or coke. There they drink champagne. Go to *Antoine* in downtown Lagos. It's a good

Lebanese restaurant very much crowded. And just watch. British and Americans would drink beer. The locals prefer Dom Perignon. It's not more expensive, or barely more. I sell Dom Perignon in greater quantities in Lagos than Moët & Chandon sells in France and in the world altogether."

We still had two hours to kill before we landed in Lagos. I turned on one side and fell instantly asleep.

The tires skidding on the Tarmac suddenly woke me up. I'd been sleeping for two hours. It was dark outside with little light around the airport. And it was raining.

The heat slapped us as soon as we stepped out of the plane. A strange smell of rotten material, dead animal and sewer, hit me all at the same time.

"That's the regular smell of Nigeria," Jack Mallburn said when I complained about it. "Nowhere else in the world do you find this odor. Perhaps with the exception of Calcutta. Some say that it takes a while before you get used to. I've come here for the last five years every other month and I never got accustomed to it. It's an undefined odor of rottenness, putrid cadaver, human excrements, and God knows what more."

It was horrid. I tried not to breathe. But air, even putrid, is necessary for life. We walked through the immigration and customs' checks before we passed through the gate on our way out.

The airport was a wooden construction, rather a shabby dwelling, with a corrugated aluminum roof, not quite shielded from the rain. Luggage was piled up on a muddy floor where passengers had to retrieve them.

We found ourselves outside where a vast crowd seemed to loiter idle under a large sign: *No Loitering*. "You just follow me," Jack said, "and don't talk to anyone. They are going to try to get some money from you. Don't answer them. Don't even look at them."

We found a taxi driven by a woman. "That's rare," Jack said. "Usually they stay home and make kids, and their men come to work. Unless she's a widow."

But what surprised me was the way the driver started the engine. She had no key and the ignition was dangling down to the floor with part of the wiring. She connected two wires and the engine started revving up. I looked at Jack. He shrugged. Probably a stolen car, he whispered.

Then we left the airport through a narrow muddy road lined with decaying shacks lit up with candles. No street lights, no electric sources of illumination. It was a continuous black hole for several miles. "The slums of Lagos," Jack said. Occasionally, a bigger house seemed to enjoy electric power.

And all the way to the hotel, loud music out of radio-transistors. The same terrible music for everyone.

My first contact with Africa wasn't what I expected. Since my childhood I had always thought of Africa as the country of wild animals and desert. Just like the picture I chose to illustrate my article in *Perspectives*.

That was Africa, not what was unwinding in front of my sorry eyes. "You get use to it," Jack said as if he had read my mind.

Then we passed a bridge and the taxi followed a larger road lined with streetlights and houses that looked like houses.

The Ikoyi Hotel was a huge modern construction that overlooked the bay where thousands of illuminated cargo ships were at anchor.

We stepped into a large and quiet lobby when eleven o'clock chimed somewhere in the hotel.

The attendant at the counter seemed to be sleeping on his chair. Jack approached silently, got close to the man, and, all of a sudden, thumped his briefcase on the counter as hard as he could. The receptionist jumped three feet in the air as he woke up shaking.

"Ogah!" Jack said. "I hope my room is ready."

"Yes, Masta. As usual, the same one. Number 212."
"All right, my friend. Now, Here is Mr. Borny. He has a reservation made a week ago from France. What room does he have?"
The employee stared at me as if he couldn't figure out what to do with me. "I don't have no reservation, Masta. Nothing for today. Maybe tomorrow."
I was afraid to understand too well. I opened my briefcase and showed Ogah a copy of the telex we sent from Monte-Carlo. He didn't even know what that was. "No room, Masta." I thought he was going to cry. "No room," he repeated.
I felt an upcoming qualm crawl into my body. "How do you like that," I said starting to get nervous. Definitely my first experience with Africa wasn't a thrill. Lagos wasn't Disney Land.
"That's fine," my friend said. "I have a suite. Plenty of room." He turned to the employee. "Ogah, take our luggage to my room."
"No one for that, Masta. Too late. All go home."
"I guess we'll have to carry our own suitcases," Jack said discouraged. "Okay, let's go, I know where the room is."
We were walking towards the elevator when Ogah yelled, "No work, Masta. Elevator no good."
Jack shrugged as he took a sharp turn to the left towards the stairs. "What a country!" he said shaking his head. "But what a treasure for business. Seventy millions people, rich with more oil they can use, who needs the production of the whole world. They import all the damn goods they can't produce here. And their needs are huge. I sell wines, but I'm sure I could sell anything. Offer them a product. They will buy. At any price. Not long ago, on a previous trip, I met an Italian guy who sold shoe polish and candies."
"I don't see the connection between shoe polish and candies. But I'll try to remember that for the day I run out of work. I might come back and sell them solar cream."
"They'd probably buy that too."

The suite was large and comfortable but the smell knocked me out. It was an odor of rotten wood. All the walls were veneered with mahogany. An expansive wood even by Africa standards. The builders —they were Dutch— only forgot that the humidity and the constant heat in the country do not allow the use of material subject to putrefaction.

But at least I had a place to sleep. I thought about the receptionist. "Is his name really Ogah?" I asked.

"No," Jack said laughing. "I don't know his name, but they call each other Ogah, which means, I believe something like *Brother*. You can't go wrong if you call them Ogah."

"In Algeria that word could be replaced by *Cruyah* which also means Brother. I'm not sure I pronounce it right. But must be pretty close. And what about *Masta*?"

"Oh that is the Pidgin way to say Mister. Nigeria is the cradle of the Pidgin tongue. A vernacular language spread over this part of Africa. Sometimes it turns real funny."

The next morning we saw Lagos for the first time in daylight. That wasn't a very pretty picture either. I had an alarming feeling and an uneasiness that was growing by the minute. What in the world am I doing in this part of the world? I could feel a huge depression coming through me like a sudden illness. I wasn't in a very good shape and I was lucky to have met Jack Mallburn in the plane. I couldn't imagine what I would have done if I had been by myself confronting that stupid Ogah.

We had breakfast in the crowded restaurant of the hotel where Jack met with a lot of people he seemed to know, shaking hands, saying a word to about everyone.

A tall skinny black, impeccably dressed, came to our table. He saluted Jack almost affectionately, then said, "I want to talk to you, Jack."

"I bet you do, Moses," my friend replied with a smile and a wink in my direction.

"A friend?" I asked when Moses walked away.

"Yeah! Sort of. Moses N'Guneya, the hotel manager. He buys a lot of champagne and wine from me. I charge the hotel twice as much as is decent, and he gets a kickback on the difference."

"Is that legal?"

"Of course not. They shoot you for that. But they would have to shoot half the dignitaries of the country. Everyone goes by that rule. Starting at the high social stratum. If you want to do business here and make money.... give some away. You can't lose. Who pays the bill pays the kickback. You won't believe the amount of money given away in that kind of transaction. No one knows for sure, but it's probably in the billions of dollars."

"I'm lucky not to have anything to sell."

"I have to be in downtown Lagos this morning." Jack said after a pause. "I guess you have to be some place too."

"Yes. First I have to pick up my photographer at the airport. He's coming from Duala, Cameroon. Then, I have to find out where the Convention Center is. I know it's downtown."

"So, we'll meet at *Antoine* around one for lunch. Is that all right with you?"

"That's fine. I'll take care of my guy and go figure out when the show starts and how to get our professional cards."

At the door I grabbed a taxi which looked like a real taxi with a male driver at the wheel. Ignition key was in the right place. No dangling wires.

At ten o'clock I watched the Cameroon Airline flight land on the runway and come to a stop near the airport building. I watched the passengers get off the plane trying to recognize a short guy with the name of Georges Martial.

I caught his sight as he tried to explain to the customs agent why he had so many cameras in his luggage. I saw him fishing something from his pocket and extending his hand as in a friendly gesture. He then walked through the gate and joined me when I waved a hand.

"Welcome to Nigeria," I said with a wince. "I'm François Borny."

"Nice to meet you," he replied with a back glance towards the customs agent. "That's all they know. Money. But at least it's easy. Give them two dollars and you can bring in a truckload of cocaine."

"Let's go to the hotel. I hope you have a reservation."

"I do, but that doesn't mean anything."

"You tell me?"

The trip to the hotel looked less sinister than the night before. At least it was daytime and, if the music was still loud and sickening all the way to Ikoyi, the sight of those dwellings was less terrifying in broad daylight.

Georges had indeed a reservation. The employee at the counter wasn't the same as the previous night. This one looked more civilized and his English fluent. My new friend went up his room as I waited in the lobby.

Two minutes later he was down and we walked to the front door looking for a taxi.

The Convention Center was a large one-story-high-ceiling building surrounded by stately trees I didn't recognize. It was true that my knowledge in botany could be written on the back of a postage stamp. Anyway, I didn't come to Nigeria to study the flora which, I was sure, must be very interesting.

Inside, the center looked like a beehive. Hundreds of people were working around the huge room. There were cubicles arranged in such a manner that they left space in between for the traffic of visitors who would come to the center. Most of the countries of the world would be represented in this first International Tourist Convention.

I read on the booths already finished the dream names of countries like Singapore, Japan, Kenya, Morocco, Tahiti, Borneo, and even Monaco. Wow, I might meet with someone I knew from the Principality.

I looked for the management office, found it accidentally and met with a huge black man who just walked out of it. He had to be not less than seven feet and weigh probably more than three hundred pounds. But he was amenable, gracious and smiling and, definitely, proved to be a big help.

"I am François Borny from Monaco and this is Mr. Georges Martial from Cameroon," I said shaking his hand. "I know you must be terribly busy with the convention but I have only one question before we leave you alone."

"I am John Obiyan Director of the Tourist Office. Shoot your question, Sir," he said laughing and shaking my hand. For a minute I wasn't sure to recover the use of my fingers. But everything was there and all right after I massaged them vigorously my right hand.

"We just need to know how we can get our cards. I have here my invitation and my friend's I received in Monaco." I showed him the letter the Convention Center sent to us.

"Yes, I do remember someone from Monaco. Please to meet you, Mr. Borny and you Mr. Martial. We do not have many visitors from your country. Please, come in."

Once in the office, he opened a drawer, groped for a minute or two, then pulled two plastic cards with our names on. That was easy, I thought. "Here we go," he said. "The show will start hopefully the day after tomorrow at ten o'clock. Welcome to Nigeria, Gentlemen."

I thanked him and we walked out looking for a taxi. There were aplenty outside. "To *Antoine*," I said to the driver.

It wasn't yet noon but *Antoine* was already filled beyond capacity. I would have a hard time to find Jack in this throng.

It was a large room with just a few over a hundred tables set everywhere in no particular order or design, and already filled with food and drinks. Most of the tables had a bottle or two of Dom Perignon. Beer was drunk mostly at the crowded counter. A place, I believed, that would be impossible to get close to.

I didn't see Jack in the crammed corner but he saw me. He waved his hand until Georges noticed that giant making desperate signs. "Is that for you?" Georges said.

"It is indeed. This is my American friend. Thank God I met him."

We literally swam to the counter where finally we joined Jack. Georges presented himself and Jack introduced us to a gang of hilarious expatriated Brits a little inebriated. They made fun of my accent, but it was somehow sympathetic and even cute.

The food was great though I didn't know exactly what I had. Georges seemed to know and enjoyed it as the old African he was. I didn't ask. Just ate.

35

I hadn't seen Jack Mallburn since we last had lunch at *Antoine* where he introduced Georges and me to a young elegant Lebanese, Assan, who happened to be the owner of the restaurant. He was married to a very pretty English lady whom we also met. She used to work for the Foreign Office in Lagos. After the independence of Nigeria from the British ruler, she entered the private sector working for an Advertising company, OPS, short for Orbit Publicity Services. After her marriage with Assan, she quit her job to help her husband's business.

* * *

The show was a good one. About eighty countries managed to be represented for the week-long convention supposed to last until the following Thursday when a large banquet would be held with all the participants as well as the press representatives.

Each evening, after the show, Georges and I went back to the hotel where I had to clean up my notes of the day and began to write my report. Georges had found a local photographer whose lab was available, and inexpensive, any time he wanted to develop his negatives. That was very convenient for I could see every night prints of every shot he had done during the day.

As for Jack Mallburn, we didn't see him at the hotel. I had the key to the room, got in any time but had no idea of the whereabouts of my American friend. I would go to bed without seeing him and I would leave the room in the morning having spent the night by myself. I assume Jack had many friends and customers in Lagos and probably spent a lot of time with them, selling his wine.

On Saturday night, after the convention had closed at the center, I returned to the Ikoyi Palace without Georges who was developing some more negatives in downtown Lagos.

I found a note from Jack that said: I'm sorry to miss you. I'm still very busy taking orders for my champagne. I'm not sure Moët & Chandon can produce enough Dom Perignon to satisfy my clientele. Open the refrigerator. You'll find a bottle of that delicious champagne that must be just chilly enough for you and your photographer to drink. But wait for me on Monday. The hotel manager, you have met, has a very special party I'm sure you'd want to attend. I won't say more but be ready for a fantastic and unusual party. See you Monday and enjoy the champagne.

That was sort of mysterious. We shall see.

Georges came late that evening with a couple hundreds new pictures. Not only from the Convention Center, but also from around town. "Let's have dinner," he said. "I'm starved and you buy."

We went up to the last floor where an Italian restaurant served German and English specialties besides the usual pasta. But first we drank a glass of champagne in Jack's room.

We had a table near a large window overlooking the city and the harbor. Not much to see except for the thousands of ships anchored away from the shore and waiting their turn to get into the port. "Sometimes they wait as long as a month," the waiter said when I asked the question.

"Wow! And if it's perishable goods?" I said.

"Well, the insurances, I guess, take the tab. Or maybe not."

The food was correct if not great but the chat with Georges was interesting.

"I've lived in Duala for the past twenty-five years," he said, "when France ruled the country. At the time there were no air-conditioned systems. Only fans. During the rainy season, which last on average ten months a year, the heat is unbearable. So I'd drive my little Renault up north to Maroua where the rain forgets to show up eleven months a year. It's hot but dry. It's the country of elephants, giraffes, wart hogs, leopards, cheetahs, hyenas and snakes. But the nights are relatively cool, and that's is the best thing you can find in the north."

"I've seen your pictures and I remember one I used on the cover of *Perspectives* with a herd of elephants and some giraffes. I believe I would like to go there. That's the idea I have of Africa."

"If you happen to come to Cameroon, I will arrange a trip to Maroua. We can spend a long weekend outside the city, stay in a *boucarrou* —it's a hut with thatch roof built to support the heat— and wander around looking for wildlife. A few miles away we can cross over the Logone River and be in another country: Chad. Same landscape, same wildlife."

"That sounds great," I said already excited. "For now, let's finish our assignment and return home. But first I want to attend a party. I've been told it is a very special party."

"Africans are good at setting up very strange parties. We have some in Cameroon you might like to attend. For now I need to go to the bank. I made a transfer to the Nigerian National Bank downtown Lagos."

"We'll go in the morning. I need some cash too."

We returned to our respective rooms, poured myself another glass of champagne and sat down with my notes of the day. I believed that it would be an interesting paper to write. I didn't know yet how interesting and bizarre it was going to be.

* * *

First thing to do in the morning was to go to the bank. Jack had returned to his room late in the night. I didn't see him but I saw the empty bottle of champagne I had barely opened. He must be sleeping in his room. I didn't want to wake him up. I walked silently out and joined Georges in the lobby.

We grabbed a taxi to downtown. As we reached the City Square we noticed a small crowd on the sidewalk across the street from the bank. I paid the driver who looked at me with a sorry face. "Are you going to the bank?" he asked.

"Yes. What's wrong?"

"The bank is closed today, and perhaps tomorrow and the day after."

"Why? It's Friday."

"You see the man lying a few feet from the front door. He's dead."

"It's too bad for the poor guy, but what does he have to do with the opening of the bank?"

"No one gets close to him. You can see the policeman on the sidewalk with the crowd. He's waiting for someone to get close to the dead."

"Why?" You can't touch the corpse?"

"Oh yes, you can. But then the policeman would grab you and you would have to take care of the dead. Find his family and, if he has no family, make arrangement for his funeral and, of course, pay for it. There is a law in Nigeria; if you discover a cadaver you are responsible for him. That's why no one gets close to the poor guy. The bank's employees won't open the door. Some of them are across the street waiting for an idiot to show up and take care of the dead."[1]

"That could take a long time," I said with a glance at Georges.

"Right," the driver said. "You better go back to your hotel and come back tomorrow. You might be lucky."

---

[1] True

"How long he has been there," Georges asked in French and I translated.

"Probably several days. Look at the lizards on the body. The flies that are already on the corpse attract them. It takes about a day before the bugs come and another day for the lizards to join the feast. So, at least three days. And the smell doesn't get any better."

"I didn't notice any difference with the other part of the city," I said with conviction. "That's the same odor I've had in my nostrils for the last three days. Let's go, Georges, let's return to the hotel. I don't want to spent the rest of my time in Nigeria searching for the poor man's family."

I explained to Georges what I caught of the driver conversation. "Weird stuff," I said. "You want to live here, Georges?"

"I like Duala better."

* * *

We returned to the bank the next day and the following one. The only difference we had noticed was the increasing number of lizards on the cadaver. Nothing we could do and that was the bank that had our money. "We are running out of cash, Georges. The undertaker better come quick if we don't want to starve to death."

The rest of the day was even with what we had at the convention. I talked to the exhibitors, met with an adorable lady from Monaco I'd never met there, and shared my impression on Nigeria. She wasn't carried away either by what she'd seen so far. I asked the few foreigners I talked to if they were aware of that curious rule of cadaver discovery. One had heard about it. But Jack Mallburn knew. He didn't think I would encounter such a situation, so he didn't say anything to me about it. Why would he raise the subject? When I explained what was my problem concerning the cash, he just replied, "Not to worry.

Tomorrow you come with me to the bank. You'll have some money."

Jack Mallburn hadn't stop intriguing me since I met him in the plane. For the second time I wondered what I would have done without him. He was a great guy, open, sympathetic to other people's problems, and ready to do favors. I'm sure he must have a lot of friends. I liked being one of them.

Sunday evening the convention closed earlier, ready to reopen some time later in the week, but only one afternoon to nine PM. The banquet would be held at that time with what we all feared: a long list of guest-speakers, which I heard, was the usual finale for such a convention.

But I believe we had learned a lot about Africa, from north to south, east to west. Not only about Nigeria. We had met interesting people from Kenya, South-Africa, Morocco and Bali, and many other countries. I read brochures, a lot of them, asked questions, jotted down a few notes and asked Georges to shoot some pictures I would like to have in Monaco for that report I was going to write. I already had a good portion of it written down. I'd finish it in the plane on my way home. Junior Dunan would be ready to edit my prose. I'm sure. He loves to make changes to my writing. He's the boss, isn't he? But that's fine with me. Nobody is perfect."

We went back to the Bank the next morning with Georges and Jack. The dead man was still there, but no more onlookers. The cop had given up, had disappeared and the square was clear of people. No activity whatsoever, and the bank's door was still secured.

We trudged around the corner, passed a travel agency that was closed, a barbershop with a few people at the door having a conversation about the dead, and found a narrow iron gate which seemed to be locked. Jack passed an arm through the bars and knocked at the door. A man opened a crack, stared at Jack with a smile, then came out and unlocked the iron gate. "Good morning, Mr.

Mallburn," he said. "Please come on in. Mr. Abangy is in his office."

"Good morning Lawrence. How's the boss today?"

"We have had that unfortunate situation for three days now. But I'm sure this will be taken care of today."

Mr. Abangy stood when he got sight of Jack through the glass pane of his office and walked towards us. "Hello Jack," he said with a wide smile and an extended hand. "What can I do for you?"

"We need some cash and your bank seemed to be in quarantine."

"Yes. Very disturbing. How much cash do you need?"

Jack introduced Georges and me and asked how much I need. "Only to survive until Wednesday," I said. "We'll be on our way home then."

The putrid odor of the dead man drifted throughout the whole building. It was almost as bad as outside. I was ready to leave.

We thanked Mr. Abangy and left the bank through the same door we got in. I glanced at Georges who looked happy. "Now you can buy me a dinner," I said with a wink at Jack. Then, I thanked my American friend. "How do you manage to know everybody, Jack?"

"I like to make friends. It's easy if you know how and it's always convenient. You see?"

"Yes, I see. Lucky me I met you in that plane from Dakar."

Jack laughed. "My pleasure, my friend."

I have to get acquainted, I thought, if I want to travel to Africa. It seemed to be an absolute priority.

* * *

It started raining as soon as we got to the hotel. Ten o'clock in the morning and we got drenched hurrying from the taxi to the front door. That was some kind of rain. But Jack and Georges didn't seem to be stunned. We sat in the lobby and they ordered some beer.

"This is the weather we have in Duala," Georges said. "We have an average of four meters of rain a year. One of the most drenched places in the world."

"That would be one hundred and sixty inches, over thirteen feet," Jack said after he mentally made the count. "That's about the same here, in Nigeria. Not fun."

"Where are you from, Jack?" Georges asked curious.

"California, my friend. Anaheim, the country of the A's."

"And what would that be?" I said staring at the ceiling.

"What? You don't know the A's? The best baseball team in the world."

"Sorry, but no, I don't, though I heard about baseball once."

Jack had a croak of laughter close to choke. "You're kidding me, of course."

"Of course," I said laughing. "So, what is that party about? It's supposed to be held today, isn't it?"

"Yes, around noon, but the rain must stop."

"It's an outdoor party?"

"It is."

"We have to be back before six," I reminded him. "The convention has its last setting tonight. Then we have the banquet and even fireworks."

"I know. I'm also invited."

"Oh! What did you do to deserve such a fine treatment?"

"I furnished the champagne," he said with a wink and a laugh. "Unfortunately not Dom Perignon. They couldn't afford it they told me. But as I said, that won't prevent our distinguished visitors from getting drunk. They bought enough champagne to intoxicate half of Nigeria."

The rain had stopped around eleven o'clock when Moses N'Guneya, the hotel manager, approached our table. "I think we can make it, Jack."

"I think so too."

"Are you coming?" he said staring at me.

"Yes, why not?"

"Jack, did you tell your French friends what it's all about?"

"It's a surprise for them. I'm sure they will enjoy."

I grabbed Jack's arm and asked, "What should we bring?"

"Bring money. Ten *Nairas* will do."[1]

We rode, Jack, Georges and me in Moses' car that went in the direction of the airport. Thirty minutes later Moses took a right turn towards a wooden area on top of a hill.

When he stopped near a dozen of cars parked there, I looked around a little anxious. We were at the gate of a cemetery. I glanced at Jack who was smiling devilishly.

"What in the world are we doing in a cemetery," I muttered.

"I told you," Georges said. "Weird minds in Africa. Never be surprised about anything."

We got off the car and found ourselves in three inches of mud. A young girl, probably ten or twelve years old, walked to the guests, a tray in her hands. "That's when you fish your ten Nairas from your pocket, and lay them on the tray," Jack said.

We walked, still in the mud, toward a little mount under a tree. There was a hole in the ground. That's a funeral, I thought. Nothing very special.

I didn't understand why Moses invited us. Perhaps for the ten Nairas.

"Now, you look," Jack said. "You won't have many opportunities to witness such a show. For it's a show."

We approached the hole. A coffin was next to it. I stared with

---

[1] One Naira = one dollar

horror at the open casket. A dead man was there, but he must have been dead for a generation or two. He was mummified, with long frizzy hair, showing the front teeth out of his mouth, and lying on his back, his gnarled fingers intertwined on his chest.

Moses walked to the coffin holding the young girl's hand. They stopped for a few seconds, chin on their chest, as praying. It was a vague monotonous murmur among the invited people that gave me the creeps.

The prayer was over and everyone got closer to the tomb. Moses and the girl bent over, grabbed the mummy, and turned him on his right side. Then they closed the coffin and put it back in his hole. Two men approached holding shovels, and then began to fill up the cavity.

Suddenly there was laughter and loud talk among the guests as everyone joined Moses and congratulated him for a reason I couldn't figure out.

As we walked to the car, still with mud up to the ankles, Jack said, "That's a Yoruba tradition. They do that once a year."[1]

"Why do they move the dead?" I asked my hair still standing on end.

"The dead is supposed to get tired to be in the same position. So, once a year, at the anniversary of the death, they change his position."

"How long this horrible show is performed. I imagine the dead must have been dead for a century or so. He looks in good shape though. Skinny, but in good form." I almost laughed but I knew better.

"This annual ritual is carried out as long as there is a direct descendant in the family. The dead you have met—"

"No I haven't met him," I said with my spine trembling.

"Well, the dead you haven't met is Moses's father. He died many

---

[1] True

years ago. And every year, at the same time, he comes here and proceeds to the change. He is the only son of the defunct. So when Moses dies, there won't be any direct descendants left. Moses would be then taken care of by his daughter, the young girl you saw with him. She would perform for her father what he did for his."

"Very strange," I said, "but this is some experience I didn't think I would have on my first trip to Africa. In a way, I am fascinated."

36

I was relieved when the Pan Am flight 805 took off from Lagos International Airport and climbed rapidly through the thick layer of clouds. In a moment the sky would be blue, just like home. For almost two weeks I hadn't seen the smallest patch of blue in this shroud.

I left Georges at the airport, his plane leaving an hour later, with a big shake hand and a hug. We exchanged wishes, addresses and a couple of *au-revoirs*. Jack Mallburn insisted to accompany us for a last goodbye. He had some more business to take care of, but would be returning to the States a week or so later. I gave him Juliette's address in Atlanta in case he happens to be in Georgia. And, of course, I gave him my address at Saint-Laurent-du-Var and at work if he intended to travel to France. I knew he would for he was still in business with Moët & Chandon though the wine maker is several hundreds miles away from Monaco.

In a few hours I'll be hugging Aline, Susanne and Mom at Nice Airport. Junior Dunan might be there too, but I won't hug him, no matter what.

I had plenty of time to check my writing, look again at all those wonderful pictures Georges had shot for me, and think over about what I did during those two very interesting weeks in spite of my feelings about Nigeria.

I didn't like the country or at least what I had seen. Actually it wasn't much since I never left Lagos. But I enjoyed the experience, the weird things I happened to witness, and, moreover, the kindness of the people I've met. Moses N'Guneya was a charming host at the Ikoyi Hotel in spite of his periodical habit to joggle his dead father in his tomb. John Obiyan was, and still is, a very competent Director of Tourism, and Georges Martial was the best photographer I've ever met who became a very good friend.

As for Jack Mallburn, he was undeniably an exceptional human being and a very uncommon character. I could never thank him enough for what he had done for me without, I know, any ulterior motives. He was disinterested and sympathetic, and his help had always been free. I've kept for years a very special memory about him. Sometime later I had the opportunity to meet him again. Once in Monaco, where he came for a quick visit, and once in Los Angeles where I happened to be.

I knew that on my next trips to Africa I was going to miss that devil man who had entry everywhere. God bless you, Jack Mallburn, wherever you are.

* * *

It was a gorgeous day in Nice when the Pan Am flight landed in the middle of the afternoon. We had stopped again at Dakar airport on our way home. But this time there wasn't any American who embarked and took the seat next to me.

Susanne was the first to run when she saw me at the gate. Behind came Aline and Mom. Henri Dunan was there too, but he didn't move until I got sight of him. He approached with his usual smile and his special slow gait, hand extended. He let me embrace my wife and kiss Mom, then said, "How was your first trip to Africa?"

"I like Spain better," I said with laughter. "Interesting," I continued more seriously. "It's been the experience of my life. I've finished my report if you want to see it."

"We can wait. *Perspectives*' next issue is due next month. Take the weekend off with your family. I'll see you Monday. Pleased to have you back, François."

He turned around after he saluted Aline and Mom, then walked away. "Good man," I said. "It was nice of him to come today. He didn't have to do that, but I appreciate the thought."

The airport was only six miles away from home. Ten minutes later we parked the Renault in the garage. Mr. Langevin was watching from the third floor as I managed to block everybody else's car. He climbed down the stairs holding a bottle of Dom Perignon and four glasses.

"Hope you deserve the welcome," he said smiling. "I saved it for your return."

Next thing I knew Aline was unpacking my dirty laundry as I slumped into my favorite armchair in front of the TV. That was the last thing I remembered for I fell asleep within seconds.

We spent the weekend together going to the beach on Saturday in Saint-Laurent and having a barbecue on Sunday offered by our landowner.

I accompanied Mom to rue Mirabeau on Sunday evening and returned home to prepare to resume my regular work.

* * *

With the Dunans we had devoted the whole Monday morning looking at the pictures I brought back from Lagos and talking about my final report. "That's interesting," Paul Dunan said a little confused. "Interesting and bizarre that story of the cadaver on the street."

"Strange, yes, and inadequate. That law about discovery of the dead is marked by incongruity. For me it was unbelievable. To see that poor guy lying in the street is beyond all comprehension."

"Well," Junior said, "We'll go with that and also with the story of joggling around the dead year after year. That's a good report, monsieur Borny."

I was surprised. Henri never called me monsieur and I never called him anything else but Henri since those days back at Laubry Printing.

Perspectives was still in business with the printing company two blocs away from Saint-Laurent. Every morning, on my way to work, I would stop at the plant where we always had something in progress. From being Mr. Laubry's employee I became a customer who was treated differently, of course. I enjoyed it.

In my years as a student and a photoengraver, I used to come to the shop wearing a coverall and a hat to protect my hair from the bitumen and the resin. That had changed since I worked for the Dunans. I always wore a three-piece suit, a white shirt and a necktie. For a more serious appearance I had a briefcase where I usually carried my lunch. But no one but the Minotaur knew that.

Everybody showed me respect in spite of their familiar friendship, and the new employees, who didn't know me when I worked there, called me Mr. Borny. That was fun, but I believed I deserved it because of my hard work for the years I belonged to the *Perspectives* staff.

I would get in my office around nine or nine-thirty in the morning while the other employees were at work at eight. Of course, I was the last one to leave most of the time, sometimes well past nine P.M. But still, the elder Dunan seemed to be desperate to see me in the morning. Martine had told me on numerous occasions that the Chairman of the Board came to my office and seemed frustrated not to see me there.

I could have been at work at eight like everyone, but I would miss the early visit to the printing shop where, almost every day, I had to give the imprimatur for some of our works being printed there.

This Monday morning, my first day following my return from Africa, both Dunans were waiting for me. Martine, from her desk, waved to me with a smile. "Welcome back," she mouthed silently.

"Here you are finally," the elder said.

"Sorry. Should I start earlier? You seem to be in a critical emergency."

Both Dunans laughed. "No," the father said, "but sometimes we

need you early in the morning."
"You make me feel like I'm indispensable." That's flattering."
"Come, François, let's talk seriously." We all three walked into Dunan Senior's office as Martine got up from her desk and asked if we'd like some coffee. "Sure, that's a good idea," Senior replied.
There was a brief silence while Martine poured some coffee into three mugs. I wondered what this was all about. That must be serious for the Minotaur wouldn't have called a meeting in his office. "Please, shut the door on your way out, Martine."
We sipped our coffee for a minute or so, then the Minotaur got on his feet, his bullish eyes staring at the carpet. "You might not know," he said with his gentle voice, "but I'll be retired before the end of the year. That's pretty soon, isn't it?"
I nodded without a word. That was less than three months. Was he ill or just tired of running a large company like *Perspectives Publishing*?
"I thought about it for a while now. Henri and I had talked about this while you were in Africa. I believe Henri and you can run this company with the help of the Parisian personnel who would be delighted to see the whole company transferred to the capital. That won't happen while I'm of this world. After me, it will be another story. But I'm not ready to die, my friend. I intend to live many years in Monaco and take some trips with my wife. That's what I always wanted to do."
Old Dunan, I believed, was holding back a tear. His voice had imperceptibly broken somehow. "Now," he said, "we need you here, in your office. We'll find someone who would do your job at the printing shop in Nice. He would be given your office, Henri would take mine and you'll have Henri's. Does that sound good?"
I smiled delighted though I knew I was going to miss the old man. But he lived across the street and I was sure we'd be seeing him. "What about our beer in the afternoon at Caesar's?" I asked.

"I didn't forget that. I'll work my best to maintain our relationship on the same basis," the Minotaur said laughing. "I'd give up my job, not my beer."

Henri got up as Papa sat down. "Well, he said rubbing both his hands together, "You are going to move to Monte-Carlo. Saint-Laurent is a nice little city but too far from our office."

"I'm sure you know the cost of a rent in Monaco," I said a little frightened at the thought of moving here.

"We're aware of that inconveniency," the Minotaur said. "We have a solution. We'll pay for it and we'll increase your salary. And as long as you work for the company, you can live in the apartment."

"We have found one on Boulevard d'Italie, Henri said. "It's a large apartment on the top floor of a small three-story building, with a nice front and backyard and an uninterrupted view on the ocean. The beach is just a flight of stairs down from the house. You'll like it."

I did like it and so did Aline. We moved at the end of the month with the blessing of Mr. Langevin, our landlord at Saint-Laurent who, once more, watched me driving away from his house.

It was Susanne's eighth birthday and Aline was pregnant with our second child.

37

I have a more pleasant memory of my second trip in Africa. *Perspectives* had been asked to produce an article about a French company in Fort-Lamy, Chad. It was common knowledge that large companies, operating in the Third World, paid *Perspectives* for an article accompanied with pictures. It was a good deal for us, and a good advertisement for the company.

The name was *COTONFRAN* —short for Cotonnière Française— It was a multibillion giant that grew cotton all over Chad and some other places else in the world. The country was the fifth global producer of cotton.

I found myself on a *UTA* flight from Nice to Fort-Lamy, the capital.

I had sent a telex to my friend the photographer Georges Martial in Duala to join me at the *Hotel du Chari* where I made a two-room reservation.

It was a surprise to me when I caught sight of Georges at the airport. He was already there waiting for me. The flight from Duala was only two hours long and had arrived in the morning before *UTA*.

The weather was extraordinary. The sky was of a deep blue, the air dry and the temperature around eighty degrees. Ideal weather for a stay in Chad. The rainy season, that lasts about a month with its usual flooding and heat, had been over for a few weeks and the gorgeous season was back to last almost a year.

Georges was ready, two of his cameras around his neck and his desert hat on his head. "Glad to see you again, Georges. How's your life since Lagos?"

"Better since I left Nigeria. Hope we won't have to go back there soon."

"Not a chance, my friend. But I think I'm going to like it here."

"This is a different world, François. Dry like a chickpea, desert everywhere around, but still not very hot and not humid, except for the rainy season which is over now.

"That's my Africa," I said jubilant.

"I have a taxi waiting for us at the door. We have indeed a reservation for two rooms at the Hotel du Chari. No problems here. The manager is a Jewish guy who seems to be competent. His wife works with him and the hotel is better maintained than I ever saw it before. I believe the man is from Nice, but he's been around Africa for a while. He comes from Libreville, Gabon, where he managed a small hotel."

"At least we won't have any surprises at the hotel."

I didn't know at that time how wrong I was.

I picked up my piece of luggage and followed Georges to the taxi. The city was bathed with sun. There was just enough breeze to keep the air cool and the top of the palm trees swaying gently.

"The hotel is only three minutes from the airport," Georges said, "but nothing is far away here. COTONFRAN is just down the river, about two blocks."

"We'll go there in the morning. For now I want to rest a little, then a good dinner and meet with Roland Poireau, our correspondant in Fort-Lamy."

The lobby at the Chari was large and well ventilated which was a change from Ikoyi in Lagos. No smell of rottenness, no putrid wood and no cadaver next to the front door.

On the wall, above the counter was a huge print of a black and white picture representing a horse playing with a dog. It was vivid as if the animals were there. I read the signature. It was one of Georges

Martial's pieces of art.

A young lady came to the counter smiling. "Good morning, Mr. Martial," she said addressing Georges. "And this is Mr. Borny, right?"

"Right," I said. "Nice to be recognized as a customer."

"I am Elisa. We received your telex a few days ago, and we were expecting you this afternoon. Mr. Martial already has his room. The rooms are adjacent. 201 and 202."

The building combined three aisles open to the river and set around the swimming pool, next to a terrace with the bar at the end of it. The restaurant was busy in spite of the late hour of the afternoon. The crew of the *UTA* flight was already in the hotel and most of them were in the swimming pool.

The rooms were on the second floor with a large balcony overlooking the pool. Beyond, the Chari River rolled its water down to Lake Chad. A few fishing boats were moored on the opposite bank, next to a small agglomeration of thatch-roofed huts. Kids were in the water as women occupied themselves around the houses.

It was a nice and peaceful sight. Those kids playing in the river, the fathers working on their fishing pots, and women doing what all the women in the world do: work.

An agreeable smell of grilled meat drifted to my room. Georges looked at me as he smelled the same odor. "What do you think?"

"Why don't we have dinner now. It's still daylight but I'm starving," I said. "Let's go down to the restaurant, have a drink or two, and by then it will be time for a nice dinner."

We walked down, crossed the lobby and stopped at the counter. The young lady was gone and replaced by the manager. I dropped my key on the counter as the man raised his head and stared at me in silence.

"François?" he asked with a broken voice.

I looked at him. He was a young man about my age I guessed. I never saw him before. But there was in his eyes something I recognized without being sure. "Yes," I said scrutinizing that face that wasn't totally unknown to me. I knew I'd seen those eyes somewhere in the long gone past, but I couldn't put a name or a place.

"François Borny," he said. "I've been waiting for you since I received your telex."

Oh! I thought, that was all. He knew my name from the telex and waited for my arrival. That was a good managing job. But still, an idea was crawling into my mind.

"I wasn't sure," he continued, "it would be you. Obviously you don't remember me. I remember you, François Borny. Rue Mirabeau in Nice, the war, the Germans, the Gestapo and the SS's."

And then it came to me like an explosion in my head. "Sylvain, Sylvain Bénichou," I yelled. "Yes, I recognize you. That was twenty years ago, my God, but I've never forgotten my childhood friend."

He jumped over the counter before I could move around. We hugged each other for a time that seemed endless, until the young lady came out from the office. I went suddenly into a quiver and I could feel Sylvain shaking in unison. "I wasn't sure it was you when I read the telex. François Borny revived suddenly some old memories I never could erase totally from my mind."

He was crying, and I was crying in front of Elisa and Georges who wondered what was going on. He knew something out of the common had happened. "This is my wife, Elisa," Sylvain said turning to the young lady.

"I knew who you were when I saw both of you embracing," she said a little pale. "Since we had received the telex from Monaco we have talked about you. I know a lot about your childhood, the life you two have shared before and during the war. The ordeal you both had experienced."

"It was nothing in comparison of what Sylvain and his parents had known. I remember the night—"

"It was Christmas Day 1943," Sylvain cut in, "and I can't forget the terrible night when the Gestapo came to arrest us."

"What happened to your parents?"

Sylvain remained silent for a few minutes, tears rolling down his cheek. His wife took his hand and brought it to her heart. "Come to our apartment," she said. "We'll talk better."

I turned around to Georges. "This is my friend Georges Martial. He works for my company as a photographer."

"Would you like to come too?" Sylvain asked.

"Thank you, but I rather let you recover from the surprise. I'd bet you have a lot to talk about."

"As you wish," Sylvain said, "but tonight you are my guests. We'll have dinner on the terrace around eight."

"See you then. Pleased to meet you," he said smiling to Sylvain and Elisa. He turned around and shuffled away.

* * *

It was an unforgettable evening. My blood was still boiling inside me. I could believe Sylvain was still among the living, I repeated to myself. I had thought of him thousands of times but never imagined that he was alive and well somewhere in the world. Why did he disappear from Nice never to return?

He was alive, yes, but the story of his life was a sad one. We sat in his apartment drawing room facing the window that overlooked the restaurant and the river. He had suddenly slumped into a leather armchair, both hands holding his forehead, eyes closed.

"That was a terrible night," he said, "a night followed by days and days of fright, hunger, unawareness of where we were going, of how long this ordeal would last, and what would happen to us.

"We were gathered, I believe, in the prison in Nice, but I'm not sure, as daylight broke in the cold of this Christmas Day. We were two or three hundred people there, freezing to death. I talked to a few.

They were all Jews. At that moment I didn't know where my parents were. We had been separated when we went down our building, rue Mirabeau. Two military trucks were waiting. We were loaded like cattle and it was then that I lost sight of Mom and Dad.

"I was thirteen years old, François, and, all of a sudden, I was an orphan. Some time in the morning, I don't know what time it was, we were thrown onto more trucks and moved to the train station that was surrounded by a cordon of SS's in arms. Inside the station were several hundreds of people, all Jews I learned later, ready to be thrown onto a cattle train."

There was a pause. Sylvain had closed his eyes again, chin on his chest and tears running down his tanned face.

Elisa and I waited in silence. I was sure that Sylvain's wife knew about the ordeal. Her eyes were wet and, from time to time, her shoulders were shaken with sobs.

"What a disgrace to be a Jew at that time," Sylvain pursued. "Rats, when caught in a trap, were treated better. We were forced into cars at a point where we couldn't move inside. We could only stand. No room for sitting and much less for lying down.

"The doors were locked and, after a moment, the train began to roll out of the station."

"My poor Sylvain," I said. "I remember the night. Dad had showed up in the wee hours of the morning defying the SS's patrols, but he had already left when we heard in the staircase the recognizable quick steps of the Gestapo. For a moment I thought they were looking for Dad and I was glad he had departed. I was wrong. The Germans were gathering that same night all the Jews of the city who hadn't fled in time. In my college years I met a professor, Dr. Schwartz. He was arrested that same night and sent to Mathausen. He made it back and I had the honor to be one of his students."

"Mathausen. That's where some of us ended up," Sylvain said. "We were directed to Dachau. What a nightmare it was. The trip lasted three days. People died in the car. Mostly old people. I believe there were eight or ten who didn't finish the voyage. We piled them up in a corner of the car which gave some of us a little room to sit down. We switched position by standing and lying in turns.

"The door never opened until we reached our final destination. We had been confined in the same car for three days amid a horrible smell of cadaver, excrement and urine. No food, of course, no water for the length of the trip. So we were almost happy when we reached the end of the journey.

"I never saw my parents again. I never knew if they were sent to Mathausen or with me to Dachau or if they died in the train. In my years in Dachau I never met anyone who knew them."

"It lasted a very long time," I said. "When did the misery end?"

"I was fifteen at the end of the war. I never knew how I survived. I didn't do anything for that. Just let things go and other people take care of themselves and forgot about myself. I survived because I believed it was a god, the God of Abraham that had an eye on me. It couldn't have been otherwise."

I got on my feet, walked to the window and looked outside. Those memories, I thought, have been a terrible experience for Sylvain to renew. "This was twenty years ago, Sylvain," I said. "You must erase that from your mind, though I know it must be next to impossible."

"It's impossible and no one wants to forget. But talking about it makes me feel better. With Elisa we talk once in a while. And when I saw your name on that telex, I knew all those memories, good and bad, were coming to me in a rush."

He got up and came close to me putting his hand on my shoulder. "I'm so glad, François, you were the one on that telex. I would have been terribly disappointed if it hadn't been you. Now, you have to tell me the story of *your* life."

"Nothing in comparison with yours. After the Germans had cleared Nice and the Americans replaced them rather beneficially, everything was easy. I went to school, then to college. I traveled a few times to Spain to learn the language. I got married, had a kid and I'm waiting for a second one. Do you have kids, Sylvain?"

"Not yet. Elisa and I have met in Libreville, Gabon, a year ago. We got married when I was offered this job in Chad six months ago. I like this country, I like the way we work here, and the money is good. Now, we have to work out how to have kids."

"I can explain to you how we do that."

Elisa and Sylvain laughed as we stared through the window at the restaurant.

Georges was sitting there, his hat rammed into his head, a drink in his hand and one of his cameras on the table. I had learned when we first met in Nigeria that he never parted with all his cameras at the same time. He always kept at least one at arm's length ready to be used. I saw some of his unusual snapshots and knew he had a lot of talent and a very fast reflex. I remembered a funny portrait of a French President. Georges got a shot, of course without the president's knowledge, catching him the index finger stuck deep in his right nostril. It was a rare picture, and Georges had to be there and have the extra-quick reflex to take advantage of the situation. He never sold the picture and I'm sure he could have made a lot of money with it.

"You didn't tell me who save your butt in Dachau," I said.

"Russians. They reached Dachau just before the Americans did. So we were sent to a so call liberation camp behind the Soviet line. It wasn't much better than the concentration camp, but at least the gates were open and we could leave whenever we decided to. That's what I did when finally the Americans stepped into the muddy camp and told us that we were really free. Which we weren't quite sure so far.

"A Swiss commission invited some of us, mostly young people, to go to Switzerland where we were treated as royalties. I'm happy I went there. That reconciled me with the human gender. I was fifteen years old, weighed less than a hundred pounds, but ready to start a new life in a country that hadn't known the horror of war. I went to school in Zurich where I studied . . . German. What a derision. I'd spent two years in Dachau and I couldn't learn a damn word spat out by those rogues we had as guards. And there I was, in Zurich, a German-speaking city, studying a language I abhorred.

I finally graduated from the Swiss high school and, as I spoke French, they sent me to a boarding school where I learned how to run a hotel. That's why you see me here. I made a career of it and love it. I work with my wife and we have a good life in Africa. I have my boat to go fishing on the Chari, sometimes to race other boat owners, I have my car to wander around when the hotel is not too busy, and new friends I would like to introduce to you.

"This weekend, we'll have a big party, here, in my hotel. Most of my friends have their own boats. We'll probably go catch some big *Capitaines*."

"Is that a fish?"

"Yes, my friend. Some are huge. Elisa is very good at fishing them. I'll show you later one she caught last Sunday without any help besides getting the monster on board. It's in our cold room. It's over ten feet long. I don't believe I've seen fish that big before. In Gabon we used to go for tarpons. Great fish too. But *Capitaines* are very special. And, besides, very good to eat."

"I'll be here Sunday. Do you mind if we invite Georges."

"No, of course not. We'll be about fifty people. That's the average in Fort-Lamy. I had arranged all this in my head even before you came. I took the risk of dreaming about it."

It was nice to sit outside on the terrace, staring at the slow flow of the river, under a bright moon and a cool breeze, and sipping a Dom Perignon 1958 that Sylvain had saved for an extraordinary occasion. And that was an extraordinary opportunity. "To our childhood," Sylvain said raising his glass. "To twenty years of wasted times."

I raised my glass. "No, it wasn't wasted," I said, "For you have been all the time in my mind. I just wasn't sure if you were alive."

Sylvain shrugged, smiled and said, "To those twenty years."

The supper was excellent though we didn't have fried termites. Sylvain laughed when I told him about the bugs. "I've heard of that delicate dish," he said. "Never tried and never will. I like better a slice of grilled *Capitaine* and a spit-roasted gazelle leg like the one we had tonight, the whole thing pushed down with a Château Lafitte 1949."

"You are a connoisseur."

"I had to study all those French wines in Zurich, and I'm glad I did. Makes me appreciate what I eat and what I drink."

"I'm open if you want to teach me."

Georges took some pictures, of course, smoked a large cigar that bothered everyone for thirty minutes, and offered, in compensation, to buy the liquors. After champagne that wasn't the ideal choice, but Sylvain agreed and called the waiter, a tall lanky black man who seemed to walk bent in three parts, like a zigzag. His name was François, which made me smile. "That's an unusual name for an African, isn't it?"

"Not in Chad," Elisa said laughing. "Their president is François Tombalbaye. Most of the young people nowadays are called François, even if their birth certificate says differently."

That was a very pleasant evening. Elisa was a charming host, cultivated, witty and very much in love with her husband. Sylvain looked happy with his life. That was a change from twenty years ago.

"What are your plans for tomorrow?" He asked.

"I have to work. That's the object of my coming here. I have a report to write about COTONFRAN and its production. We will probably have to go up north to shoot some pictures of cotton fields and people at work."

"I'll join you. We're not too busy and Elisa is a competent person to run the Chari." She looked at him, and then smiled. "Sure," she said. "Enjoy your friend's company."
"I know the country south, north, east and west of Fort-Lamy. Interesting area. We might come across elephants. There are plenty of them a few miles away. They are usually peaceful, but sometimes dangerous without any reason. Everybody heard about that guy who got killed last week in his 2-hp Citroën. You know, the kind of car that seems to be made of corrugated board. He came across a herd of elephants traveling on the road a few miles away from here. He stopped his car about fifty yards from the herd. We could tell the distance by the tract —mainly dung— the animals left on the road and the position of the car with the dead guy in it.

"For a reason no one could figure out, an elephant, probably the oldest male, approached the Citroën and smashed it into pieces. The man was barely recognizable. This is a very exceptional incident, but we have to be cautious on those trails.

"I'll drive you around tomorrow. What's your first objective?"

"First, pay a visit to our representative, Roland Poireau."

"Oh, I know him. It's a crazy guy who bought an old motorboat, threw away the motor and mounted in its place a 280 hp Chevrolet engine on it. Of course, he wins all the races with his boat flying at some eighty miles an hour. But one day he will be killed in this racing coffin. He's one of the regulars at all the Fort-Lamy parties. Loves champagne and Scotch as well. And beer and wine. His wife who must be no more than four foot six tall, is a ballet teacher, sells advertisement for the local newspaper, and takes care of her deranged husband. They'll be here Saturday night, you can count on it."

"I've never met him but we have talked on the phone and we wrote each other a few times. Once in a while we publish one of his articles in *Perspectives*. His writing is correct and often interesting."

"We always have something fascinating to talk about in Africa, no matter where we are," Sylvain said.

Georges Martial agreed, his contribution being the photographic part which was often more explicit than a thousand words.

"Let's go see Roland Poireau first and then COTONFRAN. The big man there is Jean Rigaux. Never met him either but we have talked on the phone a few times. He'll tell us where to go and what to shoot for the illustration of the article.

It was past midnight when Georges and I returned to our respective rooms. It had been a long day but so full of surprises and so emotional I was in a euphoric state. I couldn't find sleep before two or three in the morning.

It was about six the next morning when Georges knocked at my door. I was out of the shower a minute before still with a towel around the waist. I opened the door and there was Georges holding two cups of coffee. That was nice. "Sylvain is ready whenever you are," Georges said. "He's almost desperate. His car is already revving. You can hear it from here."

I got dressed while sipping the coffee as Georges checked his bag and his half dozen cameras. I always wondered why photographers need so many of them. He also had a leather box full of lenses. 35, 50, 85, 100, 120, 300 mm, a wide angle and a zoom that must be no shorter than 600 mm. He must carry about a hundred pounds of equipment on a normal working day that included about a hundred rolls of film, all sizes and speed, three tripods for simultaneous utilizations and a bag of filters for all kinds of weather and light. Plus a few flashes that could be mounted on his cameras. But the results of his work could fill any artistic gallery and attract a large crowd.

We went down to the restaurant where Sylvain and Elisa were waiting for us. Breakfast was smoking on the table with the waiter François smiling, still folded in three parts.

"Good morning," I yelled before I got to the terrace. "I'm starving."

Sylvain laughed. "We're waiting. The roast of gazelle is still good with mayonnaise. Even cold. The coffee is homemade by Elisa and the eggs are François's work of art."

That table looked good and mouthwatering, I thought. And it was indeed great.

After a lavish breakfast we left the Hotel du Chari around 7:30 in Sylvain's Land Rover. "It's a good car for Africa," Sylvain said, "even in a sandstorm. "Few cars are good in that weather. This one is the best. Sandstorms can last several days. No one drives at that time or tries not to. You don't even want to go out which doesn't prevent you from having sand all over you, in your mouth, your hair, your nose, your ears, and in your food."

"That happens often?" I asked.

"We had one storm two months ago that lasted the whole week. Friends said it was the first since 1960. A long time."

We arrived at Poireau's home ten minutes later. He expected me after the phone call I gave him from the hotel, drinking some coffee on his front yard and smoking a small black cigar I could smell even before I got out of the car. He got up and walked to meet with us. Roland Poireau is a short guy, bald though still in his thirties, and walked with a gait that let me believe he had a problem with his right leg he dragged badly.

I approached extending my hand and said, "Please to meet you Mr. Poireau."

"Call me Roland," he said with an engaging smile. "Like some coffee?"

"Sure. What's wrong with your leg?" I asked.

"Oh, a stupid accident," he said with a shrug. "Still hurts."

I turned around and introduced Georges Martial. "You know Sylvain Bénichou," I said. Of course he knew him. The French community had, for a long time, created a colonial group that almost never parted. There was not much to do in those colonial times but get together as often as possible and live the life of the expatriated. Everyone knew everybody.

"I've heard about your boat," I said as we sat down. "How do you like the life in Chad?"

"There are good things . . . and bad things," he added after a short reflection.

"What for instance?"

"The life is easy. We have a house that goes with the job. In my case it's *Perspectives Publishing* that pays for it. I have another job, a part time one, working for Cameroon Publicity in Duala that pays for the extras. The domesticity is cheap, so my wife doesn't have to cook or to do anything in the house. We have a gardener, a cook, and a laundry boy who serves as a driver or a gun bearer if I go hunting. My wife has her ballet school which keeps her out of trouble. Once in a while, at least once a week, we gather together at someone's home, get drunk and sometimes decide to go on the river with our boats at two in the morning. We race, break our boats, fall into the water and someone has to pick us up before we drown. Then we returned to the party forgetting our watercrafts on the river. We'd find them a few days later and miles away near Lake Chad. They would be stranded in a sandbank but lacking anything valuable that could be taken away. No more radio, binocular, fishing rods, oars, antenna, anything that can be dismounted. And the next day we start over the life of the desperados. That's the life of the colonials."

"Well," I said, "that sounds crazy, but I guess it's the kind of life you have chosen."

He chuckled then pulled a drag on the cigar and started coughing. "That damn cigar's going to kill me," he said with a wince. "That's one of the bad things. Drinking too. We all drink way too much in the colonies."

"Chad is no longer a colony," I interrupted.
"You really believe that?" he said with another fit of coughing.
"We are still the bosses here. People need us. We supply them with a home —my staff lives in a house in the back with wife and children— with a secured job and with food they wouldn't have if we, French, weren't be here. They have their national independence to play with. They have their own National Assembly, their deputies, and their senators who gather once a year to change all the laws. But no one would dare to change the rules as far as we are concerned."
"In a word you're happy with your life."
"Pretty much, yes."
"And what are the bad things?"
"Oh, there are a few. Malaria for one. We all have the virus more or less. We have to keep taking those damn pills, Quinine, every day, we have to get some shots once a year for yellow fever, cholera, smallpox, typhoid, typhus, and I don't know what more. And we better not forget to do that. Africa is a dangerous place to live. Then, there is that damn whisky we all make a large consumption of as well as wine, liquors, beer. We eat too much and not very healthily and our liver must look like a sponge. You never live too old in this continent."
"But you like that, don't you?" Sylvain spoke for the first time. "We all like that life. If we had to go back to France, we'd be miserable."
"You're right. Dangerous life but so exciting" Roland replied. "I wouldn't return to France unless some crazy guy kicks us out."
"It might happen sooner that we think," Sylvain said. "Look up north. Moammar Gaddafi is eyeing Chad, a country he'd like very much to add to his territory."
Mrs. Poireau walked out of the house with a tray and a coffee pot. Roland introduced us and she sat next to her husband. She was a petite woman, not particularly pretty, with small round blue eyes and blond

hair cut short. She smiled non-stop that bothered me for that smile looked like a commercial one. Not really sincere. She spoke with a grating voice but didn't say much. I decided not to like her. After several trips to Chad I kept my first impression on that little lady. Yes, I know. I'm a terrible guy to judge so quickly, but it happened that my first feeling was right, though I won't say why.

Mr. Rigaux, the big man at COTONFRAN greeted us in his vast office of the third floor overlooking palm trees and the river. He was a huge man with gray hair and very thick spectacles sitting on a rather large nose. He got up when we stepped in, shook our hands and offered us some coffee. I introduced Georges who was the only stranger besides me. Mr. Rigaux knew, of course, Sylvain and Roland, being part of the French community.

"All we want to know," I said, "is what do you need in your article. What pictures do you want us to shoot and where?"

"I gathered some information about our company," he said pointing at a stack of printed material on his desk. Here you have enough to write a novel on our company."

"Ten to twelve pages would do," I said with a chuckle.

"Here is a map of our headquarters up north. I'm sure Sylvain and Roland know the country. Ask for Paul Bonnin. He's the manager there. They call him Chief Paul. I talked to him this morning on the short-wave radio to announce your arrival. He's waiting for you. Be careful up north. Elephants have been terrible lately."

We left Mr. Rigaux after he had explained to me what he needed in the article. When we shook hands, he promised us to be at the party at Sylvain's.

* * *

Lake Chad loomed suddenly in front of us under the midday sun.

A few curious flat-bottom boats sailed across the lake under the light breeze. Their owners stood as they held a long stick with which they pushed their small crafts.

"Those boats are made out of papyrus," Roland said. "They call them *Kadei*. You can see those boats everywhere. As there are no forests around the lake, so no lumber, the stalk of papyrus has been used for centuries. People move from one bank to the other, pushing their boats for miles. Then they stop somewhere on a sandy beach, build a few huts with mud and papyrus thatch and live in those villages as long as they are not destroyed by tornadoes during the rainy season. They spend their days fishing which is their main occupation.

You can find that kind of village all around the lake. Some are abandoned after their destruction by the tornadoes or simply deserted because of a bad omen."

"Like what?" I asked curious.

"Oh, they have plenty of those. Like seeing a hyena in the morning around the hut, or a *varan* too close to the kids."

"A what?"

"A varan. It's a monitor lizard of the varanidae family. A rather big flesh eating ugly lizard that can grow up to a formidable ten feet." So, they abandon the village and even the poultry. They just take the goats, the sheep, the wives and the kids and push their boats twenty or thirty miles away and build another hut."

"How do they make a living?"

"They don't. Their only production is the *tilapia*, a fish they catch in the lake. An excellent food fish. Also a little gardening and a little poaching. They raise a goat or two for the milk and a sheep or two for their worship at the time of the *Aid-el-Kebir*."

"Aid-el-Kebir?"

Sylvain was watching me with a smile. He had known all those funny customs for a long time, since the day he came from

Switzerland with a degree in hotel management. "You have always lived in a civilized country," he said. "You are not aware of the weird things the world has produced since its creation."

"I don't believe, I'm from a such civilized part of the world," I said. "I remember the Krauts. That wasn't civilized as far as I knew."

"No, you're right. That wasn't a time of civilization." His smile had faded away from his face."

"All right," Roland Poireau said feeling that the conversation had taken a bad turn. "Aid-el-Kebir is one of the Moslem rites, one of the holidays that comes up once a year. Muslims are supposed to sacrifice a lamb to the glory of Mohamed. Or perhaps it's to the glory of Allah. Who knows? Hence a little flock of sheep that follow the family wherever they go."

"Are they really Muslims?"

"Forty-five percent of the population around Lake Chad and in the north are. They are *Hausa* coming from the north under the domination of the Moslem Libyans."

"And the whole flock follows the master on the *Kadei?*"

"They walk around the lake and, if they get lucky and do not encounter any hyenas or varans or crocodiles, they might arrive safe to the site of their new home."

While we had the conversation with Roland, Sylvain had driven away from the lake. The road now was a simple trail with animal footprints of all kinds, mostly elephant, Roland said. "Let's walk a few yards and check that dung over there."

Georges was first to get out of the car. He had all ready pulled three cameras, two around his neck and one ready to be used.

The sun was going down fast on to the horizon. We had passed the lake a few hours ago and the landscape had changed drastically.

A hundred yards away was the edge of a dense forest. "We'll walk to the woods," Roland said. "Sylvain, follow us as close as you can. The animal excrements we've seen are elephant manure. And it looks very fresh to me. We might encounter some specimen in the forest."

"Let me change my camera with a wide angle," Georges said with a chuckle. "We might be too close to them."

"We don't even have a gun," I said a little worry.

"Oh yes we do," Roland said with a smirk. Never come here without a firearm."

The Land Rover was behind us finding its way through the trees. We found some more dung but no elephants. "Somehow we have lost them," Roland said a little disappointed. As for me I was relieved. I love elephants. They are gracious animals, funny, beautiful, but for me only in a zoo.

We got out of the forest and resumed our trip on the corrugated trail.

The sun was low in the horizon when we reached a small village of four or five huts. As far as the eyes could see, there was an immense cotton field behind the village. "That must be the northern headquarters of COTONFRAN according to the map Rigaux gave us."

A lanky black man barefoot and dressed with a long short and a torn T-shirt approached us holding a big stick as a cane. "Where is Chief Paul?" I asked.

"Him in the cotton gin."

"Good." That simplified the situation. "Where is the building?"

"There," he said pointing in the direction behind the village.

"Where would that be," Poireau asked.

The black man turned around and we followed him. In the field, two or three dozens of workers, women mostly, were picking cotton dragging huge bags behind them.

We perceived the plant about a quarter of a mile away. Trucks were loading bales and I wondered how those big trucks could find their way through the bush. We had some difficulty with the Land Rover that could barely get through difficult passages.

Paul Bonnin was a short fat man, with a lot of blond hair on his bare chest but none on his head. He was almost as dark as the men working around him. When he noticed our presence he walked towards us rubbing his hands on his shorts. "I was expecting you," he said with a curious deep voice and a sympathetic smile. "Rigaux called me on the radio. Welcome to Koro-Toro, the capital of COTONFRAN. How long are you going to stay?"

"As long as necessary," I said. "Hopefully not too long. We have a lot of documentation and we know what Mr. Rigaux wants. We need some pictures of the fields and of the cotton gin. Perhaps some workers, but I let that to my friend Georges. He's an artist with cameras."

"We have a camp behind the cotton gin." Paul said. "It's a big tent with a dozen of cots, more than enough for you. The noise of the gin might disturb you. We're working around the clock at this time of the year. Cotton must be shipped to Duala. A long way down the African continent. And you know the quality of the roads."

"Yeah," Sylvain said rubbing his back.

"We'll have a good dinner tonight. I killed a nice gazelle two days ago. Should be perfect for the roast. My men are preparing the fire. It's going to be dark in thirty or forty minutes. Night drops as a stone in those latitudes. You can have a shower and we'll have a good drink while the men prepare everything."

"That sound terrific," Roland said. "I could make it without a shower but not without a drink."

That was the first time that I spent a night in the bush, the real African bush with the sounds and the odors particular to Africa. The occasional hysterical laughter of hyenas, and the roar of a lion in the distance kept us, at least me, awake for a while. A little breeze, blowing through the windows of the tent freshened up the air.

We had an excellent dinner of roasted gazelle accompanied with good wine from Paul's reserve. In Africa no one forgets his wine and whisky, even in the boondocks.

The sun was still missing at Koro-Toro when Georges shook me up from my cot and offered me a cup of coffee. That was a friend who reminded me of my mother who used to wake me up every morning with a cup of coffee. She told me once that I'd never get that treatment once I got married. Sorry, Mom, but Aline has done that for years.
Almost everyone was awake in the camp. Paul Bonnin was giving orders to his men before he entered the large tent where Sylvain, Georges, Roland and I had spent the night.
After a series of quick orders to his staff and a cup of black coffee, Paul accompanied us to the field where cotton flowers were in bloom. Georges shot a little over two thousand pictures with each of his cameras, and then we walked back to the cotton gin where he got some more photographs inside the plant.
Georges managed to take a picture of a hyena pilfering in the dark around the camp. "We have many of those," Paul said pointing at the wild animal. They are all right as long as they don't gather in packs. Then, they must be destroyed. We go in the bush in the middle of the night with a few of my men and kill a dozen of them. I hate to do that but it's a must when the hyenas become a little too bold for my taste. I don't like to see them inside a tent or a hut. Besides, blacks believe those animals are a bad influence in their life. We have to get rid of them before they dare to attack their sheep and their goats. I've lost good workers because they believe they can't live where a hyena had urinated. People just leave everything behind and start over another life somewhere else."
I joined Georges and Paul in the large tent. "Enough pictures?" I asked.
"That was easy," Georges said.

Quickly done. In less than two hours the pictures were taken, all the information gathered and we were on our way down to Fort-Lamy and a more civilized country, though I enjoyed my first night in the wilderness.

We thanked Chief Paul for the excellent gazelle, for his welcome and for the help he provided us. He offered us some gazelle meat to take with us which was accepted by Poireau.

"I haven't gone hunting since my stupid accident," Roland said with a wince. "Still difficult to walk for hours."

"What happened to Roland? I whispered to Sylvain.

"Oh, nothing major. He got caught in the middle of a herd of water buffaloes he was following. One of them wedged him against the only tree in the middle of nowhere and gored him several times on his right thigh very close to his femoral artery. He lost a lot of blood in the operation."

"How did he get away with the water buffalo?"

"He just thrust the barrel of his shotgun in the mouth of the bull and shot two twelve-gauge deep in the throat. When his friends found him he was almost dead. An hour later he might have been. But I told you, that guy is crazy."

We left the Koro-Toro encampment about noon with the satisfaction of a job well done.

We didn't see any elephants on our way back to Fort-Lamy but we came across a few hyenas that fled frightened in front of the car. It was dark when we reached the Hotel du Chari where Elisa was conscientiously at the front desk waiting for the night guard.

I was exhausted but happy after that day in the bush. Georges found a photographer in downtown Fort-Lamy where he could develop the few dozens of rolls he had shot at Koro-Toro. I would see the pictures before I went back home. My notes were very much cleaned up by now, so I could finish the article at the hotel and on the plane.

We had a light snack though Sylvain and Roland were ready to open their homes for a last dinner, which would have meant for a last party. "It's enough for the day," I decided. "Tomorrow is Saturday and you have your party, Sylvain."

We had a beer, Georges, Roland, Sylvain and I, and then we all went to bed.

Saturday night the front yard of the hotel was illuminated a giorno for the occasion of my reunion with Sylvain. The whole French community was there and the restaurant closed to the usual customers except for the UTA crew who spent the night at the Chari. "No business today," Sylvain had said. "Only my friends." And the stewardesses were very friendly.

I met every expatriate living in Fort-Lamy. They looked happy, overweight, making enough money not to worry about it, cirrhotic, and not willing to change their life style. In a few years they would retire early in their life for they would not be able to keep up the tremendous pressure of being happy under those conditions. They would return to France and enjoy their retirement drinking sodas and visiting their doctors two or three times a year to get rid of the different viruses they brought from the colonies.

I returned to Chad a few times and every time I enjoyed the sojourn. Until 1975 when François Tombalbaye, the president, was assassinated by General Maloum backed up by Moammar Gaddafi, the Libyan leader. A mess followed the death of the president. The airport was closed to air traffic and the city's name was changed with the new and more African appellation of N'Djamena.

Chad has never been the same since. Tribal feud deteriorated the confidence people had in the country as new names came out from nowhere to complicate the political situation. Muslim Arabs from the north and Christian blacks from the south didn't get along.

Sylvain left N'Djamena and the Hotel du Chari in a hurry with his wife and his two children. I did the same, but as the airport was closed, we had to drive up to Nigeria, cross the border unlawfully, make a curve towards the south to enter Cameroon near Maroua — again unlawfully. From there we flew to Duala before we took the *UTA* flight back to Nice. No more Chad for me, I decided, and I believed for Sylvain either.

For me it wasn't a problem since my job was in Monaco. For Sylvain it could have been. But I heard sometimes later that he had returned to a more civilized Gabon with his former employer. I'll meet him there at the first opportunity, I decided.

The first article I had written on the cotton company was published when I returned to Monaco. Georges' pictures were great as usual.

COTONFRAN was a powerful company but not powerful enough not to be nationalized by the new government in Chad in 1975 and its name changed to COTONTCHAD.

38

My son Jean-François was born on February 17, 1964 in Monaco, two days after my return from Haiti. I almost missed his birth day for he was expected two weeks later. The hospital was only three minutes away from home and five from my office. So, when Aline called me that morning around nine I rushed home, picked her up and drove straight to the Hospital Princess Grace.

I'd spent a week of my life in Haiti trying to prevent the dreaded *Tontons Macoutes*[1] of Papa Doc Duvallier, the Haitian president, from grabbing and throwing me in prison. But it took me two weeks to reach the island following tortuous and illegal routes.

In France, of course, we had heard about Duvallier's secret police but being so far away we had no real idea of the horrid situation in the island.

I flew a Pan Am to Miami, spent a day at the airport trying to find a flight to Port-au-Prince or anywhere else in Haiti. Couldn't make it, so I found a cruise ship to Fort-de-France, Martinique, and left two days later. I called Juliette in Atlanta and told her that I had two days with nothing to do and I was going to fly to Georgia for a quick visit.

It was my first trip to America, in January 1964. I didn't see much of Miami since I stayed at the airport waiting for my flight to Atlanta.

Juliette was at the airport with her eight year old son, Jeremy,

---

[1] Haiti Secret police

whom Mom and I had never met. Jimmy Gunn was traveling north to Omaha for his company. "He travels more and more," Juliette complained. "Well, I know it's his job, but we spend a lot of time at home without him. Eventually he will stop traveling or at least slow down. There is a chance we'll move to New Orleans. Another job with the same company. A promotion."

"That is good news. A promotion is always welcomed. How is he?"

"Gained a lot of weight and doesn't have time to work out. Perhaps in New Orleans he will settle down. Less travel and more office work."

The house in Marietta was the one we had seen on pictures years ago when Juliette first came to America. It was a nice house in a pretty area surrounded with woody hills. When would I have such a house? I thought. Not in France, and certainly not in Monaco. The apartment we lived in was superb, large, and modern with an extraordinary view over the ocean, but it was a rented one and I knew I couldn't afford to buy that kind of housing if it were for sale. And it was not.

Jimmy came back from his trip to Omaha the next day. He had indeed gained some weight but also a few years. He looked mature with his receding hairline, his mustache that had turned a little grayish, and a few wrinkles around his eyes. But the gentle look in his blue eyes had remained the same I'd known twenty years earlier.

We spent the evening in a Mexican restaurant and for the first time I drank a Margarita. Not crazy about it but it was a first. And the last.

Juliette and her family were happy without a doubt. Jeremy was a nice young boy and Jimmy remained the quiet man we had known in Nice during World War II.

Mid-morning, Juliette took me to the airport and I was back to Miami in time to ride in a taxi to the harbor and sail on a cruise ship whose name I've forgotten. Jimmy was already gone somewhere else up north.

* * *

Fort-de-France looked like Nigeria with a big difference in the weather, in the smell, in the sky that was of a deep blue, which never happened in Lagos when I was there, and the little breeze from the ocean that was charged with agreeable odors of vanilla and wild flowers. Typical of Martinique, I was told. Well, I'd rather breathe that than the decaying smell of rotten material.

Fort-de-France was alive and well. But I had to stay for a while at the Lamentin airport and try to find a plane to Haiti. Nothing was to leave Martinique towards either Port-au-Prince or any other city in Hispaniola. I might have to give up the idea to write something about Haiti. But I was far away from home and I would hate to have flown from Nice for nothing. I don't believe the Dunans would be very happy. No matter what, I had to find a way to go to the damn island. Dad would have said: swim. Yeah, right.

I rented a car at the Lamentin airport and drove towards, or what I thought was towards downtown. I drove off, made a right turn and found myself where I'd picked up the rented car. I tried again and was finally out of the airport headed south instead of north. Another turn, another formal imprecation against that damn road I couldn't figure out, and finally I was on the right track.

I picked out a hotel on the beach near a marina. It was almost dark when I opened the room overlooking the ocean. It was nice, clean and relaxing. I had a shower, changed my three-piece suit for shorts and a T-shirt and walked down to the lobby. A pretty black woman smiled at me and, with her unique accent, asked me if she could help me. I didn't remember hearing such a pleasant accent before, a singing intonation where the R's eluded.

"You sure can, Beautiful," I said. "How can we go from here to Haiti? Any means would do."

"There are no communications between the two islands. No regular flights or cruises. Sometimes a crazy sailor goes there just for fun. But he would be right back in the civilized world with his hair still standing on end."

That was a way to summarize the situation. I laughed. "Where can I find a crazy guy who wants to meet with the *Tontons Macoutes* and have his hair standing on end?"

"You might try the store *Ship-Shop*, Ernest Deproges Street. It's a sort of mailbox for the sailors away. They keep the mail there until it is picked up. They might have an idea where to find such a crazy guy. But I doubt."

I thanked her and walked down two blocks to the marina. The store was on the pier next to a small restaurant already crowded. That reminded me that I was close to starvation. I first entered the store, looked for someone to talk to and found a young Creole who looked at me as if I was lost. Perhaps my pale face clashed with the normal faces he usually saw in the island. "Yes," he said with a girlish intonation as his long eyelashes fluttered.

"I'm looking for a boat available to go sailing for a few days, and I've been told that I might find one here."

"Well," he said with his mezzo-soprano voice. "Not exactly here, but we are a mailbox for those who want to receive their letters in Fort-de-France but are often off the island. We have one of those sailors who picked up his mail this morning. He should still be in the marina. His boat is *Eole VII* and must be in his mooring for only twenty-four hours or so. Number 215, south pier."

"What the sailor's name?"

"Maurice Hamon, a real crazy fellow," the young Adonis said with a gracious chuckle.

Maurice Hamon? I thought. That was weird. I knew a Maurice Hamon years ago when I worked part time at Laubry's printing shop. He was a plate maker. It couldn't be the same. But, thinking over I remembered that he was nuts about the ocean. He even had a small boat, a very small sailboat with which he went to Majorca. The Spanish coast guards were lucky to find him alive thirty miles offshore, his nutshell capsized amid a ten-foot swell. The following week he showed up at work saying that he had to buy a bigger boat. Twenty feet would do. I hoped, if it was the same guy, and why not, that he would have gotten rid of his twenty footer. For I was not going to sail anywhere on an insane man's nutshell.

I thanked the ephebus but didn't dare to get too close to him. Scared to be hugged. I walked down the pier thinking of Maurice. He was born and raised in Paris. He happened to be one of those good Parisians —there are some— who refused to stay all their lives in a narrow horizon between the Eiffel Tower and the Arc de Triomphe. They wandered throughout the world and discovered that there are other things than Paris. And usually, those Parisians remained at large the rest of their lives.

South pier was a stroll away from the store. *Eole VII* was there, all sails furled, beautiful and majestic, with her long two masts pointing to the darkened blue sky. A man was on board cleaning the deck with the help of a young black boy.

At the favor of a light illuminating the starboard side I recognized Laubry's plate maker who, I remembered then, had disappeared from the shop after his misadventure near the Spanish coast. It was he, no doubt about it. Damn Maurice. He had always acted as insane as he looked. And here he was, in Fort-de-France, doing what only God must know.

"Ahoy!" I yelled. Maurice turned his glance around, holding his hose. "Maurice," I said, and then I laughed. He stared at me for a minute then cried, "François. What in the world are you doing in Fort-de- France?"

"Looking for you, my friend."

"Looking for me? Well, you almost missed me. I arrived last night from Venezuela. Come on board, come." He went to the footbridge and removed the chain. "Come on in. Oh my God!"

I stepped on the deck and we shook hands then hugged. I was happy to see that scoundrel, always up to something insane. "How long have you been in Fort-de-France?" I asked.

"You mean before I came from Venezuela? A few years. Before that it was Cuba, Puerto-Rico, the Grenadines, Trinidad and Tobago, and finally here in this marvelous island of Martinique. Nine years ago I left Laubry's shop, bought a restaurant, made a lot of money and acquired this ketch. I left Nice, France, my friends and, all of a sudden, I was sailing up the oceans. A life I wouldn't change for all the gold in the world. A dream. Let's go down to the low deck and have a drink.

"That's some surprise," he said after a silence as if he couldn't believe it. "François in Fort-de-France. Praise the Lord."

"You have here a magnificent craft."

"A nineteen meter, sixty-four foot floating palace."

"And you sail solo?"

"Most of the time. Sometimes my girlfriend, Monique, joins me, but she gets bored if we sail nonstop for more than three months."

"Who wouldn't? I said with a wince.

"Then, she returns to France, waits for me to show up wherever she is, and we start over. On short sailing sprees, I take Guillaume with me." He pointed to the young black on the deck. "He's sixteen, a school drop out and an orphan. With me he eats every day, and I believe he has fun." He called the boy. "This is my friend François," he said. "Almost as crazy as me."

"Not quite though," I insisted laughing.

We sat down in the nice and cool stateroom. "I have some wine, I brought from France," Maurice said. "That will be all right?"

"Sure, fine with me."

"So, tell me, my friend, what are you up to, in Martinique?"
"I'm trying to go to Haiti and can't find a way."
"Haiti. No one wants to go to Haiti. You know what happens over there? They kill people."
"The Tontons Macoutes? Yes, I've heard. But I have a paper to write about it and I didn't come this far to give up a few hours away from my final destination."
"A few hours? You're kidding. We're talking about five days of sailing from Fort-de-France. That is if you find someone crazy enough to go to Haiti."
"I found someone."
"You're lucky. Who is that guy?"
"You."
"No. Definitely not. I don't want to be nowhere close to that."
"We don't have to go to Port-au-Prince. Anywhere in the island will do."
"I might think of a way, but it's a long way" he said after a moment of reflection. "But you must be sure you want to do it."
"Shoot," I said now excited.
"Well, I won't go to Haiti but Santo Domingo is much more hospitable. You could go to Puerto Plata, on the northern coast, and from there cross over the border anywhere and find yourself inside Haiti. The lowest profile you'll keep, the healthier you'll feel."
"I need to go to the countryside where people are not afraid to talk, where I can find the origin of this people, their language, their traditions and their beliefs. I want to see voodoo."
"That's much easier than in the big cities. Tontons Macoutes seldom crackdown in mere villages. That's the only solution I can see. Now, as I'm by myself, Monique being in Paris, I have plenty of time to devote to that insane adventure. I'll take you to Puerto Plata in Santo Domingo but you are on your own to Haiti. Be sure, I repeat, be sure you won't regret it. Don't blame it on me if something goes

wrong."

"That would be about a week before I get somewhere in Haiti, right?"

"About correct, yes. You want to do it?"

"Let me call my company. A week to get there and another week to write something about it. Then back to Fort-de-France and fly to Miami for a return home. That's about three weeks."

"Yes, but you don't have to come back here, in Martinique. We just keep going westward and I get you to Miami faster than a roundtrip. What about that?"

"You're sure you can do it?"

"I can, though I'm not sure I want to do it. Call your boss first and let's have dinner downtown after that."

I talked to the Minotaur who still hadn't retired. "It won't be long," he answered to my question. "As soon as you are back you won't see me at the office."

"Yeah! Right," I said. "You were supposed to be traveling the world for two years now. So what happened?"

"Did you call me to ask when I'll retire?"

"Sorry, Sir, just want to let you know where I am."

"And where in the world are you?"

"Martinique, Sir. That the closest I could get to Haiti. It might take another week to get there. I found a demented friend of mine who agreed to take me there and bring me back to the civilized world. If you agree it would take at least two more weeks."

"Hold on, François, Henri is here. Talk to him."

"Good morning, Henri," I said when I got Junior on the line. I explained to him what I'd told the Minotaur.

"That's fine," Henri replied. "*Perspectives* is due next month and the other articles are closed and ready for editing. Are you sure you want to do it?"

"Not really, but I'm here."

"If you don't feel like it, forget about the whole thing and come back."
"I'll be fine, Henri."
"All right. Do whatever it takes."
"Can you call Aline and tell her I'm all right?"
"I'll do that. Good luck, François."

* * *

A Creole band was playing out of tune West Indian music in the garden of the hotel *Paradis,* downtown Fort-de-France. The palm trees swayed gently under the breeze coming from the north driving the mosquitoes away. The temperature was as ideal as it was perfect that evening somewhere in the middle of the New World.

Maurice lit up his pipe and relaxed, his back resting on his armchair watching, through the dangling foliage of a giant banana tree, the moon's reflection on the ocean.

"I think I am happy," Maurice said closing his eyes. "I was prepared to a boring week or two before I decided or not to go pick up my girlfriend in France. You have decided for me."

"I'm sorry I've messed you up." Then I thought better: Maurice is messed up by nature. He didn't need any help. Since I met him, years ago, he had done weird things and never seemed to be happier than when he pulled out of one of these deeds. I recalled he enrolled in a spelunker's club and started exploring caves as a hobby. All by himself. This was before he started sailing. They found him one weekend, stuck two hundred meters under the surface of the earth and, as it had been raining nonstop for three days, he got mired in four feet of water, and the rescuers had to dig and pull him out to safety.

He also suddenly began to like equestrian sports. He went to a club and started jumping as soon as he figured out which side he had to mount the horse. He broke his collarbone twice and decided then to devote more time to sailing.

I reminded him of all these activities that had vanished little by little. But he got stuck to the ocean and didn't do anything else. He was entitled to a partial retirement, but I knew Maurice had always had enough money to do what he cared for. He made a little fortune in the restaurant trade for which he had no knowledge at all. He bought, for a mere one thousand dollars, a small bistro, with the curious name of *Pet au Diable* that was closing for bankruptcy. The restaurant was in the little village of the *Matelles* near Montpellier, in south France.

The village of the Matelles was, and still is, a classified national monument. No one had the right to change anything in the hamlet. For that's what it was: a hamlet proud of its three houses and its restaurant dating from the seventeenth century.

Montpellier is a large city with an important university of medicine, forty kilometers from the village. About two thousand students live there ten months a year. The day those students discovered the *Pet au Diable* —French for Fart of the Devil— there wasn't enough room in the miniature bistro suitable for everyone. Tables for twelve were set outdoor with two pretty waitresses serving only grilled food. And the cook was no one else but my friend Maurice.

After five years working hard, Maurice sold the then successful restaurant, for two hundred thousand dollars, to an Italian couple. An enormous profit in only five years. He bought the ketch, named it *Eole VII*, for he had six previous smaller Eoles, and decided to spend his life on the oceans. All of them. [1]

---

[1] True story

39

As usual Mom, Aline and Susanne were at Nice airport when I arrived on a rainy day. It was cold too and sad but I was happy to see them again, a thought that had evaded me for a while when I was in Haiti. Maurice was right; no one wanted to go to that island, not until the *Tontons Macoutes* and the likes of Papa Doc Duvallier would be kicked out.

Monaco was refreshing and civilized in comparison to the trip to the New World I'd just completed.

Aline was close to give birth and Mom ready to be there and help.

My office didn't look different from the day I left it and though Martine looked at me from the corner of her eyes, I knew that everything would be fine as soon as I talked, wrote and showen something that would turn a common stomach inside out.

I had begun my article when Maurice and I escaped from Fort-Liberté up north near the Dominican border.

Maurice didn't take any risk entering the Haitian national waters. We moored at Puerto Plata, On the Spanish side of the island, and found our way to Haiti across the border near Cap-Haitien the most important city in the north.

Maurice had changed his mind when we reached the Dominican city. "I can't let you go in that hell by yourself," he said scratching his nose as if he were thinking. I was sure he had already made up his mind during the four days of sailing. Maurice never took too long before he decided to do something. Mostly when that something was crazy. He always had been a spontaneous action man. Most of the times he went deep into trouble, but he never regretted it and he never learned from it either. He would make the same stupid mistake over and over and would laugh about it.

It was in the Dominican harbor that we found *Eole VII* gently pitching and waiting for us. Guillaume was there, a little bored, but faithfully on board. We set sails the next morning westward with Miami in our minds.

* * *

"So, how was it?" Henri asked when he stepped in my office the next day.

"Scary, but fun. With my friend Maurice —you know Maurice?—

"No, I don't believe so. Who is he?"

"He was a plate maker at Laubry's years ago."

"The curly hair guy always joking? The one who almost drown on the Spanish shores?"

"That's the man."

"Where in the world did you find him?"

"In Fort-de-France, arriving from Venezuela. That man is insane, foolhardy and reckless. That is why it was scary to be with him. I always expected the unexpected. But he helped me in more than one way. He even took some pictures while we were running like rabbits on the Haitian countryside in front of the Tontons Macoutes."

"I saw the pictures you left with the Minotaur. Good photos. We'll use them. I don't have your article yet. When will it be ready?"

"I'm just reading it one more time. I'll bring it to you in a few minutes."

Henri Dunan walked to the door then stopped and said. "By the way, Dad is retiring at the end of the week. I'll be here this weekend to fix my new office."

"I'll be here too."

One more time I found myself alone, the last article I wrote in my hand. Martine had done a good job with her typing. No matter how meticulously I read and checked her copy, I couldn't find any misspelling or mistakes in her job. She had always amazed me for the years we had been working together.

As I stared blindly at the copy, the memory of the trip came back to me slowly, and as I thought about some episodes, a shudder shook my spine.

We had arrived at Puerto Plata, I believe it was on Tuesday January fifteenth. Four days before, we had left the marina in Fort-de-France with a strong wind that turned out to be a dangerous storm as we hugged Saint Thomas and Puerto Rico. But Maurice didn't seem to be worried. That was the problem with my reckless friend. You don't know his limit and sometimes I wonder if he has any. When does he start being anxious? I was frightened the whole time we were at sea. But that was nothing in comparison of what we were going to experience on the land of the voodoo.

"That will be fine," Maurice had said as he skipped Eole VII. "If we keep that kind of breeze, forty knots winds, for a few days it may save us time. Hurricane season is long gone, so no problems with that."

We landed on a narrow wooden pier just in front of a shaky building that could be the harbormaster's office and the police station. We left Guillaume on board and walked to the building. It was nice to feel something still under my feet.

We found a slip for the duration of our stay and, as I could speak Spanish, we got along very well with the office personnel. We had our passports checked, stamped and were charged ten dollars to have the right to set foot on the island.

We even had a good meal in a small restaurant on the beach whose owner, a big black lady named Susanna, grilled for us a couple of

huge lobsters for the price of a breakfast in Martinique.
"First things first," Maurice said. "We have to cross the border to Haiti if it is there you want to go."
I chuckled.
"This shouldn't be too difficult. There is a constant smuggling operation along the frontier and Dominicans and Haitians mingle every day on both sides."
I asked Susanna if she knew someone who had a car that could take us to Haiti. "Sure," she said, "mi marido, my husband." He has a big truck, with which he goes to Fort-Liberté where he exchanges his vegetables and his sugar cane against lobsters. The best time is by night to avoid the Tonton Macoutes. Those are real bad people."
"What time could he be ready?" I asked.
"Nine or ten. You wait here in the restaurant. He'll pick you up. It will be two hundred dollars."
"Tell him one hundred for both of us. After we get there."
She smiled and shrugged. "Be here at nine," she said. "He'll be here if he's not too drunk."
We left Susanna and went back to *Eole VII*.

It was almost ten when I was waking up from a short nap I had on my chair at Susanna's. I was tired waiting for her husband and decided to close my eyes and sleep.
Eugenio was a large black man who must have some difficulty fitting into a regular car. He shook our hands graciously and pointed to a Ford truck that must have been built the same year as the model T. A tarpaulin covered the top and the rear down to the tailgate. I walked to the rear, pulled the tarpaulin aside and saw a mountain of sugar cane that had probably been cut the same day. "Is that what you sell?" I asked.
"For lobsters."
"I like lobsters better too."

"You know it's going to be two hundred dollars."
I smiled with a glance to Maurice. "Yes, one hundred dollars. That's what I said." I fished ten bills of ten dollars and waved them in front of his round eyes. He snatched the money before I could prevent him from doing so. "Get in," he said as he slid onto the driver seat laughing.

It took almost eight hours to cover the seventy-five miles from Puerto Plata. We had first to climb the Cordillera west of the city, then to ford a stream, the *Yaque del Norte*, hoping that the last rain didn't increase the volume of the current. Eugenio stopped on the muddy bank, looked around a little worried about the strength of the stream. Maurice and I got off the truck to stand next to Eugenio. "Do you think you can go through this flow?" I asked with my quivering voice.

"Don't know," the black man said. "There is a bridge south from here but that is twenty miles away. You want to try to cross over?"

"It's your truck, my friend," Maurice said. "If the current carries your truck away, we might be able to swim. I don't know about you."

"I can swim. The river at this point is only a hundred feet wide. One way or another we'll find ourselves on the opposite bank."

"Yes, but not your truck," I said.

We made it to the other bank safely, but the truck picked up some water and it refused to go further once it had landed on a little sandy beach.

Eugenio grabbed a flashlight in the glove compartment, pulled the hood up, looked at the engine, and shook his head. "I don't know what's wrong."

I looked too, right and left, up and down which didn't give me any idea of what the truck needed. I've never been able to recognize a carburetor from a generator. I looked again and couldn't even find the sparkplugs.

Maurice looked at his turn. "I need a wrench, a screwdriver, and rags. Then he began pulling parts from the truck, which scared me.

But with Maurice fright is common place. After a thought, he had a boat with an engine that has to work, and besides, Maurice was capable of doing about anything he needed in his life.

An hour later, all the parts were back where they belonged. At least I thought. Eugenio turned the ignition and the engine revved. "What about that," I said. "We are going to charge you for the mechanic job," I told Eugenio. We climbed back into the truck and took off.

Dawn broke when we reached the suburbs of Fort-Liberté under the rain. That, in a way, was good. Not many people in the street and the traffic was quite light. I looked around and so did Maurice. We have been told that the Tontons Macoutes were easily recognizable. They all wore gray suits and dark sunglasses at any hour of the day and of the night.

We went straight to the police station to show our passports, but Eugenio stayed behind, not having any paper suitable for the French-speaking part of the island.

Right away we recognized the Tonton Macoute at his desk. He was a handsome guy as much as we could see of his face. He wore sunglasses though it was dark in the office that smelled like rotten something. The Tonton got to his feet. I could tell that he topped over six feet with broad shoulders and long arms he extended with a smile. "Welcome to Haiti," he said. "Where do you come from?"

"France," I replied. "We were sailing before we stopped at Puerto Plata. We decided to come across your border and visit the country."

"May I see your passports?" He looked at Maurice who hadn't say a word yet. I hoped he would stay silent for a while for I wasn't sure the Tonton Macoute would appreciate the kind of humor Maurice used when he didn't like somebody.

The man spoke a perfect French with just a slight accent to classify him as a native islander.

"I see you don't have any entry visas. No one had checked you at the border."

"There was no one at the border," I said. "This is why we're here in your office. We didn't want to wander around without the authorization to do so."

"And that you don't have. I keep your passport to check while you can stay at the *Hotel de la Plage* for the night. Tomorrow you'll come back here and I'll let you know if you can have a visa. Before that don't leave town."

He looked at the passports one more time and laid them on his desk. "I'll see you in the morning," he said in a suave tone.

We walked out after we asked for the address of the *Hotel de la Plage*.

"We'll see you tomorrow, Sir," I said with a smile.

As we moved away from the police station, two Tontons Macoutes were dragging a black man rather harshly. He had a bloody face and an ear was hanging on his cheek almost completely torn off. People nearby watched the spectacle with no more emotion than if it were a dog passing by.

"Look at those poor guys," I said. "They stare at the misery of this man in the hands of the Tontons Macoutes with no concern. I would say, happy not to be him. Let's go to the hotel."

"First let's find Eugenio and let's get the hell out of here."

"We can't do that, Maurice. Remember, they have our passports."

"No they don't," he said laughing and waving his hand and our two passports.

"You crazy son of a gun. How did you do that?"

"You saw the guy when he laid our papers on his desk before we walked out?"

"Yes, sure."

"Well, I picked them up right away behind him. We would never get them back if I didn't do that."

"That's what I said. You are totally insane and you are driving me on the same mental level. I should have known better before we left Martinique."

"There's not much we can do now, my friend, but one thing."

"What would that be?"

"Run, anywhere but run and put the most distance between the Macoutes and us. We'll come across some more of them. Let's just try to avoid the encounter."

We found Eugenio on the beach dealing with an old fisherman who held a conical lobster pot with a few crustaceans wriggling inside. Next to him was a stack of sugar cane Eugenio had unloaded from his truck.

"We have to go. Now," I said with a back glance at the police station. I wondered how long it would take to the obsequious Macoute to find out about the passports. "Let's go, Eugenio," I repeated. "Now."

"That old guy is a crook," Eugenio said pointing to the fisherman. "He wants twenty dollars besides the load of sugar cane."

I fished twenty dollars in my pocket, and gave it to the man.

"Here. Now, Eugenio, take the lobsters, throw them in the back of your truck so we can leave. When we are through with this trip, you'll have another two hundred dollars."

The Dominican was happy and the old man was happy and we were happy as soon as the truck took off southward and disappeared into the forest.

* * *

Eugenio had driven all night towards Saint Raphael to avoid the *Mountains of the North*, then through a low valley until we reached a small village of a few huts. There were no Tontons Macoutes there but two dozen men who were idly sitting in front of their cabins, more women than men and a swarm of kids.

"Where are we?" I asked Eugenio.

"I don't know. Now it's time for me to go back home. You don't need me anymore." He turned round towards his truck, climbed into it and waved his hand goodbye. Thirty seconds later he had disappeared from our sight.

"We might have a problem," I said. "We'll have to find another means of transportation to return to Puerto Plata and to the *Eole VII*. I walked to a woman sitting on a small bench, grinding something in a mortar. "Where are we?" I asked.

"In the forest, near Maissade."

"Yes, sure, Maissade. That's the only town I know in the world, where most of the time I spend my vacation," I said then I laughed. Where is Port-au-Prince?"

The woman point southward. "Seventy kilometers this way. Behind the *Montagnes Noires*, the Black Mountains, difficult mountains. You no go Port-au-Prince. Over there, no good. Tontons Macoutes no good."

"We don't want to go to Port-au-Prince. We just want to know where we are and how we can get to the next city in this part of the country." I had hard time making myself understood. The woman could speak but patois which was Hebrew to me.

"Does any one speak French?" Maurice asked aloud looking around. A young man, his back against the thatch of a cabin, waved his hand, then got up and ambled towards us.

"I come from Port-au-Prince," he said. "It's no good there. Papa Doc, our president, is crazy. Tontons Macoutes are everywhere. Very mean."

"All right," I said. "You speak French. What are you doing here? Hiding?"

"Yes, hiding. Tonton Macoutes after me."

"Well, they will be soon after us too. This is Maurice. He wants to take some pictures of you and your friends here. Your houses, your fields, your poultry, your goats. Tell us how you survive in the countryside. Then I need someone, perhaps two or three people, coming with us, people who can show us the country and the traditions."

"Voodoo?" the young black said simply.

"Yes, voodoo.... and Tontons Macoutes."

"Tonton Macoutes no traditions. Murderers. Soon no more Papa Doc, and his secret police would be gone too. We know for sure."

"How do you know?"

There was a pause that lasted a few minutes. I waited for his answer but I had an idea what it was. Finally he muttered, "Voodoo."

That was what I had in mind. They were going to get rid of the president, Papa Doc Duvallier and his horrid Tontons Macoutes with the help of some voodoo priests and their tricks, some black magic and, probably, some murders.

"What's your name?" I asked.

"Toussaint."

"Well, well, is that a common name in Haiti," Maurice asked. Of course he heard about Toussaint l'Ouverture, one of the early heroes of the independence of Haiti. But that was at the end of the eighteenth century and we didn't know that the name was carried over for the past hundred and sixty years.

"No, not common. Only me. One of my ancestors was Toussaint l'Ouverture. You know him?"

"I sure do. A slave who became a general in your first Army of Liberation in the late eighteenth century. He was taken prisoner by the French general Leclerc on behalf of Napoléon Bonaparte, sent to Pontarlier, France, thrown in a filthy jail, where he died of boredom in 1803 at the age of fifty-six. There were rumors he was assassinated by one of his prison guards who stole his golden watch."

He looked nicely surprised that I knew his ancestor who probably wasn't. "Now more slaves everywhere, in Port-au-Prince, in Cap Haitien, in Mirebalais. But no more army of liberation."

"And you are trying to build that army anew but in the rural areas of the island?" I asked matter-of-factly. "Poor idiots," I whispered.

He didn't answer, lowering his glance to the ground, and then he shrugged. "Listen," I said, "I don't have much money, but if you come with me, and show me the country and tell me the story of your life, and the story of your friends, I'll promise you'll have five hundred dollars when you get us back to the border with the Dominican Republic." I looked at him right in his eyes, and waited.

He had a sudden grin that illuminated his face. "I come with you," he said after the short pause. "I take two friends with me." He walked back to a cabin, stepped in and got out after a minute or two with two men one of whom was a giant way past seven feet. "This is Clément," he said pointing at an old man with a red scarf around his head, "and this is my friend Samson." The giant approached, looked at Maurice, and me then smiled and offered his hand to shake. I wasn't sure I wanted to take that friendly hand, but we complied, Maurice and I.

Toussaint had an object in one hand he was trying to conceal. "What is that?" I asked indicating his back.

It was a doll. A rag doll, a man in a black suit and a top hat. He looked familiar to me but I wasn't sure. I looked again. The doll had three needles stuck where the heart was supposed to be. "Papa Doc Duvallier?" I asked. Of course it was. "You're killing him?"

He nodded without a word. [1]

"We are going to talk, my friend," Maurice said now fully interested. He took a few pictures of the doll, then of the three men.

---

[1] President Duvallier died in 1971 presumably of a massive heart attack

Night had suddenly fallen on the hamlet. Torches and candles were lit all over the place. We sat at a table outside a hut with the three men and the woman who spoke patois. Someone brought a calabash and set it on the table. "What is this?" Maurice asked.

"Beer, homemade beer. Women do that. You drink."

"Thank you, but I'll pass," I said preventing a wince to show on my face.

"I'll drink," Maurice accepted. "Yeah! I'll try."

I watched him as he brought the calabash to his mouth. He had a sip, then another one, and looked the gourd-like fruit as if he were reading the label. "Not bad," he said.

After a short silence I said, "So, why are you killing the president?"

"Papa Doc no good," the giant said bringing his enormous hand to his throat as to strangle himself. "No good. Him dies."

"Just like that?"

"We have prepared a voodoo ceremony for tonight in the *Montagnes Noires*. There is a clearing in the forest where we, voodooists, gather when the moon is full. You can hear the drums in the valley."

I listened looking at the sky. Toussaint was right. We could hear the drumbeat coming from everywhere. "That's the call," Toussaint continued. "Tontons Macoutes will try to infiltrate our ranks, but we know them too well. We are leaving in an hour, but first we eat."

A woman brought some fruit and a grilled chicken. I didn't notice but I was starving. The chicken was tough and cold but no one cared.

Suddenly, through a cloud, the moon showed her full size face round like a pocket watch. Toussaint stared at the sky, smiled and got on his feet. "We go now," he said.

* * *

The clearing was large and well illuminated by the moonlight and a series of torches stuck in the ground. We arrived around two in the morning with Toussaint, Samson and Clément, the man with the red scarf.

There was a huge crowd mumbling some lament and swaying from one foot to the other. They kept their heads down and their eyes closed. "How many people do you think they are here?" I asked Maurice.

"Four or five thousand."

"That's what I thought. What are they going to do?"

"Have not the faintest idea. Voodoo, I guess. Let's ask Toussaint."

The three men we came with had retired a few feet away isolating themselves from us. They were talking with volubility and with what looked like a great passion. Finally Samson laughed with his extraordinary deep voice.

"They are happy, I believe," Maurice said as he walked to the giant. "What's going on, Samson?"

"Good happening, last night," he said with a burst of laughter.

"I'm happy for you. What is it?"

Toussaint approached wearing a serious face. "We caught a Tonton Macoute last night about a mile from here. He thought he could mingle with the crowd after he removed his glasses and changed his clothes. They always try. The crowd recognized him. He's in bad shape but he will be much worse tomorrow morning."

After a long silence, Toussaint added, "No white men have ever witnessed what is going to happen to him. You want to be there?"

I felt a sudden uneasiness. "What are you going to do," I said. "Kill him?"

"Oh no, we won't kill him."

At that precise moment, looking at Toussaint's face, I sensed a tremor coming from the end of my back and crawling slowly like a snake up to my neck. What were those three devils up to, I wondered?

Clément hadn't said a word since we met at the village. He turned towards me and smiled. "We won't kill him," he uttered with a smirk, "but he will die."
That was a little obscure to me. We won't kill him but he will die. Of what? Natural causes? Toussaint looked at me, then put one hand on my shoulder and said, "Today we'll have a very simple and generally well known voodoo ceremony."
Toussaint explained pointing to a rock fifty yards away. "Clément is our *Boko*, our priest, and he will perform the ritual on that flat boulder over there. It's our altar. Red is the voodooist's color so, everything will be covered or dressed with red cloth. The altar, the ground where the initiation will take place, and the heads of our initiate."
A man arrived, his head and shoulders covered with a red cloth, hands clasped on his chest. "What is Clément going to do to him?" I asked.
"Nothing bad. That man had been cursed by an enemy and he might lose his soul—"
"His what?"
"Soul. His soul might be lost for ever, so Clément will take it away for a period of two or three weeks before he will put it back once he's sure there is no more danger."
"What's the procedure?"
"Simple as I said. We dig a hole in the ground, a foot deep, the initiate kneels inside still covered with the red cloth and Clément will sacrifice a chicken he will behead with his machete letting the blood flow on top of the initiate's head until not a drop is left in the bird."
"Yes, simple," I said with a glance at Maurice. "May we take some pictures?"
"No, sorry, you're not supposed to be here in the first place."
"If you want us to help you in your struggle towards freedom, you might want us to tell the whole world what is happening in your

country."

"Let me talk to the *Boko*." Toussaint walked to Clément as the *Boko* was preparing for the ceremony. I could see the two men having a discussion but Clément was still shaking his head.

"Not a chance," I said to Maurice nodding towards Clément and Toussaint. The *Boko* is not hot to share his secret. What can you do?"

"I'll try a trick," Maurice said with a smile. "I just won't use a flash. Nothing to it."

Toussaint was back. "Sorry," he said, "no pictures. But tomorrow you can take all the photographs you want to."

"Well, that would be nice," Maurice said and winked at me.

Maurice managed to take a few pictures of the initiate man losing his soul draped in red and drenched with chicken blood.

"Not particularly mouthwatering," I said.

"Better than chicken shit," Maurice said with a muffled laugh.

It was my first voodoo ceremony, and, at that moment, I'd have bet that it would have been my last one. [1]

The next day, if I understood the three scoundrels, it wouldn't be a voodoo trick. It would be an assassination.

* * *

A reddish glow over the hill started the day. The Montagnes Noires above the deep valley of the Artibonite got the first light of the morning. Dawn was minutes away, and life on the mountaintop was resuming. I was tired and so was Maurice. We hadn't slept for over

---

[1] This kind of manifestation is well known by all the visitors of Haiti. Most are organized solely for the visitors. Of course they are fake voodoo.

thirty hours now, hadn't eaten much either, and walked a great many miles starting at the small village near Maissade.

The Artibonite River meandered lazily among the lilies and the giant iris of the valley. Maurice and I were standing there amazed by the beauty of the scenery. The sun was still hiding, and on the hills it was cold. It had rained the previous night while we were climbing the mountains, and the ground was soaked and muddy.

When I saw Clément stopped near a giant cactus down in the valley, I couldn't figure out what was in his mind. I asked Toussaint what the Boko was doing.

"Pick up some thorns," he had replied. "Those cactus are called *chandelles*, candles. Their thorns contain a rare lethal poison. If you get scratched by one of them while passing by, you better run to the next doctor as fast as you can. During the war for our independence, the French Riflemen would strip their prisoners, tie them to those *chandelles* and let them die.

Toussaint stared at the Tonton Macoute who had been brought to the hilltop and tied up naked to a stake. He had no sunglasses, which was considered by the secret police to be the supreme insult.

Clément approached the prisoner with a deprecating face while he fished a red handkerchief from his pocket. Slowly, keeping an eye on the Macoute, he unwrapped a few thorns he had picked up from the cactus in the valley. He slowly grabbed one of the thorns, stared at it, and turned to the victim with a wry smile on his face.

Standing fifty yards away from the prisoner, Maurice and I watched Clément laying the thorns carefully on the ground on top of the handkerchief like a surgeon laying his instruments on the operation table.

"Those thorns are going to kill the Tonton Mcoute, slowly but surely," I said.

"Maurice nodded. "Yes, I heard and they don't even bother with a semblance of a trial."

"Expeditious justice," I said. "There is no room for Tontons Macoutes on this island, I believe. After Papa Duvallier dies — remember the rag doll?— the Macoutes will disappear."

I looked at the horrible setting. Everyone was enjoying themselves. The crowd from last night, or most of them, had followed the Boko up the mountain and was now jubilant. Maurice had already taken two rolls of film. "Check those savages," he said nodding towards the throng.

Not a word of apology or regret had been uttered by the Tonton Macoute, not a complaint and not a moaning while Clément and Toussaint had stuck the first thorns into the prisoner's body. They had started by the tongue, piercing through it with three black thorns stuck in a triangle design.

"What's that guy's name?" Maurice asked.

"No one knows, I presume, and no one cares either."

"I don't know what kind of crime the Macoutes are charged with," I said, "but this way of justice is unbelievably cruel."

"No, it is not," Maurice replied. "The Haitians have no idea what cruel means and have no respect for human life. During their life as slaves they endured the worst treatment, and often death was the best thing that could happen to them."

The torture had stopped for a few minutes as Toussaint and Clément seemed to confer what to do next.

They decided for the face, the neck, and the penis. Not a word or a cry came out of the Macoute's mouth until Toussaint pushed in the last ones into his eyes.

Maurice shrugged and I turned my glance. It was terrible but nothing we could do. It was the law of the voodooists. Nothing and nobody could save the policeman.

"I asked Samson a few questions on our way up here," Maurice said. "The giant told me that the man will die, yelling his pain, and cursing his god Dambala for not helping him. I asked who was Damballa?"

After a few seconds, Samson answered: "The God of the Universe, he had said proudly. "Our voodoo god" He will die tomorrow or the day after, the giant had explained. All will depend on his resistance to the poison.

"It's inhuman," Maurice said, "but it's their problem. I wish we weren't here on this magnificent mountain where we just witnessed a serious case of murder. Come on, François, and let's join our friends of the civilized world. It's time to leave this land of horror. Let's find the little village near Maissade and pray we find a way to the Dominican border."

40

"I read your report on *Perspectives*," the Minotaur said opening my door. "Gave me the creeps."

"I thought you had retired," I said laughing."

"I have. I'm just here for our little trip to Caesar's. Like a beer?"

I didn't like beer as much as I loved the old man. We could spend hours together and never get bored. One of the rare persons of whom I can say that. Besides Aline.

We sat down as usual facing the harbor. Prince Rainier's yacht was at anchor in the same place I'd seen her for years. Raising my glance I could perceive the national flag flying over the palace. "The Prince is home," I said as if this was very important. The Minotaur smiled, stared at the flag for a moment, then shrugged.

"Who cares?"

"I would if he made me a Monaco National."

"You'll never be."

"I know, but my son might be one day. He was born in Monaco."

"Not enough, my friend. It's much more complicated than that. You are born in America and you are American. You are born in France and you are French. You were born in Monaco and you are anything you want but Monegasque. Let me explain to you, if you ever care to know."

"Yes, sure. I never knew the exact rules."

"Well, there are a few cases. Your parents are Nationals and there is no problem. You were born Monegasque. That what they call the Nationals."

"That's not my case."

"Right. Second case: Your father is a Monegasque but not your Mother. You were born a girl; there is no problem either. You are a female Monegasque since the first day of your life. Now, that gets a little complicated. Your mother is Monegasque and your father is not. If you are a girl, that's fine, but if you were born a boy, you might be a National only after you have served in the French army as a French soldier. Makes sense, right?"

"No, but it's all right. In my son's case, what are the rules?"

"That's even more difficult. If your son married a Monegasque and they have a female child, she would be Monegasque at her birth. If the child is a boy, then we return to the aforementioned rule; he would be Monegasque after military service in the French army. Your son might have a daughter and a son and a wife of the Monegasque nationality but he would never be a Monegasque himself. That's about all the rules they have in this country."

"And what are the benefits to being Monegasque?"

"Ah ah. That is a very big deal. Citizens —there are about two thousand in the Principality— have all the rights. First they are taken care of from their birth or from the day they become citizens. Like after the military service for the boys. They will never pay income taxes no matter how much money they make. They will have priority on any vacant jobs in the local administration where they will enjoy higher paid jobs in the Monegasque hierarchy. They live in luxurious apartments for the cost of an efficiency. They won't have to pay for the telephone. No taxes on cars or TV or any luxury taxes. They would be invited to the palace with the Prince several times a year. Their children would have free tuition as long as they are in school with the certitude to have a job when they graduate. There is probably more benefit than I can recall now."

"That's interesting. I've just learned something new today."

"Doesn't everyone do that? I've learned a lot reading your report on Haiti."

"I've discovered an unknown world there, Sir. A terrifying world of which I had no idea. We had to run and hide when we left the Montagnes Noires. Half of Papa Doc's Tontons Macoutes were after us. Probably to retaliate for the killing of one of them. We separated from the crowd and started our way down to the village. Only Samson came with us. When we arrived at the huts, they were burning, some were already to cinder. Bodies were all over. What a gruesome sight! Not far from the huts, we recognized Eugenio's truck still on fire. We approached to watched with horror that Eugenio was in the cab. Dead of course. They must have arrested him on his way home and forced him to show where he brought us. The lobsters were still in the back of the truck. Cooked. We had to leave right away. I went to Samson who was watching the disastrous spectacle with tears in his eyes. Such a big man crying, what a moving scene."

"He didn't cry when they torture the Tonton Macoute."

"They apparently had their reasons."

"The Tontons Macoutes also."

"You're right, Sir, but I couldn't be judge. However we had reached the eastern part of the island, found a car with a driver and joined Puerto Plata the next day late at night. We didn't stop at Susanna's restaurant. We wouldn't know what to tell her about Eugenio. The next morning we were sailing westwards to Miami where we had the films developed. You have seen the pictures. Unappetizing."

"Good pictures by Maurice. Did you fix his salary with Henri?"

"Yes, Sir. We sent him a check in Martinique. He'll be happy."

"That's good."

We had spent over an hour at Caesar's, our beer getting warm. We got on our feet and walked towards the office. "I won't go upstairs," the Minotaur said nodding to the fourth floor where my office was. "I think I'm going home. See you tomorrow."

* * *

As soon as I stepped in the vestibule I knew something went terribly wrong. Mom was there, a tear on her face. "What happened," I asked worried.

"I didn't want to call you at the office," Aline said. She had in her hands a telegram. I hate those. They always bring bad news. This one was a terrible one. Jimmy Gunn's plane crashed in Jamaica on a business trip. There were no survivors.

Juliette, Jimmy and their son Jeremy had moved to New Orleans a few months prior. They had found peace and stability after Jimmy had been promoted to Agency Director with few occasions to fly, which made both of them happy. My brother-in-law had been traveling almost nonstop for the last fifteen or twenty years. Now, he was getting more relaxed preparing for his retirement which he expected to enjoy in no more than four or five years. Well, so much for a nice retirement.

I called Henri Dunan at home to inform him that I was flying the next day to New Orleans. I would be absent three or four days."

Mom had decided to come with me. She loved Jimmy and it would be an opportunity for her to visit Juliette whom she hadn't seen for at least three years.

It was hot and dark in New Orleans when we landed at Kenner. We had flown a TransWorld Airline from Nice to Paris, to New York and, finally, to New Orleans. Mom was tired but she had enjoyed the flight and mostly the nice attention she got from the flight attendants. It was her first flight, but a nice one.

A lady, friend of Juliette's, picked us up at the airport. She was holding a sign with my name on it. "Sorry," she had said, "Juliette is at the funeral parlor, of course. She asked me to pick you up. I hope you had a good trip."

"It was all right, considering."

Juliette was wearing sunglasses to hide her eyes. She had been crying since she heard on the newsreel channel that Jimmy's plane had crashed in the Blue Mountains. "It was a small plane hired by his company for a quick trip to Kingston," she said.

"That was *quick*, all right," Mom said with a broken voice.

The parlor was crowded but the coffin was closed. They had found the seven occupants in very bad shape. Only Jimmy was recognizable. But no one wanted to see a dead man in his coffin with such wounds.

"The eulogy will be later tonight," Juliette said. "They will bury him tomorrow morning."

Juliette and Jimmy had bought a new house on Houma Boulevard in Metairie, Jefferson Parish. It was a nice two-story house, in a residential area, with a manicured front and backyard, a swimming pool and stately trees with Spanish moss all around.

Mom and I were introduced to a lot of Jimmy and Juliette's friends as well as his work pals from Atlanta and New Orleans. "Jimmy Gunn was loved by everyone," Juliette said. "He was such a good man. Jeremy is devastated. He lost his best friend."

41

I returned to Monaco after the funeral, leaving Mom behind. She asked to stay for a while to help Juliette cope with her trauma. The terrible death of Jimmy Gunn had destroyed a happy family. Juliette was lost, of course, but she wasn't in any needs money wise. Jimmy had made a good living for the past twenty years, had made smart investments and, of course, had contracted a very lucrative insurance within his own company.

Juliette wasn't left in a lurch if it wasn't for the mental torment.

Mom stayed in New Orleans for three months. And she already missed her *Cour des Miracles*, her friends and, I believed, my own family in Monaco.

On March 30th, 1975, Susanne married an adorable good-looking boy from Monaco. His name was and still is Jacky Rosati. He was good for nothing but playing drums for a Greek singer, Demis Roussos, and his orchestra, a band that traveled the world eleven months a year. However they managed, in between two absences, to give me my first granddaughter; Stephanie in 1977.

I was a grandfather and Mom a great-grandmother.

And I was still working for *Perspectives* though the Minotaur was getting old and ill. I saw him less and less in the afternoon. Then suddenly, he didn't show up all together. Henri explained that his gout forced him to stay home most of the time. I paid him a few visits at his home until he was taken to the hospital one night as I was traveling to Cameroon to write a report on the dam and the aluminum plant at Edea near Duala.

I found my friend Georges Martial waiting for me at the airport flooded by a torrential rain. "Nothing unusual," Georges said. "Nice to see you again. Heard from Sylvain?"

"Yes, he went back to Switzerland, Zurich. They visited with us in Monaco last year with Elisa and their two kids. Beautiful family."

We drove to Edea the next morning. Georges picked me up at the *Hôtel des Cocotiers* at six in the morning. We had a good breakfast and were ready for a bad drive.

The road was a little better than north Chad, but not much. My back hurt when we got to Edea. But the trip was worth the broken back. The dam was a superb realization spanning the Sanaga River with its enormous pipes, six or seven of them, that brought enough power for the cities of Edea and Duala. That was impressive.

Georges took very few pictures saying that he had about two thousands of them at home in Duala. Nothing had changed since the construction of the dam in 1960. No need of new photographs.

We talked to the manager of the dam, Antoine Moyabe, a big fat guy who never stopped laughing no matter how serious our conversation was. I felt exasperated since we didn't have any straight answers to any of my questions.

"Do you have any documentation printed about the dam," I finally asked with little hope for a good answer.

"Yes, we sure do," he said with a crack of laughter.

"May I have it?"

He got on his feet, walked to a cabinet and pull ten inches of printed material. "Here we go," he said still laughing. "We have everything about the damn dam."

Finally, after an hour of useless talking, I had what I came for. Nothing is easy in Africa. I learned that the hard way. It's very difficult to make concrete any idea you bring with you if you have to deal with an African. I lost patience a few times, and even gave up on some occasions.

"That's nice of you," I said, and I laughed loudly trying to match his stupid good humor. Georges stared at me as if I was insane. I probably was.

"If you want more ideas for your article, talk to Mr. Abassouley at the Ministry of Information. He will be willing to speak to you as a writer for *Perspectives*. He loves the magazine."

"Well, that wasn't too bad," Georges said when we got out and climbed into the car.

"I was starting to get nervous with the fat man. He was finally useful," I said showing the stack of paper. "Let's go to the hotel and call that... what was his name?"

"Abassouley. You better get used to African names if you want to work with them."

We've got the Ministry of Information on our first call. "I'd like to talk to Mr. Assoulabey—"

"Abassouley," Georges said laughing from the other side of the room as he was pouring himself a large whisky.

"Hold on please," the female voice said with a Cameroonian accent.

While I waited I read the name I wrote on a piece of paper one more time.

"This is Manuel Abassouley, may I help you?" the correspondant said with a perfect Parisian accent. That man was a Cameroonian, no doubt about it, and yet he spoke with a profound voice and a beautiful French accent. Where did he come from?

"This is François Borny from the magazine *Perspectives*. I just came from Edea where I talked to Mr. Moyabe at the dam—"

"That idiot?" he cut in.

"Sorry, Sir, but he suggested I talk to you about the dam. I have to write a report for the magazine, and I'm leaving the day after tomorrow."

"I have a some information Moyabe probably doesn't have. I like your magazine, Sir, and I know you from having read a few of your articles. Especially the one you wrote on our neighbor, Nigeria. Crazy country, isn't it? And I liked your article on our country. You must have spent a lot of time in Cameroon."

"It's the first time I set foot in your country, Sir. All I wrote about I've read from a large documentation we have in Monaco."

"I think it's amazing."

"May I dare to invite you to dinner, tonight, Sir. I am at the *Cocotiers*. It will be an honor for me."

"Sorry, Mr. Borny, but we have our Independence Day tomorrow and great festivities are planned. And I'm in charge of the organization. I'm really sorry, but we might have the opportunity to do that some other time in the future."

His diction was perfect, his amiability was obvious and so was his good will. "I'm sorry too, Sir. Perhaps another time."

"Let me tell you something. The manifestation starts at ten in the morning at the Stadium of the Independence. Let me pick you up around nine thirty, as my guest."

"I'll be honored, Mr. Abassouley. Thank you very much. I'll see you in the morning." And I hung up satisfied of my whole damn day.

* * *

We had dinner with Georges in the garden of the *Cocotiers*. Good food cooked by a French chef with the means from Cameroon. Which meant huge grilled lobsters that melt in your mouth.

"You can buy those lobsters on the beach or on the road for two dollars," Georges said.

"Two dollars?"

"Yes, the kids dive four or five meters just outside the mouth of the Wouri River and bring up ten or twelve of them. All the size you have in front of you. They ignore the small one. The bottom of the river is infested with those monsters. You can see the kids on the road waving the lobsters to the passersby."

"I wish they would come to Monaco, but I guess the prices would skyrocket there."

"I'm sorry you have to leave the day after tomorrow. I had planned for your coming here, a quick trip to Maroua. Remember, the real Africa I promised to show you. Perhaps next time."

"I thank you, Georges, but I don't know if I'll ever come back here, or anywhere in Africa. The old man is dying in Monaco. Last time I saw him he didn't look too good. He has passed eighty years and he knew that the end was near. I'm going to miss the Minotaur."

"I heard that's what you called him."

"Everyone calls him that, even his son Henri. And you know what that death will mean? The company will be going to Paris. And I'm not ready to follow."

"Who wants to go to Paris?"

"Not me, but Henri can't wait. He never said a word about it but I know. He loves the capital where he bought, years ago, a beautiful apartment in the *Bois de Boulogne*. Too bad. I like working for *Perspectives*, and I like the travels. We don't know yet when the transfer will take place. Something's sure, a lot of our employees will find themselves without a job. And finding a new job in Monaco is something near impossible."

On those sad notes we got up and left the restaurant. Georges went home saying, "We'll have dinner tomorrow night, here. It's all right with you?"

"Sure." I waved my hand and climbed to the sixth floor room.

* * *

I was waiting in the lobby around nine in the morning facing the front door. I didn't know what Mr. Abassouley looked like but I assumed he had the means to recognize me though I didn't know how.

It's was not long after that I watched a Mercedes-Benz with two motorcycles escort stopping at the curb right in front of the door. A cop in full dress walked to the counter. He talked to the concierge but I couldn't hear what they were saying. It was just funny, I thought. The concierge turned his glance to me and nodded in my direction.

I had a sudden flash that must show on my face. What did I do wrong, I thought? A cop looking for me, in a foreign country. I always try to behave when I am abroad, no matter what country I am visiting.

The motorcyclist walked to me, stopped at attention about ten feet away, and gave me the most beautiful salute I've ever seen executed by military personnel. He handed me a card that I took, read, and then smiled. It was an invitation for the morning manifestation.

"The Minister wishes you to join him at the stadium," he said still standing at attention.

"Minister? What Minister?"

"Of Information, Sir. His Excellency Manuel Abassouley."

It took me a few seconds to realize the surprise that hit me right at that moment. I got on my feet a little shaking, but finally managed a smile. "I'll be honored," I said. Couldn't find another word.

"The limousine is outside." He opened the door for me and I sat behind the chauffeur.

In the stadium it was a delirious crowd. The Mercedes stopped just under what looked like the presidential tribune. A few persons were already sitting. The cop showed me the way to my seat, stood at attention, saluted and disappeared from my sight. I was the only white in the bleachers so far. In a country ruled by blacks that was normal, I thought.

The surprise of this invitation hadn't faded away yet. I was still shaking, mostly of embarrassment. I'd talked to the Minister of

Information as if he were the guy next door in an office building. Invited him to dinner as if he hadn't anything else to do but have free lunches. That idiot of Moyabe at the dam could have told me that Abassouley was the Minister of Information. The third most important person in the Republic. I was still outraged at the thought of my screw-up.

A few minutes later another Mercedes stopped at the foot of the stand. This time it had to be big shots for the car carried two National flags on the front fenders.

I was right. The President Ahmadou Ahidjo got out of the Mercedes first followed by an African in his traditional dress. He was pretty much overweight, short and bald. Both men climbed the stairs as everyone stood while the National Anthem was played by a company of Republican Guards. The President stood for a moment when he reached his seat, waved to the crowd and, finally sat down.

The little man kept standing looking around as if he were looking for someone. The someone was me. He waved, then decided to climb the five or six steps that separated my seat from his and approached extending his hand. I recognized his velvet voice as soon as he spoke. "I'm glad you could make it," he said shaking my hand.

"I apologize, your Excellency, I had no idea to whom I was speaking. I just thought you were an insignificant clerk with information I needed for my report."

He brushed the air with a wave of his hand as if it was no big deal. "We'll have lunch here today after the manifestation," he said with his stunning deep voice.

"By the way," I said, "how did you recognize me?"

He smiled. "Look around, Mr. Borny. You're the only white man."

Stupid me.

"I like your magazines. They bring a lot of hope to the African people in general and to the Cameroonians in particular. I really appreciate your company's effort to promote this continent. Let me join the President for the moment. Later, he wants to meet with you during the banquet."

Another flash of pleasure came to my face. I must have looked like a maraschino cherry.

I met the President El Hadj Ahmadou Ahidjo at the banquet that day. He was a tall man with a noble port who spoke with a heavy African accent but with moderation and intelligence. He shook my hand and said, " I like your magazine, Mr. Borny."

It was about all, but I felt a warmth run through my body.

42

The bad news was there when I landed at Nice airport. I went straight to the office with Aline. Martine was crying. "He passed away last night," she said. "Henri is at the funeral home with his wife and his son. You may join him, he said."
"I'll do that." I put my heavy briefcase down on my desk and left the office.

The funeral was already crowded. Half the population of Monaco was there. The Minotaur had spent almost his entire life in the Principality where he was well known and respected.

The tiny church of Sainte Dévote wasn't fit to accommodate those who came to pay their last respects to Paul Dunan. On the first row was the family. Henri was there with his wife, his son and his mother. Just behind were three directors of the Paris headquarters, who flew to Monaco the same morning, Alain Pelletier, a big guy with a comic strip face, an old lady, Annette Pinoche, who must not be much younger than one hundred years, and a young editor, to whom I often spoke on the telephone, wearing thick spectacles and a gray suit horribly wrinkled, whose name was Adrien Laplanche. Aline and I were next to them wondering how long they would remain in Monaco after the funeral.

* * *

The meeting took place on Monday morning at nine o'clock on the fourth floor of our office. Henri managed to say a few words in memory of his father and everyone added something that was supposed to be nice.

Then the serious business started almost right away by the representatives of the Parisian office. After a few minutes, the Minotaur was forgotten, the office in Monaco was rapidly erased from the surface of the earth, and the one hundred and ten employees in the Principality wasted as non-valuable material. They were ignored as if they hadn't ever existed.

Henri Dunan was obviously sad and didn't say a word while Alain Pelletier recalled the life of *Perspectives Publishing* praising its long-term undertaking to the sky.

There was a short pause, then Pelletier said, "We all know that the life of the company had, one day, to end in Monaco. For years we had tried to bring a new direction, a new meaning to an already successful enterprise. Our beloved Chairman of the Board had always opposed the transfer of the company to a more convenient location. He had lived in this tiny country for an entire lifetime and we understood his reluctance to move out. His son has understood the situation long ago. He's ready to move on and take the reins for the best of the company. Unfortunately we cannot afford to move everyone to Paris. A few employees will follow if they have the desire. He looked at me, waved a happy hand, then smiled. I am terribly sorry about everybody else. We are ready to move early January. "Gentlemen, good luck."

We had lunch with Henri and the three Parisian directors at the *Café de Paris*, in Monte-Carlo. Martine was there as one of the executives sent to Paris, and one of my colleagues in charge of the documentation department, Joël Maynard.

"What do you think, François?" Henri asked. "Ready to move on?"

I kept silent a minute or two, then said, "I don't believe so, Henri. If you had moved any place but Paris I might have followed you. You know my aversion for the capital." I glanced at the directors. Only the old woman winced which didn't matter to me. She was ugly anyway.

The lunch had kept in my mouth a bitter taste and the driving rain that was pouring that day didn't warm up any heart. I was forty-seven years old and for the first time in my life I was going to be out of work. Twenty-three years in the same company. It will be twenty-four when the company will be gone for good.

* * *

It didn't take too long for my wife and me to decide where to go.

On that rainy evening I came home from my office in a bad mood. Early in the morning the whole staff was told about the layoff coming up within weeks.

Only three executives amongst us were told that relocation was available in Paris. But who wants to go to Paris if not on vacation? Paris is a great city full of very interesting and exciting venues one can find only there.

But having to work in the capital was beyond my worse nightmare and, as far as I was concerned, a matter of insanity. Working two or three hours away from home, and having to deal with the Parisian transportation system which, several times a year, went on strike, was not for anyone not Parisian born, way passed a normal state of mind. I had on several occasions experienced the craziness of life in the capital. But it had always been only for a few days at a time on quick business trips. To make a sedentary life there amid a bunch of braggarts, was the last thing I wanted to do.

Besides, the layoff allowed me to have my full salary paid for the next twelve months. Which was more than enough to look for a job anywhere but Paris.

And why not America? I thought. Aline agreed. She was ready to go anywhere in the world.

So, it was indeed quickly decided. Ten minutes at the most to figure out where to go. My wife not speaking English, we decided to settle in New Orleans where, we were told, everyone there spoke French. Yeah, right.

Besides, Juliette lived there which would be helpful for foreigners like us who barely understood the tongue.

* * *

Before we decided with certainty that we really wanted to move to America, I made the trip by myself on July 5, 1978. My worry was that I wasn't sure that I could find a job. It was out of the question to resume my managing editor's charge in a country where I barely spoke the language. My only hope was that I could accept a technician position in a printing or publishing company. I'd been a photo-engraver for a few years, though on a part-time basis, but I worked in collaboration with printing companies for the last twenty-four years. I knew how printing worked, how to impose a form, how to fold correctly a press sheet, how to bind, to stitch, to make layouts. I knew how to shoot camera, make plates and make color corrections on color proofs.

It was late that day, close to midnight, when I arrived at New Orleans airport. The Air France flight from Nice was, I believed, deliberately delayed so when we got to Paris, the plane to New York was already in the air.

I said deliberately for we heard, on our arrival in the capital, that the plane to New York was overbooked at the start in Paris, so they kept the Nice flight on the ground with not a word of excuse. That was, and probably still is, a common procedure in the French company. I've heard this story oftentimes.

The following flight was only four hours later. Four hours to kill at the airport.

We arrived in New York so late that our connecting flight to New Orleans had already landed there. One more hour and we finally boarded Southwest Airline to reach my destination around midnight.
Juliette and Jeremy were there along with a few friends, some of whom I'd met at Jimmy's funeral several years before.
Juliette had prepared a little party at home though it was late. But everyone came in and it was close to three in the morning when I collapsed in a second floor room. I'd been awake for the past twenty-eight hours.

The breakfast, a few hours later was typically American: Pancakes, eggs, sausages and bacon reminded me of my first trip to Atlanta before my memorable journey to the hellish Haiti.
We had a nice chat with Juliette that morning. A long interesting conversation about America, the life in the country and the multiple opportunities that are offered to anyone who dares.
"My future in America," I said, "depends on finding a job. In France it's impossible to start a new carreer when you are forty-eight years old. Too young for retirement and too old to work. What should I do? Maybe die? That would have made it easier for the social services."
"We don't have any age limit in America," Juliette said with a smile. "One of my neighbor is ninety year old and still working as a dress maker. Another one works at MacDonald. She's seventy-seven. They don't retire people here. You work as long as you want to. There is a law in the States: no employers will ask for your age."
"I feel already younger," I said relieved.
"This morning I'm going to call a few friends. I'll be surprised if we don't find something for you. A friend of mine is married to the owner of a pretty good size printing company. I'll call her."
Next thing I knew, I had an appointment with the company owner that same morning.

Around eleven we were greeted by Mr. Johnson at his shop downtown New Orleans. His wife insisted on picking us up at Juliette's home.

An hour later and after visiting the plant and meeting with most of the employees, I had a job as a supervisor in the prep. department. And I had been in New Orleans for only twelve hours.

The interview went well. Mr. Johnson was a short man with receding blond hair, slightly bulging eyes, and a smile I learned later not to trust. But it was nice to be insured to have a job if I decided to give it a try. After thought, I didn't know what else I could do.

I stayed a week in Louisiana, seven days a little crazy. Juliette's friends organized parties every day. They all wanted to know me. Even a local newspaper wrote about my coming to America. I felt welcome, an impression I never had before. Except, perhaps, when the Minotaur hired me.

But the Minotaur wasn't there any longer. And I missed him.

When Juliette took me to the airport a week later she asked, "Do you think you are coming to America?"

"Yes, unless an unfortunate mishap, I definitely will be here with Aline and Jean-François as soon as we have our resident visa."

"I'll try to pull some strings. I know quite well one of the state senators and his wife. I'm sure he can accelerate the procedure."

"Mom would be disoriented for a while. She first lost you when you married Jimmy, and now she's going to lose me, Aline and Jean-François. She will still have Susanne, her husband and Stephanie, and her best friend Carmen. Besides, she can come to America for a visit any time she wants to. But she has her friends in her *Cour des Miracles*. After so many years in this pigsty I can't picture her away."

I returned to Monaco with all the application forms I could gather in New Orleans' Immigration Services to be filled up and submitted to the American embassy in France.

We would have to go one last time to Paris, say hello to the Eiffel Tower, to the Arc de Triomphe and to my father, his wife and Liliane, my half sister. On our way back to Monaco we would visit with Aline's father Armand and his wife Suzanne, Bernard and Gérard, her step brothers, and a few cousins, uncles and aunts scattered all over France whom we haven't seen for ages. A trip that would take a week.

It would be a last round for a last farewell for I don't believe we would be back in a country where I lived for almost forty-eight years, where my children and my first granddaughter were born.

I was a little bitter, of course, after all those years where I knew happiness and where my life had been rolling smoothly, mainly since I'd met Aline. We shall see, I thought.

We had our resident visas in two days in Paris after we had a serious physical checkup by an American embassy appointed doctor. Juliette had effectively pulled some strings in New Orleans as she had promised.

We could have left France that same day, but we still had business to do before leaving definitely France and Monaco. Pay taxes for instance, and sell our belongings with the exception of some memorabilia we couldn't leave behind. A big wooden box would be filled up to the top and sent to New Orleans before we even left France. It was September 1978 and we gave ourselves three months to start our new life in America.

But I was wrong when I thought that the trip to Paris was the last one. The following month I had a phone call from Liliane. Dad had passed away in the morning of a heart attack. He was eighty-two. We left Jean-François with Mom and flew to Paris for the funeral.

On December 20, 1978, Aline, Jean-François and I, boarded a TransWorld Airline flight in Nice to Geneva, New York and New

Orleans. Sixteen long hours over part of Europe and over the Atlantic.

43

As our plane descended smoothly in the darkening New York Airport, I leaned against the back of my seat, closed my eyes and had a retrospective thought about the life we had left behind in Monaco.

I believed I've had a decent existence so far. I tried to always do my best and remain an honest human being.

Perhaps the first ten or twelve years of my life had been a little disorderly for war had struck us and driven everything upside down.

And then, life began after the war, though Dad had forgotten to share his with us. I met Aline, Mom had a good job, Juliette got married and, seemingly, had a nice life until her widowhood. And I was the luckiest man in the world when I married Aline.

We had a daughter and a son and a granddaughter and all was perfect. Or almost.

Yes indeed, I thought I've had a very decent life.

"You're thinking about what we left behind, of Susanne and Stephanie," Aline said. It wasn't a question but a statement for she knew where my thinking was dragging me.

I opened my eyes and she was staring at me with her beautiful green eyes. That lady has such an acute sixth sense that often amazes me. She can read my mind so easily it, sometimes, scares me.

"Yes, of our life to that very same day, Darling. We've been happy, I believe, haven't we?"

"Yes, Love, happy to that very same day," she repeated after me.

Susanne, our daughter and Stephanie, our only granddaughter, accompanied us to Nice Airport. What was going to happen to them?,

I thought. They had a family, of course, but a bit of friction had developed when we saw Jackie and Susanne last together. My son-in law was most of the time traveling around the globe with Demis Roussos that fat, tall, ugly Greek singer with his rasping voice. Wasn't fun for Susanne and Stephanie. And money wasn't plethora either.

"We have left our daughter and granddaughter, but I'm sure they'll be all right," I said holding Aline's hand.

"You were thinking the same thing. I'm not sure they'll be all right. Susanne hadn't looked very happy lately and Stephanie is only fourteen months old."

"We'll think about something," I said as the plane hit the runway.

It was already dark and very cold in the Big Apple, and noisy, and frightening. Too many nervous people there who reminded me of Paris, the city I love but where I wouldn't like to live for all the gold in the world.

After thought, I wouldn't like to live in New York either. Too big a city, too active. My tranquil life in Monaco, where I used to stroll from home to my office, never got me used to that kind of feverish nervousness. I was a quiet man in a quiet village —as long as there were no bells tolling every night— who moved slowly at the rhythm of the seasons. I was not sure New Orleans would be as quiet and peaceful as Monaco, but we had taken things into consideration long before we exposed ourselves to our new home.

Too late to back up, too late to change our minds.

We managed to get out of the plane in a general melee, and found ourselves in a huge hall divided into tiny cubicles where we were shown one family at the time.

Around Christmas 1978, the Immigration Service in New York was awfully crowded. Was it the regular time for migrants to show up at the American cities or was it just a coincidence? Whatever it was, we had somehow a mild feeling of uneasiness in the middle of the throng.

We were interviewed one family at the time. Our agent was an amiable black guy who never stopped smiling, asking questions, more by curiosity I thought, about our life in France and why we had chosen to come to the States. He spoke a little French and was obviously proud to show how much he had learned in high school.

It took some time before we could walk out of the cubicle. The vast room, we had to cross to get to the gate, was crammed with luggage, kids, people, old and many looking sick. There were hundreds of immigrants, just like us, waiting for their turn to go through the formalities, their heads full of hope and fright.

Depressing, but we had made the choice several months ago when we decided to immigrate to the United States. And it would be inappropriate to complain about it. Aline was exhausted and so were Jean-François and I. The agent released us with a handshake and a nice and sympathetic *Welcome to America*.

It took a few hours to move on, go to TransWorld Airline counter, change to the next airport, and board a Southwest Airline plane to our final destination.

In New Orleans we found out, when we arrived around midnight, that none of our luggage had followed us from New York. We just had two handbags that, if we were lucky, will allow us to brush our teeth and have a quick cleanup. On the following nights, always at two in the morning, a taxi driver rang at Juliette's home and delivered our three pieces of luggage.... one at a time. That for three nights in the row. I always wondered why at two o'clock.

It was eighty-five degrees at the airport, unusual temperature so close to Christmas. Everyone at Kenner was in summer dress: shorts, T-shirts and thongs. We had left Nice on a gorgeous day but the temperatures were only in the forties.

"That is a sudden change," I told Juliette who was waiting at the airport with Jeremy and a few friends of hers who had shared with her good moments as well as bad.

"That's really unusual," she said, "but don't count on that nice weather to last. Winter is here around the corner. You better be prepared for temperatures in the twenties."

Juliette drove through Kenner's streets and then through Metairie to the home I came to at Jimmy's wake. Most of the houses were brightly illuminated with thousands of lights giving the streets a magical aspect of Disney Land. I had never seen such an exhibition of colors, of lights and even of music. People strolled by in groups stopping in front of houses displaying scenes of Christmas and scenes of religious devotion.

Before we got home we were already deep in the Christmas spirit and we were in America only for a few hours. What an extraordinary feeling. "That's America," Juliette said, then smiled.

In Europe we don't give such an importance to the holiday season, and it's too bad. I believe people's behavior changes at that time. At least it should. It's an opportunity to see the world from another angle without acrimony and resentment.

We felt at peace by this calm and serene night. Monaco and Nice were already way back in our thoughts as if we had left part of our soul thousands of miles away with no intention to bring those missing pieces of ourselves in our new country. We'll start over with a brand new one.

The small party Juliette had organized was quickly dismissed. We found ourselves alone, a little out of tune with those last hours spent over half the world. Juliette had prepared two comfortable rooms for us on the second floor.

We were still a little out of sorts, like if we weren't really here, when we got up the next morning. Juliette had prepared a huge breakfast that awaken Aline and me. We went down to the kitchen filled with the wonderful aroma of coffee.

"Saturday," Juliette said, "we're having a party to introduce you to my friends. Mr. Johnson, your future employer, and his wife will be here. He's desperately waiting for you to take over, he told me when I talked to him last week."

"I'm ready," I said. "I certainly want to get things going. No time to waste."

"However, we have a few priorities," Aline said. "First, we have to find an apartment."

"That's not a problem. There is a nice apartment building down Houma Boulevard. There are always vacancies. It would be about ten miles from your job downtown."

I caught myself thinking of the apartment building rue Mirabeau, the infamous *Cour des Miracles*.

"And we have to buy a car," I added. "We can afford to pay cash."

"You don't want to do that. You have to build a line of credit, and it won't be in paying for everything in cash that you're going to have one. Besides, you need credit cards and as a new comer in this part of the world, this might be a little more difficult. But we have an appointment with my banker tomorrow."

Juliette had prepared our coming to America very meticulously. Everything she had in mind was ready for the beginning of 1979. "I guess you'll start your new job on January 2nd. You still have a week to organize your life to take off."

"We'll also need some furniture to fill up the apartment we are going to rent."

"I have an idea about that. America is great for these kind of receptions. We organize what we call a shower and all our friends bring something that could be useful. You will have to buy two beds. I'll provide the sheets. Saturday, at the party, people will come with more articles than you'll be using for the next five years."

The following day we accompanied Juliette to the bank. An hour later we had a Visa credit card. "That was easy," I said to the owner of the bank.

"Not always that easy," he replied with a smile, "but Mrs. Gunn has her entries in this bank."

Next thing was the car. That was almost as easy. In the middle of the afternoon I was the owner of a second hand Buick Skylark. It was a big car for me who used to drive a minuscule Morris Cooper in Monaco.

"Now," I said, "I guess I need a driver's license."

"Yes, but you can drive with your French license for a month. Then you'll need an American one. I'll call a friend of mine to make it easier. The next morning Juliette took us to the Louisiana Department of Public Safety in Slidel, a few miles across Lake Ponchartrain. That was where another friend, a policewoman, worked. We were introduced, had our pictures shot, and were given a temporary license.

Everything seemed to be simple, effortless. It was a good thing I had a sister in that country.

* * *

Juliette was right. Two days after our arrival, as we prepared for the party, we had to go buy some winter clothes we had never used in Monaco. It was freezing in the low twenties. The cold fell on our shoulders like an icy shroud. And, in the meantime, the wind got into the winter party. I don't remember ever living anywhere under those North Pole temperatures.

Monaco is far from being that cold. The Principality is surrounded by mountains: the foothills of the Alps that wrap the town and work like a shield from the northern cold. So, it exists in that tiny country a microclimate that allows the temperatures to remain in the mid-forties even on the coldest days. Seldom does the thermometer pass below the freezing level. I had in memory only two, or perhaps three, exceptional occasions when it snowed in Monaco. And no one understood where that snow came from. However, it was funny to play in the streets making snowballs the size of marbles. There is an Exotic Garden in Monte-Carlo whose plants and flowers bloom year around. Five miles away, those same plants wouldn't last a month. And you better be prepared for winter.

* * *

It was a great party. Sixty or seventy people showed to get in a crammed house. Juliette's friends arrived hands full. They packed everything they brought in the garage that first had been cleared for the occasion.
The food was typical American, so I learned later. There was some cooking I'd never seen or heard of before, like sweet beans, ham cooked in honey, carrot cake, devil eggs that had nothing devilish besides a good taste, and a cake thick as a house slab with ten inches of delicious and fattening whipping cream. It was a first for Aline, Jean-François and me. And we loved it. We ate until our skinny bodies were filled up with ham, beans, potato salad and a portion of cake large enough to support a couple of ice-skaters on the top. Mentally I compared Mom's cuisine and smirked. Her Canard à l'Orange or her Coq au Vin, though the finest food, would be merely appetizers here, and you would have to ingurgitate half a dozen of each to eat one's fill. Another year of that diet and I was sure we would have to buy another scale to accommodate our new weight.
I'd heard that, coming from Europe in general, and from France in particular, it would take a while to grow the needed taste for that American food. Well, sorry, but I'd grown a sudden crave for fried chicken, onion rings, hot dogs and other ugly hamburgers after I'd

tasted those unsophisticated, but how delicious, concoctions.

When everyone reluctantly left around one in the morning, we went to the garage. We could barely walk through it. There were tables, cabinets, chandeliers, chairs, a sofa, a small refrigerator, a color TV set, and cardboards of chinaware, glassware, linen, a bicycle, a wheelbarrow, and a huge wooden box of kitchen utensils. Juliette smiled as we looked stunned at those riches.

"I knew my friends would respond to my invitation. But not in such a manner. I don't believe you will have to buy much to start your new life," Juliette said.

We were dumbfounded. How people could be so generous. In Juliette's garage was a small fortune.

"Now," I said, "We have to find that apartment we talked about to put all this in so you can park your car and your boat."

"We'll go next week. Tell your new friends at the shop you are going to move. You don't have to say more. The whole printing company will show up with more trucks than you need.

We found an apartment on Houma and we moved the following Saturday. A dozen trucks made the trip in one round. At mid-morning all the furniture was in place and ready to be used the same day.

I had to get used to that American spirit, a spirit I never had experienced in my whole life in France or anywhere else in the world where selfishness is rather commonplace.

I learned very quickly that grudging isn't an American state of mind. That took me back to Jack Mallburn I'd met in Nigeria. The champagne salesman had stunned me in more than one way. I thought that was unique for an American. It isn't.

* * *

"You have a home, or at least an apartment for now before you buy a house," Juliette said when she visited with me for the first time in my new home.

"The American dream?" I said.

"Yes, that's the American dream, François. Anyone in this country is entitled to such a dream. You work hard, you follow the rules of society, and you live according to the human rights you acquired when you went through the gates of the Immigration Services of the United States of America, and you will be living like an American."

"Give me a year and I'll have my home."

"It might take a little longer, but don't get desperate. Take your time, that will happen."

We walked Juliette down our apartment unit to her car. "What are you going to do first?" she asked, "besides starting your job."

First we had to learn the language, I thought.

That was a must though we could communicate with Mexicans, Colombians and other Latinos with our almost perfect Spanish.

However, I could find my way through that new world with my broken English but not Aline. She would have to work twice as hard. And she was ready.

We thought that French was largely spoken in this state since our ancestors came from Canada long ago, carrying their language.

But, it wasn't. Yet, I went several times in South Louisiana, on the Gulf of Mexico, and met with the descendants of the Acadians who came down in 1755. They still speak a good, perfect French with an accent that resembles present day Quebec's inflection but with a curious eighteenth century vocabulary that had disappeared from France two centuries ago. One calls them Cajuns which, I believe, is a degeneration of the word Acadian. A professor at Tulane University confirmed that for me.

So, after some consideration, people here not speaking French, there wasn't another solution for my wife but to learn, and for me to improve my knowledge of the darn language I wrongly thought I had mastered long ago. One more time: yeah, right.

I heard once a friend of mine from Texas saying that Louisianans couldn't speak English either. I don't believe that.

I've been asked several times since I lived in the Unites States, where I came from. When I replied France I was told that they thought I was from Louisiana. I wondered if it was because of my horrible accent or my broken English. "I hope," I always replied, "that Louisianans speak better English than I do."

"No!" had been the spontaneous and unanimous cry.

Common friends, give me a break. I am sorry but I've met people in New Orleans, Baton Rouge, and some places else too in Louisiana, who were distinguished scholars to whom I would like to apologize for the unkind remarks of non-Louisianans.

This being said, it's true that one cannot find many people who speak French in New Orleans, besides, of course, the French expatriated who are about five thousands, most of them working at the French Consulate, running a restaurant or a bakery.

So, one choice was left to us: learn the mandatory English.

Once this was figured out we decided, Aline and I, to attend the English Second Language School where we learned mostly.... Spanish. Evidently those classes were intended for Spanish speaking people from Mexico and South America, and the teachers spoke more the Latin language than English.

As I knew Spanish, and so did Aline, we didn't care much about wasting our time in that school. We changed our minds and tried a different approach to that elusive tongue. We enrolled at Berlitz School of Languages where we happily started to study. Yes! Italian. There were no French-speaking teachers available and the closest a Latin language could be to French was Italian.

This was definitely discouraging, we thought. If we had intended to learn Italian we would have gone to Rome, and if Spanish were our particular objective, we would have stay in Madrid when I met Aline and where she had a terrific job.

But none of those otherwise beautiful languages was our goal. So, we enrolled at Robert E. Lee College night class for the mentally retarded students.

For the following months we struggled, endured our friends' sarcasms, were ready to give up, and finally succeeded in learning the English alphabet and to count up to twenty. I could count a little higher but I didn't want to brag.

It was already an improvement, I thought. That wasn't quite true for me, but it was for Aline who couldn't speak a word of English when we disembarked from the TransWorld plane in New York.

As for our son, Jean-François, he attended the tenth grade at Rummels High School with no major problems except in the French class where he earned an *F*. I jumped on my feet, checked his copy but couldn't find any mistake of grammar or syntax. Curious that *F*. I went to talk to the teacher.

She was a pretty young lady from Cuba to whom I spoke French when I was introduced. I was befuddled when I found out that she couldn't speak a word of French. How in the world, I asked her, can one teach a language that she or he doesn't know?

We have tapes, was the reply, and we check the answers with what we have on tape.

"Did it not occur to you," I gently asked, "that there are dozens of ways to say the same thing. That happens in Spanish or in English and, I know, in any language of the world."

She was first embarrassed. She apologized, blushed and promised to change the grade into an *A*. Which she never did.

It took Aline and I another six months to dare to draw into the GED exam.

And, of course, as soon as we hung our diplomas on the wall of our vestibule —so everyone coming in could see them— we knew we had finally mastered that language someone once called English.

We ran to our neighbor —who by the way was from London— and started showing off our newly acquired linguistic knowledge. He was obviously pleased and, as he laughed, he said with his inimitable British accent, "Oh yes, sure, that's pretty good, Bloke, but that's American."

* * *

We lived almost a year and a half in Metairie, working in downtown New Orleans before we decided it was time for us to move on. Mr. Johnson's smile had changed into a smirk and the smirk into a sneer. Besides, there were a few promises that weren't kept. But I learned that this was his way to treat employees. Everybody wasn't the Minotaur.

I was entitled to a week vacation that gave us some time to think about our future while we were driving towards Florida for a first visit. We stopped at Fort Lauderdale, rented a room in a motel, and spent five days on the beach which we had missed since we had left Monaco.

"I'm saving one day of my vacation days to go to Houston," I told Aline. "John Sellers, you remember him, he used to work for me at Johnson's printing, went to Houston. He said that the shop he works for is looking for a supervisor in the prep. department."

"When did you talk to John?"

"The day before we left on vacation. He came by the shop to say hello. His father-in-law is a French Canadian and is the plant manager in one of the most important printing companies in Texas. Salary there is almost twice as much as in Louisiana."

"Are you kidding?"

"Nope, John swears that, besides, he says, the cost of living is less than in New Orleans. I'm going to give it a try."

We had a wonderful time in Florida. We rented a small boat, bought some fishing reels and some tackles, and went fishing not aware that in America we need a fishing license even for the ocean. In France there is no permit for fishing in the sea, but as there are no fish in the Mediterranean it would be a robbery to charge any taxes.

We got away with that in a candid fashion and learned only some time later that the fine for fishing without license is more expensive than to buy part of the fish market in Fort Lauderdale.

Aline had never had a reel in her hand and never before had she watched with such pleasure, a fish wriggling at the end of the hook.

We returned to New Orleans in good shape and ready to start over a new year of work.

I took the first flight to Houston on Friday morning at six, landed at Hobby Airport, and rode a taxi straight to see my friend John Seller and his Canadian father-in law.

The plant was a large one with, I thought at the time, at least two hundred employees working in shifts twenty-four hours a day. I talked to the big man and found myself with a new job after a half hour meeting. My salary was decided right away. John was right. It was nice to hear the figures. Aline would be proud of me.

"I'll be here in two weeks," I said to John. "Let me give my notice and I'll be back in Houston."

Jean-François' school was almost out for summer. The next year he would be in Houston.

Two weeks later I left Aline and Jean-François in New Orleans and looked for an apartment the closest I could from work, which meant twelve miles. The apartment was larger than the one we had in Houma

Boulevard and twenty-five percent cheaper. John was right again. More money and better cost of living.

We had a last dinner with Juliette and a few friends at Antoine. It was a nice au-revoir, but Houston is only six hours away from Metairie.

On May 15th, 1980, seventeen months after our arrival in Louisiana, I rented a U-Haul truck, stacked in our belongings, hooked our Skylark on the back, and drove to Houston with Aline and Jean-François.

At that point another life had begun, but we weren't yet conscious. Starting there, it seemed that the events had moved really fast. Houston lived twenty-four hours a day. No time out here. Most of the days we worked ten to twelve hours, made good money but hadn't much time for anything else.

My son attended one of the best high schools in Texas: Saint Thomas, which was expensive but, we found out later, was worth every penny.

On weekends, when I didn't work, we would go around the city to look for a house. We found one, near Lake Houston in a woody area we liked.

We waited to have a little more money, put a down payment, and bought the home we're still living in to this day. It was June 1980. We moved in our new home five months later on November 4th.

* * *

My new job was gripping but not easy. More work than I thought I could handle in a way I had to learn. John Seller had told me that Houston was something else. You have to follow or leave it. We liked Houston, our new home, my job, and it's there that we met our friends: Bob and Nancy Adamski, Aida and Alec Dyer, Cecilia and

Gus Lansang, among them, and my golf partner and best friend, Ray McKinney with whom I'd been working for fourteen years before I retired.

Jean-François graduated from Saint Thomas High School and enrolled at Texas A & M University, one hundred and five miles from home. For the next four years we would visit College Station almost every week.

Meanwhile Aline kept learning English, thanks to the Soap Operas she watched on TV an hour a day. That usually made men smirk, but I have to concede that the results were terrific. She rapidly could communicate with any one, on the telephone, at the grocery, so well that I let her do the talking wherever we went. She ran the house as she did in Monaco with the same easiness and the same dedication.

But news from France wasn't too good.

That was the first letter we received from Susanne for a while. Things were not doing very well in Monaco. She was struggling into a messy divorce with Jackie with all the drama that such disunion could create.

We called Susanne at work and told her to get over with the divorce and come straight to America. We'll fix everything than can be fixed here. We are American residents and you are our daughter.

* * *

Susanne and Stephanie arrived on American soil on May 1982 after a bitter divorce as divorces can be. They were confused, frightened, and a little disoriented, but happy to be here with us for better or for worse. Another page of our life had turned over.

We had been missing our daughter and granddaughter for the past three and a half years. Now we were going to make up for the time that had passed by.

I found a job for Susanne with my company. We rented a small apartment in Crosby where they could live close to us but still on their own. Stephanie began school without speaking a word of English. Susanne managed to find her way with what remained of her high school English.

We drove to work and back home together, and little by little she built up her new life. Stephanie started speaking English and forgetting French. She was six.

44

December 20th, 1983. Christmas break. It was a gorgeous day though very cold in Crosby, Texas. The yards around the houses looked pitiful in this freezing winter.

Aline woke up first, as she always did, brought me a cup of coffee in bed and said. "Five years today we're in America."

It was true. I only forgot that five years ago we were standing frightened in front of those cubicles at New York Immigration Services. Five years already. God! Where did the time go?

Jean-François came to our room, a glass of orange juice in his hand. "Five years today," he said with a smile. "What should we do?"

My son always wanted do something when not in school. Texas A & M was closed for the holidays and I could have a few days off if I asked.

"Let's go to Florida," he said.

"Why not." I smiled.

"Or Mexico," Aline offered. "Cozumel, for instance, is an hour and a half away. From the rigor of the winter to the warmth of the Caribbean. One problem though."

"What's that?"

"What about Susanne and Stephanie?"

"Don't you worry about them. Susanne met a very nice man and she doesn't seem to get bored."

"You know much more than you let on. Tell us. What's going on?"

I laughed. You know Larry Chancey. He came to the party we gave for Susanne's homecoming."

"Yes, I know Larry, of course. He's a divorcee who lives a block and a half away. What happened to him?"

"I think they are seeing each other, though I'm not quite sure."

"Well, That's good news. Larry seems to be a very decent man. Let's talk to Susanne. You know our daughter can't lie. She might want to stay here while we go to Cozumel."

"Right. Let's talk to her.

Jean-François listened for a moment, smiled and agreed about Larry. "All right, what about our vacation?"

"You have a deal," I replied. "We'll spend some days in that paradise. But, I have another suggestion when we return from Mexico."

"And what would that be?" Aline asked laughing. "I know you. You always have an idea in the back of your head."

"As soon as we're back from Cozumel, we'll apply for the American citizenship. We had to wait five years for eligibility. We are now eligible. January first will be the beginning of our sixth year."

It took several trips to the Immigration Services, and about a year before we were through with the formalities. We were summoned one morning, interviewed by a nice lady, and were told that we would be called some time in the following weeks to pledge allegiance to the American flag and become citizens.

On April 15th, 1985, the Borny family became Americans. When I returned to work that morning, I found a huge cake with an American flag on top and the word *Congratulations*. That was nice from my employer. We had a quick party with champagne and a lot of hugs.

* * *

Mom's letter arrived the day following the naturalization. Surprisingly it was a thick letter. Mom never wrote much, nor often. Just a few lines, always the same: miss you; wish I were there, kisses and love.

I recognized my mother's shaking scribble on the envelope and smiled. I hadn't written to her in a while. I had to take care of that.

Inside was another letter that made my eyebrows rise. It was stamped from Madrid, Spain, and addressed to me in Nice, rue Mirabeau. It was a letter from José de Escobar, son of Filomena, Aline and I had met on my first trip to Spain. That was long ago. Thirty-seven years I believed, when I was a young graduate from high school. Spain was so far away in my mind.

I read the letter evidently written by Jacqueline, José's Parisian wife. Her regular feminine handwriting, her words typical Parisian, and even her dark humor showed through the first lines. Filomena, she wrote, had passed away on Christmas Day.

What a bad idea to die on Christmas Day, I thought. But Filomena was unique in everything she did, even in dying, and probably over eighty years old. Her life had been but a succession of wonderment and joy mixed with sadness and worries.

She liked wine and songs and friends. She had enjoyed her existence among people, people whom she had cherished, people she had chosen around her. The reason she had picked me up in the crowd, that day at Port-Bou, had always been a mystery to me. Yes, I know, I've been told that I looked just like Mariano, her dead son. But, was it the only reason? I believed she had too big of a heart not to share it. She did it with me, but also with Robert and André, those two Parisians I met in her company some time in 1948.

I've seen Filomena crying in despair, laughing with happiness like a child a minute later, but always giving everyone around her the warmth of her presence.

Filomena had lived the life she had chosen, said the letter. She had given everyone she met part of her contentment and joy as well as part of herself.

"She was such a great lady," Aline said.

"José and Jacqueline have taken over Filomena's businesses. They have left Paris not to return."

José wrote, "Our mother's last words were that she was at last, to meet up with her son Mariano."

I could see closing my eyes, as in a silent movie, a series of images parading in front of me where Filomena held the main lead. That first encounter in Port-Bou, Spain, when the fat lady sat on my only piece of luggage in front of the dumbfounded Spanish custom agents, her gorgeous voice when she sang in the restaurant car surrounded by dozens of amazed travelers. The wedding of her daughter Maria Teresa in the little village of Chinchón was the highlight of our first meeting.

We returned to Spain and met with Filomena again and again, and always with a great pleasure that never declined.

I had a glance at Mom's letter. It was indeed unusually thick. Pictures had been enclosed and Mom had written much longer than she ever did. The first picture I held in my hand was an old black and white photograph of Dad and Alphonse Renard, his war companion. They were unshaved, rather besmeared, each holding an old French rifle Mousqueton. I turned the picture over and read: *1943, Alphonse and me in a farm above Lantosque waiting for the parachuting of armament from our American friends.* I gave the photo to Aline and checked another. It was Dad, Mom and I at the beach in 1942. I was twelve. Aline looked at it but could not recognize me though she identified Mom right away. There were a few more pictures with Alphonse, Dad, Mom and Juliette.

I finally read Mom's letter. It was a long one by Mom's standards. A whole page of small, trembling writing with misspelled words and almost undecipherable sentences like only Mom could generate.

It was another sad letter, the second on the same day. Mom wrote:

our friend Alphonse Renard passed away a week ago. The hospital called me for he had no one to be called upon. I didn't even know he was ill. I spent an hour with him in his room. He was smiling the whole time I was there, making jokes to which I had to laugh with no joy. We talked about the war, of course, the bad times but also the good times when your father was still living with us.

He reminded me of the family reunions where he always found the way to tell us an excerpt of his life. It was a crazy existence he had led, he conceded, but also an interesting and sometimes dangerous one. I always liked to spend hours listening to him. He was a funny man, a womanizer, a drunk, but such a good friend. He was eighty-two when he died without anyone around him besides me. I know we were his only family.

I would like to see you all, Mom said to end the letter. I'm a little lonely on rue Mirabeau since everyone is dead or gone to the Americas. Only my friend Carmen remains faithful. She spends a lot of time with me saying that I'm too old to live by myself. She might be right. I'll be eighty-five the last day of the year. Carmen stays home a few days, and then returns to her daughter to show up again the following week. I'm glad I have her. She's a good companion.

"That was a long letter," Aline said. "We have to send her a round trip ticket as soon as possible."

We had done just that when we returned from Cozumel. Mom visited us in August and stayed home for the following six weeks. We went to New Orleans to see Juliette where Mom spent a couple of weeks before we went to pick her up and sent her back to France where she really belonged. The Cour des Miracles was her world as long as I remembered.

We had a real family reunion before she left, a reunion where Larry Chancey appeared for the first time with Susanne. We officially met him just there though we knew him as a neighbor for years. He was the most likable man Susanne had ever met. Mom liked him and we liked him and Stephanie liked him and I knew for sure that Susanne liked him.

They got married in June of that same year in a little city in East Texas, Jacksonville.

It was not long after, that Cody, my only grandson among six grandchildren, was born.

Larry had the bad idea to introduce me to golf. Early on Sunday morning we would go to the course and hacked balls for a few hours cursing every damn golf ball, every club I brought with me, and every hole full of sand they call bunkers. As for the holes on the greens, they are way too small.

When I retire, I swore, I was going to learn that awful game and I will play golf every day. Twice.

Yeah! Right. That much for learning after all those years of retirement. The bunkers still have sand and the holes didn't get bigger.

45

Juliette called me a morning in January. Mom had just passed away. She was ninety-three. It was a bad news we all expected sooner or later. Carmen found her one morning. She was lying in her bed as if asleep. She had not been ill, never went to the hospital and I don't recall her ever going to the doctor.

We flew the next day to Nice where we arrived in time for the funeral. Mom had had a long life, unfortunately not the best one, but she never complained about her solitude and her miserable existence with my father.

She was the matriarch of our family. A page was turned forever. Now we were only orphans and the only remains were a tombstone with an enamel picture in a small cemetery on the French Riviera.

We returned to Houston thinking with Aline about retirement. I might consider it.

I couldn't wait to be sixty-five to retire. I was tired of the daily routine that had lasted now a life long. But sixty-five wasn't the right age for me. I just waited, I never knew why, until my sixty-eighth birthday, in December 1998, to take the bull by the horns and gave up all my professional activities. Or so I thought.

This was, I heard later, what all the retirees said of their after-work life. Well, twenty-four hours a day are not sufficient to do whatever we had in mind for years. We always find something unusual to do, something we had never done before. For me it was the building of a covered patio. I never had a hammer or a screwdriver, or a circular saw in my hands. With Aline we had done all that since I retired without knowing the simple rules of carpentry, alignment, plumb line, water level, but with courage and will, and numerous credit cards. We had built a patio, then, one thing leading to another, a sun deck, and a second one. We dug a big hole in our courtyard and filled it with water, plants and fish.

Our house turned out to be beautiful, from the front yard to the last feet of the back, through the center court. And all this thanks to Aline who had developed in the past years an undeniable taste and talent for gardening.

"Remember," she told me once, "Don Ricardo Delmonte's home in Barcelona? Our friend the Spanish banker had the most beautiful house I had ever seen at that time. And I told you that that was the kind of house I wanted."

"I remember," I said with a chuckle. "But ours isn't quite as beautiful."

"It is to me," she said faking anger.

Actually, it was, and still is, a very nice home. There isn't a greenhouse with exotic flowers in the back garden, there is no servant named Francisco serving refreshments close to the swimming pool for there is no swimming pool, and there isn't that vast front yard with the fountain surmounted with two winged cherubs each holding a lyre.

But it's our house, the home we had built little by little during the last twenty-three years with heart and a lot of love.

* * *

It didn't take too long for Jean-François to marry Rita Lowe, a nice young lady obviously in love with our son. Four girls were born from that union of whom two are twins. Samantha, Serina, and Katarina and Katrina —the twins.

Susanne and Larry went on vacation in the Bahamas with a stopover, on their way back, in Melbourne Beach, Florida, where accidentally, they bought a motel-restaurant just passing by.

They moved to Florida a few months later, but Larry kept his business in Texas, which makes him travel back and forth to Houston at least once a month and visit with us.

January 6, 2001. Stephanie wedded her college sweetheart, Lanny Dunham. Aline's stepbrother, Gérard Fondeville and his wife Danny came from France for the wedding. They loved America almost as much as we love it and, I'm sure, they would be ready to immigrate if we insist just a little.

* * *

On January 7th, 2002, Crosby Community Center opened to the public. It's a vast building surrounded with greenery and flowers neatly manicured, next to the post office and the library, and it's managed by a very competent Director, Marty Pipes, an adorable smiling lady open to any suggestions for the sole benefit of the center. A team of employees, with the help of over two hundred volunteers, help her run the center.

One can do almost anything there: learn German, Spanish, bridge, painting, cooking, dance, and much more. I offered to teach French once a week which brought a few more people. That was fun.

This was where I met Matra Kreig, a young English teacher, head of the English Department at Hargrave High School in Huffman, a few miles away from Crosby.

Matra had a class of creative writing for some time when I found out by a stroke of luck that we could also learn English. What I needed the most. I decided then to attend the class, at least once to evaluate my knowledge. That didn't go too far, but it was fascinating to me. So many things I didn't know about the language —and still don't know— so many rules to learn that I was struck by the easiness Matra put in, explaining the why and the what and the how, giving examples, reading to the class excerpts of great writers and analyzing each line, each word in such a simple way.

I still recalled the first assignment Matra gave to the class. Homework that was: *Write a childhood memory.*

We all wrote something. My story, a four-page manuscript, was an account of World War II in France during the German occupation. We all read our work in class, answered the questions asked by the other students and developed a kind of fraternity among us.

Matra listened religiously to all the reading and said to me, "I wish I knew more of that story."

"I can write some more if you like."

"I can't wait to read the sequel."

That was what prompted this work, but when I started I had no idea what I was going to write about and where I was going to start. I didn't know that I could remember so many things about my childhood. Strangely memories came back to me, memories I thought I had erased from my mind for a long time. How wrong I was!

Matra Kreig read a good portion of my writing. She was the one who encouraged me to continue and to propose the book to an editor, or at least to an agent. "But first learn English, for Christ sake," she said.

I wrote to a publisher, Heritage Books in Maryland, who gently answered me within three or four weeks of sending my manuscript.

I'm finishing my work now. A few more pages and I'll be ready to read it over and send my first draft to Ms. Leslie Wolfinger, Publishing Director at Heritage Books. I hope she'll like it. Everyone else who read it told me they enjoyed it. Unless it's sheer politeness.

In August 2002, I had a call home from Matra Kreig, around seven in the evening. Hargrave High School had just lost its French teacher and school was to resume on the 19th with a French class, a few students, and no one to teach. "Would you be interested with the job?"

she asked.

"Sure. Might be fun."

I talked to the principal, Mr. Robert Schnuriger the next morning about replacing the defective teacher. Within minutes I was hired for the duration of 2002-2003 school year.

It has been beyond the fun, beyond what I had known before. I was almost surprised by the welcome of everyone at school. I was a little lost in that huge crowd, not knowing where to start, where to go, and what to do. A lovable lady, Janie Webster, head of the foreign languages department, spent long hours with me, helping with everything from the way to teach, how to grade the students, and, mostly, how to get through the mandatory paper work on the computer.

I could turn in any direction and have some help by, I noticed right away, a very busy personnel. Jane Snead, Barbara Cates and Martha Quaid, all of them ready to stop what they were doing to do what I was supposed to do but didn't know how. Many thanks to all of you.

On November 2002, Matra Kreig asked me to be the guest speaker at the commemoration of Veterans Day. Captain Nelson, of the JROTC, organized the celebration.

It was a great honor to be asked and, of course, I accepted, not knowing yet what to say.

That ended up to be one of the most unforgettable memories of my life.

For fifteen minutes or so, I talked to about a thousand students, teachers and World War II veterans, a speech I improvised according to the memories I still had from my childhood.

Aline was in the front row, and I could tell that she had tears in her eyes. It was with a broken voice that I ended my speech.

But what happened next was something I will never forget. The whole audience got on their feet and I had the most emotional ovation

I ever experienced.

* * *

On February 27th, 2003, Stephanie's baby boy was born. He's our first, and probably for a while our last great-grandson, Ethan Dunham. That was the last of the good things that happened to us this year.

In a few weeks it will be twenty-five years that Aline, Jean-François and I disembarked from a TransWorld Airline on a cold and scary night in New York.

We have lived a life of peace and happiness. For a long time now the magnificent country we have chosen to live in no longer frightens us. I don't recall many bad memories since we've been here, no major problems we wouldn't have anywhere else in the world, had we made the choice to stay in France.

And thinking way back through my childhood, if that day on the beach at Nice I hadn't met Jimmy Gunn, Juliette wouldn't have met him, married him and come to America dragging us, one by one.

We came three of us first, then Susanne and Stephanie followed, and a few years later our family had increased to fourteen, each one of us being adopted by the families our children married. On a normal Thanksgiving Day reunion at Jean-François's home, we're usually around forty people.

Coming to America is the best thing we have ever done in our life. Not once, not ever, did we regret our choice. For the last twenty-five years we have been a happy family living among a happy people.

The American people.

François Borny
Crosby, TX
September 2003.

EPILOG

On March 15, 2003, I woke up in the morning around six, as I usually do, and went to the dinette where a smell of coffee dragged me. Aline had prepared the breakfast as she has done for the last forty-eight years. But what an awful surprise when I tried to say good morning. My voice was gone and only remained a hoarse tone coming from the back of my throat.

"What's wrong with your voice today," Aline said kissing me good morning.

"Don't know," I complained. I reminded her that happened to me forty-nine years ago when I first met her in Spain. But it wasn't that bad and it lasted only two days.

We waited the next morning to call Dr. Hawkins, our family physician in Baytown.

Two days later we were in the waiting room at San Jacinto Hospital. Dr. Hawkins and his adorable nurse Suzy checked on me but couldn't find anything wrong. However, the doctor said, I'll send you to a laryngologist at Bayshore hospital in Pasadena, Texas.

That was the beginning of a long and painful series of examinations, x-rays, scanning and visits to an army of physicians and other technicians in the Pasadena area.

The specialist checked out my throat but the outcome, one more time, was negative. That was good news. At least for the time being. "However," he said, "I'm sending you to the Cancer Center in Houston for a scan of your neck."

I didn't see the usefulness of the scanning since he couldn't see anything wrong in my throat.

In a way I was very lucky. The doctor's instinct probably save my life. The scanning of my neck showed a tumor on the top of the left lung. For a non-smoker it was rather infuriating, almost ludicrous. And I couldn't even prosecute Philip Morris or whatever tobacco company I would have chosen if I had decided to be a smoker.

But everyone knows that lung cancer can strike even the non-smoker.

My luck was that without my husky voice, the laryngologist might have never thought about scanning my neck. We would have found out too late that that was due to a tumor.

I was sent to a lung physician, Dr. Bernard Bradley, a middle-age redheaded man, short and sympathetic, with a large smile and a way of talking that puts anyone at ease within a few seconds.

"Well," he said checking the scanner negatives from the Cancer Center, "we have something there."

"No kidding," I said with a chuckle. "Why do you think I came to see you?"

He laughed and we laughed and the ice was broken. "That's already a good state of mind," he said.

Dr. Bradley explained what I had, what he could do, what anyone could do in the medical profession, and what was the best way to treat that stupid thing. He drew a few sketches of my lung, showing what had happened to the nerve of my vocal cord that got stuck with the tumor. It was easy, simple, and comprehensible and, when Aline and I left Dr. Bradley, we were full of hope.

Today, I'm through with seven weeks of radiation with the Dr. D'Andrea in Pasadena, and with a series of chemotherapy sessions with Dr. Mitter and his so efficient crew in the other center in Houston.

"Soon," Dr. D'Andrea and Mitter said, "we'll start a new series of scanning, and we'll check all over. For now let the radiations and the chemotherapy finish their job."

That would be an important part of my life, perhaps the most important, but I know I can count on my doctors, Sherry the smiling nurse who takes care of me, my friends and mostly on my wife Aline. A paragon of abnegation.

François A. Borny
December 31st, 1930 - January 25th, 2005

He is Gone

You can shed tears that he is gone,
Or you can smile because he lived,

You can close your eyes and pray that he will come back,
Or you can open your eyes and see all that he has left.

Your heart can be empty because you can't see him
Or you can be full of the love that you shared,

You can turn your back on tomorrow and live yesterday,
Or you can be happy for tomorrow because of yesterday.

You can remember him and only that he is gone
Or you can cherish his memory and let it live on,

You can cry and close your mind be empty and turn your back,
Or you can do what he would want: smile, open your eyes, love and go on.

Final Word from the Family

Susanne and I knew that we had to finish our father's work, his life story, his written legacy.

Our father passed away January 25th, 2005, only 2 days after the final confirmation that this book would be published. So many emotions, so many thoughts... as I sit in front of my dad's computer... the same computer that he used to write the bulk of his book... the memories of my Dad come flooding in. He was a great Dad with enough examples to fill a few books. Maybe that will be the sequel... *François Borny Revisited.*

I had the honor and privilege to be the speaker at my father's funeral. His funeral was a testimony to who he was. Mom did not want to have any memorial service, but the calls kept pouring in as people found out that François Borny passed away. A particular one flabbergasted my Mom, but confirmed to me the impact that my father had his whole life. A couple that my parents met three year ago for about 10 days while vacationing in Mexico called and wanted to know when the funeral was because they were going to attend. Their call was from Minnesota, 4 hours and two plane rides away!

The small gathering at the grave site numbered in the seventies. People from all generations and background present. As I reminisced about Dad, the faces that looked back at me told me that he was a great man, admired by many. He will be missed, but not forgotten, gone, but always in our heart.

About the Author

FRANCOIS ALAIN BORNY, born in Nice, France in 1930, worked in the printing and editing business from the time he was eighteen until his retirement at age sixty-eight. After graduating from Saint-Laurent University in France, he was hired by Paul Bory Publishing Company in Monaco where he worked as a managing editor for over twenty-three years. Part of his work consisted in traveling to Africa, including French speaking countries such as Algeria, Senegal, Togo, Dahomey (now Benin), Cameroom, Chad, Congo, and Gabon; and English speaking countries such as Kenya, Uganda, Tanzania, and Nigeria.

In the meantime, he worked part time as a proofreader for Alma Editions, also in Monaco. After both companies shut down in 1978, he decided to immigrate to the United States with his family in December of that year.

François has been married since October 1954 and has two children: a daughter, born in 1955; a son, born in 1964; six grandchildren; and a great-grandson. On May 1st, 1985, he and his family became American citizens.

www.ingramcontent.com/pod-product-compliance
Lightning Source LLC
Chambersburg PA
CBHW050834230426
43667CB00012B/1995